Boddewyn, Jean J.

Comparison
advertising

DATE			

COMPARISON ADVERTISING

COMPARISON ADVERTISING
A Worldwide Study

J.J. BODDEWYN
Baruch College (CUNY)

and

KATHERIN MARTON
Fordham University

With the Special Assistance of:
IAA National Chapters
Rita Bari • Stephen Copulsky • Helmut Soldner • Vita Toros

A WORLDWIDE STUDY SPONSORED BY
THE INTERNATIONAL ADVERTISING ASSOCIATION

Communication Arts Books

HASTINGS HOUSE • PUBLISHERS
New York 10016

Copyright © 1978 by the International Advertising Association.
All rights reserved. No part of this publication may be
reproduced, stored in a retrieval system, or transmitted,
in any form or by any means, electronic, mechanical,
photocopying, recording or otherwise, without the prior
permission of the copyright owner or the publishers.

Library of Congress Cataloging in Publication Data
Boddewyn, Jean J   Comparison advertising.
  (Communication arts book)
  "A worldwide study sponsored by the International Advertising Association."
  Includes index.
    1. Advertising, Comparison.   I. Marton, Katherin, joint author.   II. International
Advertising Association (Founded 1938)   III. Title.
HF5827.B577   659.13   78-5546
ISBN 0-8038-1249-3 (v. 1)

Published simultaneously in Canada by
Saunders of Toronto, Ltd., Don Mills, Ontario
Printed in the United States of America

CONTENTS

Review Board (NARB)–Grievance Procedures–Complaints–
NAD/NARB–Media–Regulatory and Self-Regulatory Shortcomings–
Self-Discipline–Conclusion

Part Two / COUNTRY STUDIES

Part Three / STRATEGIES & CAMPAIGNS

INTERNATIONAL
ADVERTISING
ASSOCIATION INC.

IAA SUSTAINING MEMBERS

Avon Products
Axel Springer Verlag
Bacardi International
Banco de Intercambio Regional
BBDO International
Leo Burnett
Compton Advertising, Inc.
Crain Communications
Dentsu Advertising
Gillette International
Gruner + Jahr
IBM
ITT
L'Oréal
Marsteller International
McCann-Erickson International

N.V. Philips
Needham, Harper & Steers
   International
Nestlé
The New York Times
Newsweek International
Ogilvy & Mather International
Philip Morris Europe
Reader's Digest
Régie No. 1
Rockwell International
J. Walter Thompson
Time Magazine
Uniroyal
Banco Brasileira de Descontos
Young & Rubicam International

IAA ORGANIZATIONAL MEMBERS

Asociacion de Titulados en Publicidad, Spain
Associacão Brasileira de Anunciantes
American Advertising Federation
Canadian Advertising Advisory Board
European Association of Advertising Agencies
European Direct Marketing Association, Switzerland
Instituto Nacional de Publicidad, Spain

475 Fifth Avenue, New York, N.Y. 10017, U.S.A. (212) MU 4-1583

FOREWORD

THIS VOLUME is the fourth major study in a series sponsored by the Sustaining and Organizational Members of the International Advertising Association (see list).

The first sponsored study was *Effective Self-Regulation* (1974), which is now being brought up to date. The second, *Multinationals in Confrontation: How Can Better Communications Help Meet This Crisis?* was a report of the 1975 IAA Symposium in Geneva. The third, *Controversy Advertising*, was published by Hastings House, Publishers (New York), in 1977.

In the spring of 1975, the thirty-eight Chapters of the International Advertising Association were polled on their preferences of research topics of international importance. Comparison Advertising was one of the three subjects that concerned them most. Also at the top of their lists was Consumerism; therefore, a companion study, entitled *Impact of Consumerism on Advertising*, was commissioned in late 1976. The results will be published within the next year.

The subject of Comparison Advertising is one of great interest in many countries, whether the technique is practiced widely, marginally, or not at all. It involves many differences in legal codes and in regulatory and self-regulatory mechanisms; and its development is being closely followed in all countries wherein advertising plays an important part in the sale of goods and services to consumers. While this technique is not new, it is fast evolving; it has its passionate adherents and adversaries; and it is shaped by cultural as well as legal differences, as explained in this volume.

The International Advertising Association is grateful to the many IAA Chapter officers and members, national associations and other organizations, government officials and many others around the world who have supplied valuable information. Particular thanks are owed to Professor J.J. Boddewyn of Baruch College (City University of New York), who conducted the study and is the major author of the work. He led the five successful seminars held in Europe under IAA Chapter auspices in October 1977, from which many facts and examples emerged to enrich this study. The seminars were well attended by agency, advertiser, and media representatives, as well as by prominent lawyers, consumerists, government officials, and local advertising-association officers, many of whom participated in the panel discussions.

This volume is not meant to be *the* definitive study of the subject, nor does it take sides in the controversy over the use of this advertising technique— although the authors present some of their personal views in a concluding chapter. Rather, its purpose is to put into clearer perspective the various implications of making comparisons ("naming names") in advertising, to recommend some do's and don'ts, and to point to possible future developments.

Sylvan M. Barnet, Jr.

Chairman, Advisory Council
Sustaining and Organizational Members
International Advertising Association

Part One

THE ISSUES

Comparison Advertising: The Problems

WHETHER DONE POORLY or well, responsibly or not, the use of comparisons in advertising is old; and its prohibition or restriction in many countries reveals that it was practiced but became controversial. It still is. The controversy about comparison advertising (CA) centers on the following key questions:

1. *What is it exactly?* Various misunderstandings require clarification.
2. *To what extent is it used around the world?* Some crude estimates are available regarding its growing use.
3. *Is it legal?* There are clear cases of comparison advertising being either licit (e.g., the United States) or illicit (e.g., Belgium, France, and Italy). Elsewhere, its status is ambiguous and/or changing.
4. *Is it fair?* Conceptions of fairness vary on account of cultural patterns, but some of them are evolving.
5. *Is it beneficial?* Is it helpful to consumers? Does it foster more and better competition? Does it assist or detract from the image and influence of advertising and business enterprise? The "pro" arguments are generally attractive but the empirical evidence to date has often been on the negative side.
6. *Does it work, does it pay?* Advertising is but a means toward some economic goal, and comparison advertising is only one among many techniques available to help achieve that goal. Hence, comparisons should be effective and efficient—but are they? The answer to that question is not simple nor unambiguous. Yet, we can draw from our limited experience with comparison advertising a set of guidelines about when to use and avoid it.

7. The "new" life of comparison advertising is still young. We do not have answers to many questions. Still, there are choices to be made by advertisers, agencies, media, consumers (and their representatives), and governments. So, *where do we go from here on?*

To answer these questions, this report uses the materials provided by the IAA National Chapters[1] as well as other information obtained from the fast-growing literature on the subject, from interviews and correspondence with practitioners and experts, and from the cases included in this evaluation of comparison advertising.

This report is made up of three major parts:

1. *A discussion of the seven issues* outlined above.
2. *A country section,* including a score of one-page synopses, some thirty country notes as well as lengthier analyses of Canada, the United Kingdom, Belgium, Denmark, Japan, and the Philippines.
3. *Illustrations of comparative advertisements around the world,* with short and long analyses of their special features, of the reason why a comparative format was chosen, and of their effectiveness. This section also includes two lengthier case studies of the Pepsi–Coke and Datril–Tylenol comparative campaigns.

Great interest in this topic has already been expressed by the IAA Chapters that collaborated in the collection of these materials, as well as by the audiences drawn to discussions of this topic in the United States and abroad. Yet, this relatively new advertising method, whose use is spreading, remains controversial and in great need of further research and analysis. This report contributes to the debate.

[1] The assistance of Sylvan M. Barnet, Jr. (Chairman, Advisory Council, Sustaining and Organizational Members, IAA), John S.W. Wasley (Executive Director, IAA), and Hugh Holker (World President, IAA) is gratefully acknowledged as is that of the IAA headquarters staff: Mindy Lustig-Kozin, Marie J. Scotti, and H. Earle Bristed. Fraeda Saltzman at Baruch College also helped in many ways.

2

Comparison Advertising: What Is It?

COMPARISON ADVERTISING must be distinguished from related approaches as well as from "non-comparative" or "unilateral" advertisements:[1]

1. At the limit, *everything is comparative*—as illustrated by the notorious question-and-answer: "How's your wife? *Compared to what?*" Ultimately, all advertisements include some reference point, and they are therefore at least *implicitly* comparative. To state that "Chevrolet gives you a smooth ride" suggests that others cars do not, or at least not to the same extent.
2. More direct are those ads using *meliorative* ("Always low*er* prices!") or *superlative* ("The nic*est* dealer in town!") statements. They are really more in the realm of slogans than true comparisons, and most legislations tolerate them as harmless "puffery."
3. Next are *competitive claims*. Here, the existence of unnamed competitors is directly acknowledged, and comparison with directly competing products is invited—as in the famous 1931 Plymouth commercial: "Look at all three" before deciding on the purchase of a low-priced car. Such competitive claims can also be directed at other *types* of products ("Why send flowers? Sweets are nice too!") or *systems* ("Self-service stores are cheaper than full-service retail stores"). This type of "indirect" comparison is the only one allowed in some countries. However, since "names

---

[1] *"Comparison"* is used rather than *"comparative"* because the expression "comparative advertising" is already used for the analysis of similarities and differences among advertising systems and practices in various countries, as in "comparative literature" and "comparative economic systems."

Louis Sherry vs. Breyers

V.O.: Louis Sherry cherry vanilla ice cream versus Breyers. They're both all natural.

But, as you will see,

there's a big difference between them.

Louis Sherry is loaded with cherries -- an average of over 50% more cherries than Breyers.

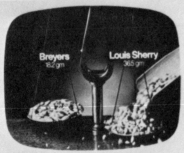

Going from fruit to nuts... Louis Sherry butter almond ice cream has an average of twice as many almonds as Breyers.

It isn't enough just to be all natural. So Louis Sherry gives you more fruit and more nuts.

Louis Sherry vs. Breyers Ad. This is an excellent example of a comparative advertisement since: (1) the competitive brand is named; (2) specific attributes are being compared; and (3) proof is provided about the claims made.

are not named," such "competitive" claims cannot be considered to be comparative in the strict sense of the term.

4. In the same vein, but differing in execution, are ads working on *innuendo*—ads in which one can readily surmise what the unnamed competing brand is (as in the famous Avis slogan "We're Number 2!"), because there are only two brands or only one well-known brand on the market to which implicit reference is made. There is also the electronic "bleep," which blots out the competitor's name ("Pepsi tastes better than *!?") in television commercials, or even "inadvertently" lets it slip through ("delayed bleep"). A more explicit form of "Brand X" advertising has recently appeared in a Carlton cigarette ad, in which, comparing itself to brands M,V,K, etc., the reference to Marlboro, Viceroy, Kent, and others is obvious.

5. The *truly comparative advertisement* is usually defined in terms of three features: (1) two or more specifically named or recognizably demonstrated brands of a product or service category are compared; (2) the comparison is based on one or more attributes of the good or service (e.g., tar and nicotine contents of cigarettes); and (3) it is either stated, implied or demonstrated that factual information (based on in-house research or obtained from independent and objective sources) has been gathered as a basis for the comparative claim(s).[2] This study deals mainly with such true comparisons.

[2] W.L. Wilkie and Paul Farris, *Comparison Advertising: Issues and Prospects* (Cambridge, Mass.: Marketing Science Institute, 1974), p. 3. McDougall's definition is much broader and also includes "competitive" claims that do not name names (e.g., "Better than all other brands!"): "Any advertisement that compares, implicitly or explicitly, two or more products, and states or implies that information has been obtained or a test has been conducted on a comparative basis, or that states or implies a particular market standing in relation to other similar products [e.g., "More women prefer Brand A . . ."], whether the other products are named or not, shall be deemed comparative." G.H.E. McDougall, *Comparative Advertising in Canada* (Ottawa: Consumer Research Council, Canada, 1976; also available in French).

3

Comparison Advertising: How Much Used?

COMPARISONS HAVE long been used in personal selling, as when car sales-men volunteer or are asked information about competing makes.[1] The door-to-door salesman who asks the lady of the house to compare his vacuum cleaner to hers is also a familiar comparison-user.

Media comparisons have a respectable history, too. Thus, a study of 1964 issues of *Advertising Age* revealed that 15 percent of U.S. media ads were ex-plicitly comparative—a proportion which by 1974 had increased to 20 percent.[2] Such media advertising usually names the competition, and contrasts the unit costs and the characteristics of the readership profile; they are therefore truly comparative in nature.

Most other products and services, however, remained largely untouched by comparative advertisements—with many countries banning or severely re-stricting the use of comparisons. In those that did not (e.g., the United States, Canada, and the United Kingdom), voluntary advertising, media and/or in-dustry codes as well as unwritten "rules of the game" strongly discouraged their use. Even international competition, in which gold and silver medals were awarded to the best wines, beers, cheeses, tools, and such, largely disappeared after World War I.

Regulations, guidelines, unwritten rules, and behavior change, of course, because of various factors. First, there is the perennial temptation of advertisers to state their real or imagined superiority in a truly comparative fashion, as is

[1] For an early history of comparison advertising, see: S.M. Ulanoff, *Comparison Advertising: An Historical Retrospective* (Cambridge, Mass.: Marketing Science Institute, 1975).

[2] Wilkie and Farris, *op. cit.,* pp. 5–6. Unless otherwise specified, statistics refer to the U.S. situation.

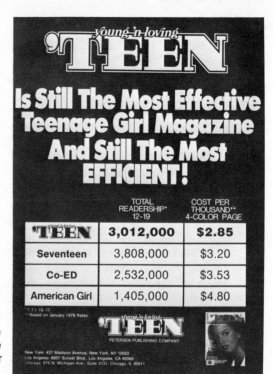

Two Examples of comparative media advertisements: one fairly traditional and the other very aggressive.

evidenced by the sizable number of complaints and legal actions in countries that ban or severely restrict this practice.

Another key factor has been the consumerist movement, which is fast spreading in developed countries, that stresses the need and even the right of consumers to be better informed in order to guide their choice among competing products. In this context, various publications (*Consumer Reports, DM, Which? Que Choisir? 50 Millions de Consommateurs, Test Achats,* and such) are now diffusing their findings among the consuming public, thereby popularizng the use of comparative product information. Advertisers, however, are frequently forbidden by law or by these research organizations from using these results in their advertisements. Hence, they have had to generate their own in order to capitalize on this growing interest for meaningful and more rational information presented in a comparative fashion.

Third, many governments have fosterd (or at least supported) this development because pro-consumerism is a political "must" nowadays. It is also a reflection of widespread prejudice among elites against emotional and non-objective appeals in advertising. Moreover, many governments are inclined to encourage competition through greater "market transparency," which is expected to result from more informative advertisements, and this policy change gives comparison advertising another boost.

Other factors at work include economic conditions. The use of comparisons may be greater in periods of economic stagnation or of slow growth (as we experience today) because increased sales must be obtained at the expense of others.

USE OUTSIDE OF THE UNITED STATES

Leaving out illegal uses of comparisons in countries that ban them, comparisons in 1976–1977 represented as much as 5 percent of total advertising expenditures in Canada and the Philippines (where it is now banned); up to 1 or 2 percent in the United Kingdom and Denmark; and minor percentages in Sweden, Switzerland, West Germany, the Netherlands, and Hong Kong. It is now emerging in Australia, Mexico, and Brazil.

The print form predominates in view of the frequent restrictions on TV advertising (often monopolized by the state). Comparative advertisements are mostly used for consumer products (food, cigarettes, soap, and cars), but also for services (e.g., newspapers in the United Kingdom) and industrial goods (e.g., earth-moving equipment in Denmark).

Interest in this practice on the part of some consumer associations, advertising agencies, trade unions, government officials, and/or jurists is keeping the issue alive in other countries that are moving toward allowing it, albeit at various paces (see country studies). Its use is unlikely to exceed 5 to 10 percent of advertising expenditures in highly developed nations, and 1 to 2 percent in less-developed ones, however.

THE UNITED STATES EXPERIENCE

In the United States, no law has prevented the use of comparison advertising. However, advertisers were reluctant to use it, and voluntary codes generally opposed comparisons. The major obstacle lay in television networks refusing such advertisements.

Television

NBC relented in the mid-sixties, but the major push came from the Federal Trade Commission (FTC). Robert Pitofsky, its Director of Consumer Protection, sent out letters in 1971 stating that the roundabout "Brand X" type of comparison allowed by ABC and CBS might mislead consumers. Consequently, these networks agreed to accept comparative advertisements on a one-year trial basis, which subsequently became permanent.

Additional informal statements by the FTC have since urged advertisers to provide buyers with more product information of a factual nature; and the Commission issued strong warnings in 1976 against industry codes and media policies that discourage or restrict this practice (see below).

Once the major television networks started accepting comparative advertisements, their use grew rapidly. Thus, a 1973 content analysis of *prime-time* network television indicated a 7 percent share of comparative advertisements,[3] and this proportion is estimated to have increased substantially to an estimated 8 to 10 percent in 1975–1976.[4] Similar information compiled by the Gallup and Robinson research firm shows that the number of comparative commercials in *prime-time* television increased from one out of thirty in the 1973–1974 television season to one out of twelve in 1974–1975 (NBC television believes that the ratio may have been considerably larger in 1976).[5] A much lower proportion, however, is provided by the CBS Television Network: they recorded only 198 comparative announcements out of 22,725 entries in 1976—a ratio of .87 percent, which is much lower than the ratios usually mentioned, but which applies to *all* television viewing (averaging well over twelve hours a day in the United States).[6]

Print Media

Very little information is available regarding the use of comparative advertisements in print. In February, 1977, the twenty-five general-circulation and

[3] Terence Shimp, "Comparison Advertising in National Television Commercials: A Content Analysis" (Paper presented at the Fall Conference of the American Marketing Association, Rochester, N.Y., 1975).

[4] E.A. Rockey, "Comparative Advertising: Fair or Unfair? Effective or Ineffective?" (Paper presented at the ANA Television Workshop, New York City, 24 February 1976). Mr. Rocky is President of Gallup and Robinson, Inc.

[5] S.I. Tannenbaum and A.G. Kershaw, "For and Against Comparative Advertising," *Advertising Age* (5 July 1976), p. 25. At the IREP conference in Paris (May 1977), Kershaw mentioned a 2 percent ratio.

[6] Letter from Ron Manders, Manager of Administration Commercial Clearance (New York, 11 January 1977).

women's magazines[7] were contacted by the authors through a mail question-
naire (with a telephone follow-up) about their policies and practices:

1. All of them accept comparative advertisements (only one magazine mentioned that it discouraged them in general).
2. With the exception of three magazines, they have not established specific
   guidelines for comparison advertising. Acceptance of such ads rests on
   the same criteria used for other advertising in such matters as truthfulness, fairness, and good taste. Two of the magazines indicated that they
   follow the AAAA guidelines; one has developed guidelines of its own.
3. Magazines could not indicate the volume of comparison advertising as a
   percentage of their total advertising volume either because the volume of
   comparison advertising was so low that no specific category was used for
   it or because separate statistics are not being compiled for it.
4. Very few problems have been encountered in accepting such ads, and
   readers' complaints have been rare—in contrast to the TV networks' experience in this regard.

Advertising Agencies

Considering the large volume of dispute and controversy surrounding comparison advertising, an *ANNY* research survey concluded that "comparative ads
are more preached than practiced."[8] In its July, 1976, survey, *ANNY* found
that out of the 278 advertising agencies with headquarters or offices in the New
York, New Jersey, Philadelphia, and Connecticut areas, 44 percent were
engaged in comparison advertising, while 41 percent were not.

Breaking down these agencies by size (measured by the annual volume of
billings), *ANNY* found that the practice of comparison advertising grows with
the size of the agency:

- of 152 agencies with billings of less than $120 million, 33 percent used it
- of 96 agencies with billings from $10 to 50 million, 60 percent used it
- of agencies with billings above $50 million, 60 percent used it

While these figures do not measure the volume of comparison advertising
utilized by these agencies, they give an indication of the acceptance of this
practice by a majority of the agencies—particularly the larger ones, even
though some of the latter do not accept them.

Users and Non-Users

Comparisons have been used with many product and service categories:
drugs, household items, cars, automotive accessories (e.g., tires), appliances,

[7] *Business Week, Forbes, Fortune, Better Homes and Gardens, Cosmopolitan, Family Circle,
Good Housekeeping, House and Garden, Ladies' Home Journal, Lady's Circle, McCall's Magazine, Mademoiselle, Newsweek, Parents' Magazine, Popular Mechanics, Popular Science, Psychology Today, Redbook Magazine, Seventeen, Sport, Sports Illustrated, Teen, Time, True,* and *US
News and World Report.*

[8] "Comparative Ads More Preached than Practiced," *ANNY* (13 August 1976), p. 1.

personal-hygiene products, foods and drinks, animal foods, pantyhose, golf balls, razors, and so on—at least sixty brands in 1973–1975.[9] Out of a total of 198 comparative ads in 1976, CBS tallied 63 automotive ads, 25 for drugs/first-aid products, 19 for toiletries, and 18 for food products and beverages.[10]

While no detailed analysis is yet available, comparisons seem to be used mostly by brand-challengers and the introducers of new or improved products. On the other hand, comparative advertisements appear to be shunned by brand-leaders and by advertisers whose products (e.g., perfume) do not lend themselves to objective comparisons. They are also avoided by those advertising practitioners who believe that it is ineffective compared to other methods, too costly to prepare and check, and wide open to litigation. Subsequent sections deal, of course, with these issues.

[9] Rockey, *op. cit.*
[10] Letter from Ron Manders, *op. cit.*

4

Comparison Advertising: Legal or Not?

WITH SCORES OF NATIONS in existence, it is difficult to answer this question completely and definitely.[1] Nevertheless, similar legal foundations usually explain the authorization, ban, or restriction of comparison advertising around the world, and similar forces are affecting the evolution of the relevant laws and regulations everywhere. These foundations and forces are analyzed here.

GENERAL PRINCIPLES

Countries vary in terms of whether they allow truthful comparisons (with some restrictions) or forbid them on various grounds (with some exceptions). Actually, very few national legislations (e.g., in Belgium) refer directly to advertising comparisons or references, or at least to denigration in competitive behavior. Elsewhere, the law is not explicit on the subject, even though there is

[1] This analysis only deals with countries that have a relatively free market system, and thus excludes centrally planned economies (e.g., USSR). It is greatly indebted to: Bernard Francq, "La publicité comparative," *Bulletin de l'Institut International de Concurrence Commerciale* (Bruxelles, Belgium: April 1977), pp. 25–78; Werner Janssen, Jr., "Some Foreign Law Aspects of Comparative Advertising," *The Trademark Reporter*, Vol. 64, No. 6 (November–December 1974), pp. 451–497 (Copyright © 1974, The United States Trademark Association, and reprinted with permission of the copyright owner); the special issue of *The Trademark Reporter* on comparison advertising (67, 4; July–August 1977); Luc Ballon, *Vergelijkende informatie aan de consument* (Leuven, Belgium: Instituut voor Handelsrecht, 1976); and G.E. Rosden and P.E. Rosden, *The Law of Advertising* (New York: Matthew Bender, 1973–), Ch. 31 ("Comparative Advertising"). The assistance of Maurizio Fusi, legal expert on the subject (Milan, Italy), and of Dr. K.H. Troxler, who provided the Swiss IAA Chapter with relevant research materials on comparison advertising, is also gratefully acknowledged.

usually some relevant body of law under which the practice—or at least its abuse—can be challenged, stopped, and/or penalized.[2]

A few general legal and constitutional principles favor comparison advertising: freedom to express one's opinions, freedom of personal development (e.g., for an advertising professional to use this technique creatively), freedom of speech, and freedom of trade and competition. Besides, business competition is generally accepted, though it is obviously an adversary relationship, with competitors "harming" each other in the process of displacing rival products through advertising and other means. Other principles, however, centering on the prohibition of harming others, on the protection of industrial property, and on the safeguarding of "fair competition," have historically predominated.

In this context, comparison advertising is considered as a particular form of *denigration,* whereby the person or reputation of a competitor is being *defamed*[3] or his products *disparaged*—whether directly (by criticism) or indirectly (by extolling the superiority or at least the equality of one's own products). Is denigration legal? A basic distinction here centers on the truthfulness of the comparison.

Typically in comparison advertising, the advantages or disadvantages singled out are true and presumably can be validated. Hence, it is *not a matter of false advertising* that is generally prohibited by one law or another. In the latter case, when actual damages can be proven, *tort law* usually provides for compensating the injured competitor, besides forcing the advertiser to stop the illicit practice.

However, some legal systems reject even *truthful* comparisons because: (1) they consider them to be fundamentally *malicious,* in that they propose to lower the public's estimation of somebody else ("No one names his competitor with any good in mind!"), and/or (2) they are *designed to gain an unfair advantage* (e.g., France). In other words, it is the underlying motivation rather than the facts that matters and that justifies prohibiting the use of comparisons in advertising. This motivation, by the way, is usually associated with a lack of objectivity, since a comparative advertiser is both judge and party regarding the merits of a competitor's product. Additionally, *truthful* comparisons may constitute deceptive advertising when the facts are not fairly selected and are therefore likely to mislead the consumer (see below). Increasingly, the literal truth is not enough, and, therefore, the overall impression conveyed is being examined.

Another legal restriction centers on *industrial property law.* The brand names of a firm's products are normally registered as trademarks—thus constituting a piece of property and part of the company's goodwill—which cannot

---

[2] It is interesting to observe that the legal literature on comparison advertising is usually more voluminous in countries that ban it than in those that allow and use it—partly as a reflection of the constant temptation to circumvent negative laws, and also because some jurists are convinced that this practice is fundamentally licit or should be authorized through some legal reform.

[3] It appears that defamation of the person of a competitor is more commonly practiced by small firms than by large advertisers.

be used by others for commercial purposes without the permission of the owner. Since such permission is rarely requested and *a fortiori* granted,[4] the issue of trademark infringement can be properly raised in such nations as Switzerland, the United Kingdom, the Netherlands, Belgium, Luxembourg, Canada and other present or former British Commonwealth countries. Others, like the United States, allow such a use if the comparison is true and told in a truthful manner.

A third body of law bans or restricts the use of a competitor's name on the grounds of its being an *"unfair competitive practice."* [5] Such commercial laws assume a variety of forms around the world, with statutory-law countries typically having a comprehensive commercial code.[6] A number of nations have regulatory bodies similar to the U.S. Federal Trade Commission (or some consumer-protection agency, as in Scandinavia) empowered to issue trade regulations and to otherwise apply the law.

Typically, such trade laws and regulations serve a double purpose: (1) to protect consumers against undesirable trade practices (such as misleading advertising), and (2) to maintain or foster "fair" competition among traders. Since most comparative advertisements are factually correct and do contribute to consumer information and "market transparency"—two very desirable objectives—, bans or severe restrictions of truthful comparisons rest on the fact that they are considered an "unfair" competitive practice *irrespective of damages caused to a competitor.*

"Unfairness" is, of course, a very subjective concept reflecting various commercial traditions, cultural traits (for example, vis-à-vis aggressive competitive behavior), economic conditions, and pressure-group configurations. In the long run, the notion of what is fair and unfair tends to evolve in the light of experience (good or bad), new values, and altered political maps.[7]

Thus, the concept of "unfair" practices increasingly includes those that are likely to harm consumers—not just traders. Besides, the recognition of community interests requires removing or altering regulations that unduly protect traders against competition. Comparison advertising provides a good test of the evolving balance between consumer and trade interests, even though the current legal reality does not yet fully reflect this new aspiration (West German courts, however, have moved in this direction).

Another dimension of the problem of "fairness" centers on the *directness* of the comparison. The law generally accepts that competing firms boost their products and services, whether comparatively or not: "We are good, we are

---

[4] A 1977 advertisement by Chrysler in France, where direct comparisons are forbidden, contrasted the Matra-Bagherra with the Lamborghini car. However, it was done with the permission of the latter, since the two cars are clearly not competitive. Meanwhile, Lamborghini received free advertisement in the bargain!

[5] Similar terms (e.g., "acts contrary to honest practice") are used around the world. Janssen, *op. cit.,* p. 457.

[6] In France, however, unfair competition is ruled by some key provisions of the Civil Code.

[7] For a general discussion of this issue, and for country analyses, see: J.J. Boddewyn and S.C. Hollander (eds.), *Public Policy Toward Retailing: An International Symposium* (Lexington, Mass.: D.C. Heath, 1972).

La loi nous interdit de comp arer la nouvelle Alfetta 2000 à ses concurrentes.

Alfa Romeo

Sorry, mais vous devrez faire appel à vos connaissances techniques.

Moteur 2 l. très souple ● 122 CV DIN ● Technique transaxiale ● 5 vitesses ● Accélération: de 0 à 100 km/h en 11,5 sec ● Vitesse de pointe: 185 km/h ● Climatisation: 11 bouches d'air renouvellent à 100 km/h. 6.500 litres d'air frais à la minute ● L'Alfetta 2000 se contente d'un entretien tous les 20.000 km seulement ● Tous ses accessoires-confort sont standards ● Prix: 258.970.-F + 25% TVA.

Alfa Romeo Benelux s.a. - chée de Zellik 65 - 1080 Bruxelles - Tél. 02/465.00.64.

Consultez la liste du réseau Alfa Romeo dans les Pages d'Or.

Dealing with comparison in a country where it is forbidden ("The law forbids us to compare the New Alfetta 2000 to its competitors. Sorry, you'll have to rely on your own technical knowledge."). This ad appeared in *Selection du Reader's Digest* [Belgian Edition], (January 1978).

better, we are the best!'' The problems then typically center on: (1) whether the competition is either clearly identified (''naming names'') or readily identifiable (''We are Number 2: We try harder!''), and (2) whether the comparison is general (''The best car on the road'') or becomes specific as particular attributes are compared (''The most *durable* shoe''). Regulations and legal opinions differ as to when these points have been reached and whether they constitute acceptable practice.

In Switzerland, Austria, Italy, the Scandinavian countries, the United Kingdom, and the United States, a direct comparison can be said to exist only if, by reference to one or more competitors, consumers are incited to make a concrete comparison of attributes. A direct comparison does not legally exist, however, if a reference to competitors becomes recognizable only by use of the imagination or by an association of ideas. The French and Dutch views are rather formalistic: they understand by clear recognizability only a reference to competitors by name or by some other clearly distinguishable means; they do not regard as such any reference to unnamed competitors. In contrast, West Germany and Belgium consider that a direct comparison exists if the readers or listeners have their attention generally drawn to the services of others, and can ascertain from the advertising text who might be meant. Yet, German legal authorities have of late no longer been regarding every instance of advertising of a comparative nature as a direct comparison just because it points at one or more competitors—particularly if the reference is only made indirectly, or if the direct statements are confined to giving information about the advertiser's own products or services.

Assuming a case of direct comparison, the reference may be *positive or negative*. The former points positively at others in order to take advantage of the good reputation of the competitor or his product and so arouse an image of equivalence (e.g., "ABC liqueur tastes like Benedictine"). Considered to be essentially parasitical, such advertising is generally prohibited in continental Western Europe. In the United States, United Kingdom, and Canada, it is thought to be actionable only if the implication tends to mislead the buyer.

The most frequent and thus most important case is the negatively implied comparison, whereby critical statements tend to diminish competitors in the eyes of the consumer. In West Germany, France, and Belgium, critical comparisons are basically prohibited, and only compelling grounds can justify a departure from this principle, such as self-defense or using such comparisons to illustrate an advantage that cannot be explained in any other way. Austria, Italy, and the Netherlands also have such a prohibition, but the application procedure is less rigid. If the grounds are adequate, critical concern with the goods or services of competitors may be admissible, as when the comparison constitutes a functional act of advertising, is suitably formulated, and does not set out directly to prejudice a competitor as in the case of informatively worded comparisons of goods and prices.

On the other hand, truly critical comparisons are in principle allowed in Switzerland, the Scandinavian countries, and the Anglo-American countries. In borderline cases, however, even true comparisons may be inadmissible if they are likely to mislead consumers or are unnecessarily derogatory. Swiss law alone recognizes this last mentioned proviso.

Even when explicit and truthful comparisons are forbidden, there are various legal exceptions and "gray" areas:

1. *Puffery* or the use of superlatives claiming some supposedly exceptional positioning ("The most erotic novel of the year" or "The most beautiful car on the road") is usually tolerated on the grounds that consumers do not take such subjective and hyperbolic claims too seriously, and that they do not significantly affect competition, since specific or easily identifiable competitors are not named. Many such claims are merely slogans. However, in West Germany, they cannot be used if worthy of belief; in Austria, if otherwise provable (e.g., "The most durable shoes"). Extreme cases of puffery really fall under rules forbidding misleading or false claims, rather than under those bearing on denigration based on correct facts.

2. Most nations allow the manufacturer of *replacement parts* (supplies, services, and so forth) to mention that his products satisfactorily fit or service the specifically named products of a competitor (e.g., "Goodyear

tubes fit Michelin tires''). In fact, this is the major exception allowed in countries that ban comparisons.

3. Typically, the law is more lenient regarding *oral comparisons made by salesmen,* although some countries (e.g., Belgium and West Germany) allow it only when comparative information is requested by the potential customer. This is really more a case of salesmanship than of advertising, but this tolerance also applies to printed comparative information sent to customers at their request.

4. Comparisons made in *self-defense* against unfair references are also generally allowed. Thus, in a famous German case, the sellers of regular coffee retorted that "Coffee without caffeine is like a car without gas" to counteract the slogan, "Coffee Hag [without caffeine] spares your heart and your nerves."

5. *Comparing systems and methods* in order to illustrate an advantage or to introduce some technical progress that cannot be explained in any other way (but without mentioning a competitor's name or ridiculing competition at large) is usually authorized (e.g., to state that one's car with front-wheel driving is safer than other makes without such a feature).[8]

6. For an ad to claim that one product is *"as good"* as another—even when lauding the latter—is considered in a number of countries (e.g., Austria) as undesirable "parasitic" behavior that exploits someone else's property by association. Countries that authorize truthful comparisons (such as the United States) do not make such a distinction.

7. Where comparisons are allowed, *even correct facts may be considered misleading* if the similarities and differences are real but not significant, if they are taken out of context, or if their presentation implies more than is warranted ("Deception can occur by silences as well as by statements").

   Increasingly, the literal truth is not enough, and the "net impression" conveyed is being examined. Consumer protection is more likely to be evoked in such a case. It then becomes a complex legal issue in view of the lack of legal obligation to be completely truthful—even to the point of listing one's own relative disadvantages (Sweden and the United States are moving in this direction). Besides, investigation and/or litigation is usually necessary to stop such practices, for which an interpretation or adjudication must then be provided.

8. *Scientific comparative tests* made public for advertising purposes are prohibited if there are no compelling or adequate grounds for them in West Germany, France, Belgium, Austria, Italy, and the Netherlands. In contrast, they are allowed in Switzerland, the Scandinavian countries, and Anglo-American nations. Comparative tests, published by a neutral body with no intended advertising object, present no legal problem, and civil law at most may be invoked.

---

[8] Nevertheless, there have been many suits about system comparisons—for example, butter vs. margarine, and bottles vs. cans.

ARE YOU SMOKING TOBACCO LEFTOVERS?

Compare your cigarette to L&M Lights, the only cigarette made with 100% virgin tobacco.

BRAND	TOBACCO CONTENT IS 100% VIRGIN ALL-LEAF?	CONTAINS ADDED STEMS?	CONTAINS RECONSTITUTED TOBACCO?	"TAR" CONTENT
MARLBORO	NO	YES	YES	17 mg.
MARLBORO LIGHTS	NO	YES	YES	12 mg.
WINSTON	NO	NO	YES	19 mg.
WINSTON LIGHTS	NO	NO	YES	12 mg.
KENT	NO	NO	YES	16 mg.
KENT GOLDEN LIGHTS	NO	NO	YES	8 mg.
VICEROY	NO	YES	YES	16 mg.
VICEROY EXTRA MILDS	NO	YES	YES	14 mg.
VANTAGE	NO	NO	YES	11 mg.
MERIT	NO	YES	YES	8 mg.
BENSON & HEDGES	NO	YES	YES	16 mg.
REAL	NO	NO	YES	9 mg.

As you can see, most cigarettes are more than just "leafy tobacco." They contain reconstituted tobacco and chopped up tobacco stems in their mix. The only one that doesn't is L&M Lights. The choice is yours.

REALLY REAL TASTE. ONLY 8MG."TAR." L&M LIGHTS

Warning: The Surgeon General Has Determined That Cigarette Smoking Is Dangerous to Your Health.

Flavor Lights: 8 mg. "tar", 0.6 mg. nicotine, av. per cigarette, FTC Report (Aug.'77). Long Lights: 8 mg. "tar", 0.6 mg. nicotine; av. per cigarette, by FTC Method.

This ad goes beyond the regular "Tar and Nicotine" comparisons to include tobacco content and other additions—but it leaves nicotine-percentage out of the comparative table.

Comparative advertisements definitely lead to litigation as is well revealed by the numerous court cases cited in the legal literature—particularly in Europe. In the United States, the Federal Trade Commission has also issued a number of injunctions: and "consent orders" have also been accepted that prohibit various comparative advertisers from making false and unsubstantiated claims for their products.[9]

The law on truthful comparisons and court decisions on the subject are slowly evolving in the direction of greater permissiveness or at least of broader exceptions in favor of this advertising technique. Several factors account for this evolution:

1. *Consumerist pressures* are favoring marketing and advertising techniques conducive to providing more and better information to the consumer.
2. Most *national governments* support this demand,[10] and many also want to foster a type of competition wherein a firm's success rests on real eco-

[9] See, for example: "FTC Accepts Consent Order Citing General Electric," *FTC News* (31 January 1977).

[10] Besides the U.S. Federal Trade Commission's support of comparison advertising, see the similar pronouncements and initiatives of Christiane Scrivener, French State Secretary for Consumer Affairs, in 1976.

nomic superiority. This requires greater "market transparency" about comparative advantages.

3. *The example of "pilot" countries* such as the United States, Scandinavia, and even West Germany (long associated with a ban on comprisons but now accepting broader exceptions) is definitely and positively affecting regulatory attitudes toward comparative advertisements.

4. *The International Chamber of Commerce's 1973 relaxation of its Advertising Code* tolerates comparison advertising (see below). This works in the same direction since its moral authority is great, and it has historically influenced national voluntary codes as well as legislation in many countries (such a relaxation has definitely affected legislative revisions in Scandinavia). Several international organizations dealing with unfair competition (LICCD) and industrial property (AIPPI), have recently passed resolutions also favoring "fair" forms of comparison advertising (see below).

5. Similarly, the *pronouncements and initiatives of various European institutions* (European Economic Community, Council of Europe, European Parliament) are supportive of truthful and fair comparisons (see below), and they could ultimately mandate their authorization in member countries. Since former colonies often imitate European legislation, this relaxation could spread to these countries, too.

Each one of these factors is complex and should be qualified in many ways. Still, the likely outcome for the next ten years is greater *authorization of comparison advertising but coupled with restrictions*—and the latter are likely to be major in some countries. The net legal result may not be very different from the present situation, wherein there are many national bans with various, and sometimes major, exceptions. Nevertheless, this evolution of the law reveals that attitudes have changed toward making legal room for a technique that, though as old as advertising itself, has been severely constrained for many decades in numerous countries.

INTERNATIONAL TREATIES

Various aspects of advertising are affected by international treaties,[11] and some supranational bodies (e.g., the European Economic Community, EEC) have addressed themselves to the topic of comparison advertising, recently tending to favor it.

The 1883 (Paris) International Convention for the Protection of Industrial Property does not readily apply to truthful comparison advertising, since its revised Article 10. bis forbids only "false allegations in the course of trade of such a nature as to discredit the establishment, the goods, or the industrial or commercial activities, of a competitor." However, the general clause of this same article also forbids unfair (contrary to honest practices) competitive acts—

---

[11] Janssen, *op. cit.,* pp. 452–53.

which brings one back to the problem of determining what is considered fair or unfair in trade practices.

Similarly, the 1929 (Pan American) General Inter-American Convention for Trade Mark and Commercial Protection only refers to acts or deeds "contrary to commercial good faith" in its Articles 20 and 21.

The 1968 Central American Convention for the Protection of Industrial Property designates as an act of unfair competition "the use of a trademark, trade name, advertising expression or symbol identical or similar to another registered to a different person or corporation, without the consent of that person or corporation, in relation to products, merchandise, services or activities protected by the registration" (Article 66. f.).

The Benelux Uniform Law on Trademarks (1969) has an Article 13A (2) that forbids "other uses" of trademarks and thus of registered product names. This prohibition seems to apply to their use in comparative advertisements. If so, it would definitely hamper the relaxation of regulations in Belgium, Luxembourg, and the Netherlands—notwithstanding the EEC Commission's proposed directive discussed below.

EUROPEAN INTERNATIONAL ORGANIZATIONS

Consumer "rights" are very much on the minds and agenda of legislators and regulators in several European bodies, with various resolutions having already emanated from the Council of Europe and the European Parliament. They carry mostly moral weight, but they are affecting the regulatory activities of the EEC and the revision of national laws (e.g., in Belgium).

Council of Europe [12]

Some of its resolutions and draft directives bear on consumer protection against unfair and misleading advertising, and it has recommended positive measures such as comparison advertising and the elaboration of professional codes of marketing and advertising practice not only to complement government regulations but also to provide less expensive and more flexible ways of coping with variety and change in member countries. [13]

In particular, Article A. (b). (v). of the Council's Consumer Protection Charter states that: "An advertiser in any media shall be required to provide on request a proof of the validity of claims made in an advertisement. An advertiser unable to provide such proof shall, if so requested, issue at his own ex-

---

[12] The Council of Europe is a parliamentary forum for the free expression of European public opinion on major issues. Some eighteen Western European parliamentary democracies (including all nine EEC countries) are represented on this Council.

[13] See for example: Council of Europe, Committee of Ministers, "Resolution (72)8 on Consumer Protection against Misleading Advertising" (Strasbourg, 18 February 1972). The Council also adopted a Consumer Protection Charter outlining consumer rights to state protection and assistance, redress against damage, information, education, and representation and consultation. Consultative Assembly of the Council of Europe, "Resolution 543 (1973) on a Consumer Protection Charter" (Strasbourg, 17 May 1973).

pense equivalent corrective advertising." This clause has already found expression in a number of countries (e.g., Belgium and France).

Article B.(iii) urges that consumer associations be empowered to initiate redress actions—another development evident in several national legislations. Article E.(vi) even encourages professional codes of trading practices that "while basically conforming to national laws, shall seek to promote higher standards, and shall be submitted—together with proposals for a private and objective enforcement of such codes in collaboration with the consumers—to national consumer authorities for approval. The authorities shall give public support and backing to approved codes." This latter recommendation has not yet resulted in any national implementation, however.

EEC Institutions

The European Parliament[14] and the European Community (EEC) have also addressed themselves to advertising in the context of consumer protection and information, and of unfair competition. Essentially, their emphasis is on misleading and unfair advertisements that prevent consumers from making the right choice and from fulfilling their function of final arbiter in the market economy, and that give unscrupulous producers an unfair advantage over their competitors.

The EEC is also interested in the "harmonization or approximation" of national advertising laws in order to reduce competitive distortions of this type: "An advertiser in Country A can use his campaign in Country B, which has similar regulations; but an advertiser in Country C will not, if the rules in his country are substantially different from those in Country B." Also, the unintended spillover of radio, television, and print campaigns from one country to another may create legal problems in the second country, and oblige the advertiser to tone down his campaign in his national market, with a possible loss of competitive advantage there.

EEC Commission Draft Directive

Following various resolutions and studies going back to the 1960s, the EEC Commission in 1973 submitted a preliminary program for consumer information and protection to the EEC Council of Ministers (who must approve all proposals of the Commission). This program establishes principles for assessing the extent to which an advertisement is false, misleading, or generally unfair.[15]

[14] The European Parliament provides some degree of democratic control over the executive branch of the EEC. Delegates from the parliaments of member countries comment on most Commission proposals, and address questions to it. Standing committees also discuss major EEC policies such as consumer protection.

[15] These various efforts and proposals are discussed in: Commission of the European Communities, "Memorandum on Approximation of the Laws of Member States on Fair Competition; Misleading and Unfair Advertising," Working Document No. 2, X1/C/93/75–E (Brussels, November 1975). The EEC draft directive includes proposals that would have significant bearing on the conduct of advertising in general—including the matters of fault and intention, the burden of proof, the parties that could be sued, class actions, corrective advertisements, and other penalties. See also:

After November 1975, an EEC Commission draft directive set out a minimum number of rules that would have to be respected in revising national legislations and in settling disputes in national courts. This draft directive had already gone through several versions, and has been discussed by government experts and interested parties (advertising and consumer associations, and such). It is very important because of the likelihood of its passage (in 1979?) and implementation in nine member countries that are major advertising nations—plus its likely impact on the legislation of associated, postulant, and otherwise related countries (e.g., Greece, Turkey, Spain, Portugal, Israel, and Lomé-Convention underdeveloped countries linked to the EEC).

The latest version, prepared in the fall of 1977 and sent to EEC Member States in January, 1978,[16] purports to "protect consumers, persons carrying on a trade, business, or profession, as well as the interests of the public in general against unfair and misleading advertising." This objective reflects the modern tendency to consider a multiplicity of interests rather than simply those of tradesmen.

Article 4 states: "Comparative advertising[17] shall be allowed, as long as it compares material and verifiable details, and is neither misleading nor unfair."[18] Clearly, this permission revolves around the definitions of "misleading" and "unfair." in Articles 2 and 3 of the draft directive:

Article 2

For the purpose of this Directive one understands by:
1. "Advertising," the making of any pronouncement in the course of carrying on a trade, business, or profession for the purpose of promoting the supply of goods and services;
2. "Misleading advertising," any advertising which is entirely or partially false or which, having regard to its total effect, including its presentation, misleads or is likely to mislead persons addressed or reached thereby, unless it could not reasonably be foreseen that these persons would be reached thereby;

Council of Ministers, "Resolution of 14 April 1975 on a Preliminary Programme of the European Economic Community for a Consumer Protection and Information Policy," *Official Journal of the European Communities, XVIII, C92 (25 April 1975), pp. 1–15.*

[16] This latest version has not yet been officially released but was sent to member states on 17 January 1978. This draft directive is now being handled by the Consumer and Environmental Protection Service, which also issued the previous version: Commission of the European Communities, "Preliminary Draft Directive Concerning Misleading and Unfair Advertising," Document ENV/311/77-E (Brussels, June 1977). An earlier version had been prepared by the Internal Market Directorate (X1/C–3): "Second Draft of First Directive Concerning the Approximation of the Laws of Member States on Unfair Trading Practices; Misleading and Unfair Advertising," Document X1/C/204/76-E (Brussels, September 1976).

[17] The June, 1977, version included the following definition: "Comparative Advertising means any advertising which draws a comparison between the goods or services of the advertisers and the goods or services of another person" (Article 1.2.d.).

[18] The wording "shall be permitted" reveals the Continental European tendency to consider as illegal what is not specifically allowed, while in the Anglo-Saxon tradition, everything is legal that is not specifically forbidden by law.

3. "Unfair advertising," any advertising which:
   (a) casts discredit on another person by improper reference to his nationality, origin, private life, or good name; or
   (b) injures or is likely to injure the commercial reputation of another person by false statements or defamatory comments concerning his firm, goods, or services; or
   (c) appeals to sentiments of fear, or promotes social or religious discrimination; or
   (d) significantly infringes the principle of the social, economic, and cultural equality of the sexes; or
   (e) exploits the trust, credulity or lack of experience of a consumer, or influences or is likely to influence a consumer or the public in general in any other improper manner. . . .

In this definition of unfair advertising, the key term as regards comparison advertising is "defamatory" as used in Section (b). Actually it is a poor choice of words, since defamation applies to persons, while disparagement is applied to firms, goods, and services.[19] One can also wonder about the meaning that could be ascribed to "any other improper manner" in Section (e), because some laws still consider comparisons as "improper."[20]

The Commission's definition would seem to tolerate "puffery," that is, comparative statements not based on any set of stated facts (e.g., "Beer refreshes best"). On the other hand, comparisons made in self-defense would have to comply with the new rules in order to avoid compounding any existing or alleged abuse or offense.

It is important to realize that the EEC directive would no longer require—as is traditional in commercial legislation—that the plaintiff show that he or she actually suffered an injury, whether as a competitor by losing customers or as a consumer by purchasing an article. Also, the techniques used in presenting deceptive information could be considered constitutive of misleading advertising—such as the partial presentation of the truth in a way that is misleading, or the use of comparative claims that are not substantiated but put forward as

---

[19] The International Union of Advertisers Associations (IUAA) and the European Association of Advertising Agencies (EAAA), in discussing an earlier version of this section, which used "disparaging" instead of "defamatory," proposed that only *unjustified* disparaging comments should be considered unfair. This resembles the wording of "without justifiable reason" that appeared in the second draft of this directive. These two associations have made numerous comments about the successive drafts, but they had little to say about comparison advertising, which they appear to support for lack of opposition to it. For a summary of their position, see: Gilbert Lamb, "A Directive in the Wrong Direction," *Campaign* (2 September 1977), p. 19.

[20] *Article 3.1* states that in determining whether advertising is misleading or unfair, various matters shall be considered, including: "the category, qualifications, and rights of the advertiser, such as his identity, solvency, capabilities, ownership of intellectual property rights [trademarks, among others] or awards and distinctions." Under *Article 3.2:* "Advertising is in particular considered as misleading when it omits material information and, by reason of that omission, gives a false impression or arouses expectations which the advertiser cannot satisfy." *Article 6* provides: "Where the advertiser makes a factual claim, the burden of proof that his claim is correct shall lie with him."

positive truths. Corrective advertisements (already allowed in some countries) would also become more prevalent.[21]

This latest draft directive now looks more like a set of guidelines that allow member countries to comply in a variety of manners—rather than requiring specific legislative and regulatory changes. It is not expected to be enacted until late 1979 at the earliest, since it must still be examined and discussed by the EEC Economic and Social Council and by the European Parliament before the EEC Council of Ministers finally approves it. Member states will then have eighteen months to comply with the enacted directive. However, they can also take or maintain other measures for the protection of consumers against misleading or unfair advertising to the extent that these measures are in conformity with the Treaty of Rome (Article 8). Should this directive be adopted, comparison advertising done in a fair and non-misleading manner would have to be allowed in all nine EEC countries.

THE UNITED STATES EXPERIENCE

There is no U.S. legislation dealing specifically with comparison advertising, but several bodies of law are applicable,[22] and the government has tended to support this practice. Thus, the increase in comparative advertisements has been credited partly to the Federal Trade Commission's (FTC) encouragement (since 1971–1972) of this technique as a means of providing consumers with more information.

This FTC support complements the United States laws and regulations that allow truthful, fair, and non-misleading comparisons.[23] A number of federal

---

[21] *Article 5* requires: "Member States shall adopt adequate and effective laws against misleading and unfair advertising. Such laws shall provide persons affected by misleading or unfair advertising, as well as *associations with a legitimate interest in the matter,* with quick, effective and inexpensive facilities for initiating appropriate *legal* proceedings against misleading and unfair advertising. Member States shall in particular ensure that: (1) the Courts are enabled, *even without proof of fault or of actual prejudice* (a) to take a decision on the prohibition or cessation of misleading or unfair advertising; and (b) to take such a decision under an accelerated procedure, with an interim or perpetual effect; (2) the Courts are enabled: (a) to require publication of a corrective statement; and (b) to require publication of their decision either in full or in part and in such form as they may judge adequate; (3) the sanctions for infringing these laws are a sufficient deterrent, and, where appropriate, take into account the financial outlay on the advertising, the extent of the prejudice, and any profit resulting from the advertising.

[22] This section is based on Steward E. Sterk, "The Law of Comparative Advertising," *The Trademark Reporter,* 67, 4 (July–August 1977), pp. 351–406; Steve Tanner, "Advertising Self-Regulation: The National Advertising Review Board Clips the 'King of Beards'," *Publishing, Entertainment, Advertising, and Allied Fields Law Quarterly,'* Vol. 13(1975), pp. 185–213; the special issue of *The Trademark Reporter,* 67, 4 (July–August 1977) on comparative advertising; and Rosden and Rosden, *op. cit.* The use of comparison advertising is prohibited for prescription drugs by the Food and Drug Administration.

[23] The strongest positive opinion may well be that expressed by Stephen Nye when he was a member of the FTC: "As long as the advertiser's claim is true, his comparison may be disparaging, it may be derogatory, it may be downright nasty." "In Defense of Truthful Comparative Advertising," *The Trademark Reporter* (July–August 1977), p. 353. The following article in that issue (pp. 358–406) is not so positive however: Albert Robin and H.B. Barnaby, Jr., "Comparative Advertising: A Skeptical View."

and state statutes as well as a growing body of legal precedents, however, contain various restrictions as well as ambiguities about the conditions under which this practice is legal. Thus, an advertiser may discover that he had committed a common-law tort, violated a state or federal statute, and/or failed to comply with FTC standards. Litigation can be started by either affected competitors or consumers;[24] but the Federal Trade Commission can also act in the public interest, by negotiating consent decrees, issuing cease-and-desist orders, and suing violators in court. FTC orders can be challenged in the courts, but the FTC usually prevails.

Common Law

While tort law varies from state to state, in general an advertiser cannot damage a competitor's personal reputation (that is, "defame" him), nor make deliberate and demonstrably false attacks upon his/her products (that is, "disparage" them).

Clear-cut cases of defamation are rare, so that disparagement is usually the issue. The burden of proof under tort law is heavier, though, because disparagement requires not only that the statement be proved false and that specific damages be proved, but it also must be proved that there was intent to do harm to the plaintiff on the part of the defendant. Still, a preliminary injunction can be obtained if the plaintiff can show that the advertising statement is at least probably untrue.

Not all disparagements are actionable, however—particularly when they amount only to "puffery," even when misleading. United States courts are generally reluctant to make decisions as to which of two products is "better" in any vaguely defined sense, unless the accuracy of the comparison can be readily ascertained. Thus, there is a difference between stating that one's product is better than another and specifically claiming that the latter is only 40 percent as effective as one's own. Also basically immune from prosecution are: (1) exaggerating the merits of one's own products (rather than disparaging competing ones) and (2) disparaging a vaguely defined group of competitors ("Better than all other cars!").

Under tort law, damages may be granted, but not injunctive relief to "cease-and-desist" from the practice—as is possible under unfair-competition legislation.

State Unfair-Competition Laws

Disparagement is usually actionable under this type of *state* legislation, which, however, does not require that special damages be proven but only that certain "unfair" practices have been used.[25] Besides, falsifying the merits of

---

[24] In those unusual cases where he/she feels that his/her rights have been violated, a consumer may sometimes sue under a tort or breach of warranty theory. In practice, it is the task of the FTC to represent the public interest. Rosden and Rosden, *op. cit.,* 31/16.

[25] Still, it is necessary in order to maintain an action for unfair competition that the plaintiff allege and prove that the publication complained of is false, untrue, dishonest, misleading, intended to deceive, or that it contains misrepresentation, dishonest or deceptive statements of fact.

one's own products (rather than those of the competition) also constitutes an unfair practice (this is not the case under tort law). Unfortunately, these state laws are not particularly clear and consistent as to what constitutes "unfair" behavior, and they are not well suited to the problems posed by nationwide advertising campaigns.[26]

Deceptive Trade Practices Acts

A Uniform Act, which grants a cause of action in cases of disparagement and in cases where an advertiser misrepresents the quality of his own goods, has been adopted by several states. Anyone likely to be damaged by a deceptive trade practice of another can sue—without any proof of monetary damages, loss of profits, or intent to deceive having to be given. However, these acts, which exist but in a few states, provide only for injunctive relief ("cease-and-desist"), but not for damages.

Trademark Protection

United States jurisprudence gives no right to a trademark owner to exclude others from the use of his trademark unless that use is likely to cause confusion as to the source or sponsorship of the advertiser's goods. The real issue is the scope of protection that should be afforded to the goodwill developed by the trademark owner in his mark. Opinions are divided on this subject, but do not appear to constitute a major deterrent to the use of someone else's mark in comparative advertisements in the United States.

The Lanham Act

Section 43(a) of the 1946 Lanham (federal) Act protects both consumers and persons engaged in commerce against the deceptive and misleading use of trademarks as well as against other forms of unfair competition. It applies particularly to misrepresentations of *one's own* products that amount to some appropriation of a competitor's goodwill, reputation, and the commercial values embodied in his trademarks (e.g., "Taro exactly duplicates Arpège's scent," if

---

[26] In the Spring of 1977, a "system-comparison" advertising campaign (prepared by Kenyon & Eckhardt) was voluntarily withdrawn by the Savings Banks Association of New York State at the urging of New York State's Attorney General, who is empowered to impose injunctions and levy fines against deceptive advertising. The commercial banks had complained that these ads were "totally deceptive in trying to make viewers believe that commercial banks did not care about people when in fact they did large amounts of consumer business." Linda Greenhouse, "Savings Banks Withdraw TV Ads That State Finds Unfair to Rivals," *New York Times* (21 June 1977). A television version went as follows:
  1. 1ST MAN: Why did I go to a savings bank for my home improvement loan?
     Well, commercial banks are mainly for business,
     Savings banks are mainly for people And I'm not a business, I'm a people. (SFX: Choir)
  2. 2ND MAN: I got my college loan at a savings bank
     Because they specialize in people, And me, I'm a people. (SFX: CHOIR)
  3. ANNCR: (VO) Commercial banks are mainly for business,
     Savings banks are for people
  4. WOMAN: Hi, I'm a people. (SFX: CHOIR)
  5. (SFX CHORI): Savings Banks are people banks.

it does not in fact). Both damages and injunctive (cease-and-desist) relief are available, but the former requires proving the damages and the fact that the buying public was actually deceived.[27]

In the past ten years, the Lanham Act has been increasingly used in comparison-advertising litigation, although the criteria and limits of its applicability are still not completely clear. In the 1974 case of Skil vs. Rockwell, the court enumerated five requirements: (1) the defending advertiser made false statements of fact about his own product, (2) his advertisements actually deceived or have the tendency to deceive a substantial segment of their audience, (3) such deception is material, in that it is likely to influence purchasing decision, (4) the defendant caused its falsely advertised goods to enter interstate commerce, and (5) the plaintiff competitor has been or is likely to be injured on account of the above, either by direct diversion of sales from itself to the defendant or by a lessening of the goodwill that its products enjoy with the buying public.

In a more recent case (1977), the makers of Anacin were permanently restrained and enjoined from using any advertisement or other promotional material which contain any representation that, at normal dosages, Anacin or aspirin (made by American Home Products) provides superior analgesia to acetaminophen including Tylenol (made by Johnson & Johnson's McNeil Laboratories), either (1) generally, (2) for conditions associated with inflammation or having inflammatory components, or (3) because Anacin or aspirin reduces inflammation.[28] The court found that in violation of the Lanham Act: (1) false representations had been made for Anacin, (2) there was substantial evidence that consumers had been and would continue to be deceived as to the relative efficacy of the two products,[29] and (3) this deception had injured and would continue to injure Tylenol's reputation among consumers. The court, however, also stated that the Lanham Act applies to disparagements of a competitor's product, thereby renewing the controversy about the exact reach of this law.

The Tylenol vs. Anacin court case is important because it proved that relatively fast (4.5 months) court relief can be obtained under the Lanham Act before an advertising campaign has run its course.[30] Prior to going to court, the makers of Tylenol had complained to the three television networks, to the print

[27] Misrepresentation of the *competitor's* products is actionable as disparagement (see above). Both types of misrepresentation are thus covered. Sterk (*op. cit.,* pp. 380–85) discusses this Act at great length. Actionable representations may be the product of affirmatively misleading statements, of partially correct statements, or of failure to disclose material facts.

[28] American Home Products Corporation (original plaintiff and makers of Anacin) vs. Johnson & Johnson and McNeil Laboratories, Inc. (makers of Tylenol; original defendants, and subsequent counterclaimants). U.S. District Court, Southern District of New York (18 August 1977). See *Advertising Age* issues of 22 and 29 August, 1977, for further comments.

[29] In reaching its decision, the court analyzed at length consumer surveys that supported Johnson & Johnson's contention that Anacin commercials had made a false overall superiority claim— particularly regarding anti-inflammatory action.

[30] Nancy Giges, "Judge Rules for Tylenol; Anacin Ordered to Halt Inflammation Ad Claims," *Advertising Age* (22 August 1977), pp. 1, 62; "Anacin Yanks Ads Knocking Tylenol," *Advertising Age* (29 August 1977), p. 4. In February 1978, J & J filed another suit charging AHP with violating this court order in subsequent ads.

media, to the Proprietary Association, and to the National Advertising Division (NAD) of the Council of Better Business Bureaus, protesting the Anacin ads ("Your Body Knows") on the ground that they were deceptive and misleading. However, only the ABC network had required some modification of the Anacin ads, while NAD was moving too slowly in its investigation of the complaint, according to Tylenol's makers.

The court case was expedited because Johnson & Johnson did not file for damages, and therefore did not have to prove how much it had been hurt by false claims. Injunctive relief under the Lanham Act also appears to be faster than the more cumbersome FTC route. Johnson & Johnson is likely to use this court decision to persuade the media to reject similar claims made by Bufferin and Bayer's Aspirin that they also have anti-inflammatory effects that Tylenol lacks (see the Datril-Tylenol case in Part III for further details about this case).

The Federal Trade Commission Act

1. General Principles

The FTC Act of 1914 declared unfair methods of competition in commerce to be illegal, and the Commission was charged by the 1938 Wheeler-Lea Amendment with the task of regulating advertising to prevent unfair or deceptive acts or practices.

If the FTC finds an advertising practice to be unlawful, it issues an order directing the advertiser to cease and desist from using the advertisement found to be deceptive. Temporary injunctions are available only in the case of foods, drugs, devices, and cosmetics; but the FTC may also order a corrective advertisement to eliminate false impressions. The Commission also renders advisory opinions concerning *proposed* advertisements.

The consideration under which all advertising is evaluated is the advertisement's *capacity* or tendency to deceive: actual deception of the public need not be shown in FTC proceedings. Such a standard makes misleading almost anything less than the complete truth.[31]

In order to be proven truthful, advertisements must be substantiated as to their claims. Since 1971, the FTC has required advertisers to provide it with complete documentation for advertising claims, but such substantiation must have been prepared *before* its use in advertisements. It appears that the burden of proof is now on the advertiser, for the Commission need not introduce evidence to show that the claims are less than completely true. On the other hand, comparisons that can be substantiated are not unfair nor unlawful under the FTC Act.

2. Price and Quality Comparisons

a. The FTC has strictly regulated the use of such expressions as "regular price," "list price," and "comparable value," which are frequently used in making comparative *price* claims.

[31] Tanner, *op. cit.*, pp. 192–93.

b. Unfortunately, it is much more difficult to regulate *non-price* comparisons because the outcome is more likely to depend on the use for which the product is purchased, on the precise needs of the purchaser, and on other subjective factors (e.g., taste) that depend on who does the evaluation. Still, the FTC has been particularly sensitive to comparative health and nutritional value claims.

c. The FTC is as unwilling as the courts to get involved in settling *puffery* disputes revolving around vague claims of superiority. Even when the comparison is fairly specific ("Save one half of the cost!"), there remains the question of what statements can be considered to be deceptive, since patently false claims are rare.

d. A more important problem here is that of the *half truth,* wherein a significant fact or interpretation is left out (e.g., there is a difference, but it is really a minor one). The general tenor of some key court opinions (FTC orders can be appealed) is that while an advertiser does not have to faithfully reproduce every finding made by an independent research body, the basic conclusions of the study must not be misrepresented.

e. More common, however, are the cases in which an advertiser makes a product comparison that—while literally true—tends to *deceive* the consuming public because of factors left out of the comparison (e.g., stating that a slice of one's bread contains fewer calories when this difference rests on its being thinner than those of competing breads—but without mentioning it). Cases of not properly following the competitor's usage instructions, or of using "manipulated" representations (pictures and such) of the competing product, also fall under this heading.

f. A related case is that of television commercials where *special effects* may be used to illustrate a claim. It appears that for a demonstration to be acceptable, it has to be performed without embellishment in the studio.

g. There are also claims that contain no untrue statements but that lead consumers to believe that a *broader and possibly false claim* is being made (e.g., a "fat-free" claim implying that the product is "calorie free").

h. *Immaterial or insignificant differences* can also be considered as misleading when they do not affect product performance (e.g., the fact that a competing razor blade has a rougher edge does not necessarily mean that it gives worse shaves).

i. The FTC seems to be moving in the direction of requiring *"more truth"* in advertisements—possibly all the way to requiring the disclosure of negative or unfavorable information. Until now, such requirements have been limited to health and safety matters (e.g., warnings in cigarette advertisements), but the Commission is considering additional applications as well as requiring performance disclosure requirements in all ads.[32]

[32] C.J. Collier (FTC Chairman), "What's Good about Advertising?" (Speech before the Peoria Advertising and Selling Club, 13 September 1976).

In the official Environmental Protection Agency 1977 Gas Mileage Guide, the

U.S. GOV'T.
REPORTS:

The VW Rabbit has better fuel economy than:

EPA Estimated Fuel Economy (MPG)		City	Highway
American Motors	— Gremlin	18	24
	Hornet	18	23
	Pacer	18	23
Buick	— Skyhawk	19	26
	Skylark	18	25
Cadillac	— Seville	14	19
Chevrolet	— Camaro	17	22
	Monza	21	28
	Nova	18	23
	Vega	21	28
Ford	— Maverick	18	24
	Mustang II	21	29
	Pinto	23	32
	Thunderbird	15	19
Lincoln-Mercury	— Bobcat	23	32
	Comet	18	24
Mazda	— Cosmo	18	26
	RX4	18	26
	808	23	30
Oldsmobile	— Starfire	21	28
Pontiac	— Firebird	17	25
	Ventura	21	29
Toyota	— Celica	22	29
	Corona	22	29
VOLKSWAGEN RABBIT		24	33

No need to list all the cars that are bigger than compacts–the Rabbit beats them all in fuel economy.

EPA estimates with the author's chemprotection. Actual mileage may vary depending on speed and where you drive, your car's condition and optional equipment.

The VW Rabbit has more trunk space than:

Interior Volume Index/Trunk		(cu. feet)
American Motors	— Gremlin	9
	Hornet	11
	Pacer	11
Buick	— Opel by Isuzu	9
	Skyhawk	10
	Skylark	14
Cadillac	— Seville	13
Chevrolet	— Camaro	6
	Chevette	9
	Monza	8
	Nova	14
	Vega	10
Datsun	— B-210	12
	F-10	14
Dodge	— Colt	7
Ford	— Maverick	12
	Mustang II	8
	Pinto	8
	Thunderbird	14
Lincoln-Mercury	— Bobcat	9
	Comet	12
Mazda	— Cosmo	10
	RX-4	11
	808	10
Oldsmobile	— Starfire	10
Plymouth	— Arrow	10
Pontiac	— Astre	10
	Firebird	7
	Sunbird	7
	Ventura	14
Subaru	— Subaru	11
Toyota	— Celica	8
	Corolla	10
	Corona	10
VOLKSWAGEN RABBIT		15

The VW Rabbit has more interior space than:

Interior Volume Index: Passenger		(cu. feet)
Buick	— Opel by Isuzu	78
	Skyhawk	79
Chevrolet	— Chevette	76
	Monza	79
Datsun	— B-210	66
	F-10	71
Dodge	— Colt	74
Ford	— Mustang II	72
	Pinto	77
Lincoln-Mercury	— Bobcat	77
Mazda	— Cosmo	73
	RX-4	72
	808	67
Oldsmobile	— Starfire	79
Plymouth	— Arrow	73
Pontiac	— Sunbird	79
Subaru	— Subaru	72
Toyota	— Celica	72
	Corolla	76
VOLKSWAGEN RABBIT		80

Who are we to argue?

Visit your N.Y., N.J., or Conn. authorized Volkswagen dealer and find out why there are over 4½ million Volkswagens on the American road today.

This ad is misleading to the extent that its title implies that all of the data provided in the advertisement come from the U.S. Government. In fact, only the "fuel economy" statistics do.

3. Prospects

The FTC has not yet come up with specific standards for comparison advertising although they have been considered, and a report is expected in 1978. The FTC's inclination appears to be that the same standards of fairness and non-deceptivity should apply to all advertisements so that no special rules need be devised for comparative ones.[33] Hence, their regulation is largely left to the media and to self-regulatory bodies which the FTC is scrutinizing, however, for possible anti-competitive restrictions by some industries.[34]

[33] "FTC Says Guides Near on Ads That Name Names," *Advertising Age* (28 June 1976), pp. 3ff.; and "Comparison Ads Will Get Little FTC Interference," *Advertising Age* (5 July 1976), p. 8.
[34] S.E. Cohen, "Widespread FTC Probe Will Seek Codes That Hinder Comparative Ads," *Advertising Age* (23 February 1976), pp. 1ff; and "FTC Memo Urges Look at Media Practices in Ad Self-Regulation Area," *Advertising Age* (12 April 1976), p. 3.

In the matter of enforcement, the FTC has been criticized for being slow—especially since its decisions can be appealed.[35] On the other hand, it can issue broad cease-and-desist orders that apply to *all* the products of a manufacturer, and/or to the *techniques used by an advertising agency.*[36] Actually, the vast majority of cases are resolved informally, with the advertiser signing a consent decree rather than entering into litigation. In any case, the FTC has fully evaluated only a handful of comparative ads.

Advertising self-regulation has proved to be a useful and effective complement to FTC action in the public interest,[37] and adversely affected companies seem now more willing to go to court to obtain fast injunctive relief—as in the recent Tylenol vs. Anacin case (see above, under the Lanham Act).[38] The threat of court action has also stopped various comparative ads such as the one captioned: "How to improve a bottle of Chivas Regal." Beneath it was shown a hand filling an empty Chivas bottle with Cutty 12 Scotch!

A LAWYER'S ADVICE[39]

When a client brings a lawyer an advertisement for so-called "legal clearance," the lawyer proceeds to ask his client whether each statement in the advertisement and the general impression of the advertisement are true, not misleading nor deceptive.

It is not easy, notwithstanding the views of consumer advocates, to answer those questions—particularly when the criterion which one must use may be the credulous man, and when the onerous burden of strict liability is imposed in this area of the law. Such difficulties are compounded in comparison advertising.

In advertising your own products, you have a relatively detailed knowledge of them. You also usually possess the enormous benefit of experience gained over years of producing, selling, and servicing your own

[35] The FTC works through cease-and-desist orders against advertisers and/or agencies. There are penalties for violating such orders but a civil action must be brought to recover the penalty (up to $10,000 per violation). There are no penalties for transgressions committed before the order was issued; and FTC orders can be appealed, thereby delaying enforcement. However, the 1975 Magnuson-Moss Warranty-FTC Improvement Act allows it to automatically apply similar penalties to firms guilty of comparable violations. The FTC can also enter into consent orders.

[36] See, for example: "FTC Accepts Consent Order Citing General Electric," *FTC News* (31 January 1977). GE failed to have adequate substantiation for the claim that its color television sets required less service than RCA and Zenith color TVs. Certain conditions must now be met before GE may cite any evidence as support for its advertising claims for TV sets *and other household products.* Matsushita Electric Corporation of America, and the California and Hawaiian Sugar Company (C & H) were similarly enjoined in 1976.

[37] Tanner (*op. cit.*) provides an excellent discussion of the respective and complementary roles of the FTC and of the National Advertising Review Board. The FTC has also been criticized for not releasing the results of the comparative product tests it sponsors.

[38] Other government bodies such as the Civil Aeronautics Board can also intervene, as when TWA was ordered to stop running an ad (using CAB data in a midsleading manner) claiming that its flights were more often "on time" than those of United Airlines and American Airlines.

[39] Based on a paper by K.W. McCracken, Legal Counsel, Association of Canadian Advertisers, Inc. (Address to the ACA, Toronto, 6 May 1975). It is reproduced here with the author's permission. For additional legal advice, see Rosden and Rosden, *op. cit.*

products. Finally, you know the timetable for future changes in your own products or their prices. That knowledge and experience are invaluable in developing supportable claims in advertisements for your own products.

However, when you decide you wish to advertise comparatively, you introduce the variable of your competitor's product. No longer are you likely to be on the relatively firm ground you possessed when you confined your claims to your product. Instead, it is your *competitor* who knows about his product in detail—not you. Once this is recognized, the legal hazards of comparison advertising become clearer.

For example, it is objectionable in law to fail to state a material fact in an advertisement, if that failure deceives or tends to deceive. However, in comparison advertising it is unlikely that a client knows all the "material facts"—whatever that phrase means—about the product being compared. He probably does not have his competitor's test results; he certainly does not know all of his competitor's experiences with the product being compared; and he is probably in the dark about his competitor's timetable for changing his product's characteristics or prices.

He usually knows the advantages and disadvantages of his own products, but I have frequently concluded that, under questioning, he only imagines he knows some aspects of his competitor's product. If a competitor's product or price is changed once the advertisement is running, the advertisement may become untrue after the fact. In a nutshell, the advertiser is preparing an advertisement in a difficult legal area, while possessing relatively incomplete knowledge and information.

I want to point out one additional problem in this area. An advertiser may suffer from the "normal" psychological phenomenon of downplaying the favorable aspects of competitive products while exaggerating those of his own. In this regard I am not talking about a deliberate conscious attempt to downplay or exaggerate. Rather, in my experience, advertisers—naturally and honestly—tend to be "sold" on their own products. It is somewhat like a normal parent's attitude about his own child. He begat it, he suffered the problems in raising it, and naturally he frequently is proud of the ultimate result. The parent will admit other children have merits, but when pressed, he concedes that his is the best!

From a lawyer's viewpoint, however, this means that in the final analysis, one does not always have a detached client. In such circumstances, deceptive or misleading representations and comparisons are more likely to occur, and failure to state a material fact—especially about a competitor's product—is more probable. But remember that in this area of the law, good faith and an innocent mind are irrelevant, because there is usually strict liability.

What are then the precise legal results which should be achieved in a comparative advertisement?

First, the comparison should be on a factual basis only. Facts can be tested and researched, while impressions, opinions, and feelings cannot be with the same precision.

Second, products compared should compete with each other. If not, deception or misleading of some member of the public may occur.

Third, apples should be compared with apples, not oranges. Compare competitive products that are similar in price and that the consuming public considers to be of the same general quality.

Fourth, do not compare insignificant elements in your product and that of your competitor. It may be tempting to create the impression that because your product is superior in an insignificant respect, it is a superior product. But it may also be illegal.

Fifth, do not imply overall superiority unless that is your message and you are willing to stand behind that general claim on a factual basis.

I would add the suggestion that you have the facts on your competitor's product before you see your lawyer. Otherwise, his response to your desire for a "legal clearance" may simply be to ask a number of questions he needs answered. That will probably delay your progress, and make you somewhat exasperated with your lawyer.

Finally, I suggest that you remember a brutally practical fact. In undertaking a comparative advertisement, you are exposing yourself to the very real likelihood of getting involved in legal proceedings if you are less than perfect. Consumers may not have the interest, the will, or the funds to take you to task should you slip. I suggest that your competitor *will* do so!

A related set of questions is raised in the National Advertising Review Board report on comparison advertising: [40]

SOME QUESTIONS FOR ADVERTISERS WHO ARE CONSIDERING WHETHER TO IDENTIFY COMPETITORS

From a study of the NAD/NARB records and from other experience, certain questions emerge, which an advertiser should ask himself before deciding to identify a competitor.

1. Is the claim of *superiority* in the contemplated comparison provable under circumstances in which the product is generally used?

   Example: If we claim superior traction for our tire, and prove that fact on a dry test track, will the same superiority hold true under other "normal" usage situations (e.g., wet, slippery surfaces)?

2. Have we refrained from claiming or implying *overall superiority* on the basis of a single advantage or a limited group of advantages?

   Example: If we claim superiority for our detergent in the removal of oily grease stains, are we implying *overall* superiority for the product, when there are other equally important areas (e.g., water-borne stains, perspiration stains, safety for colors) in which its performance is not provably superior?

[40] National Advertising Review Board, *Identifying Competitors in Advertising* (New York, 1977).

3. Are we comparing grades within our product line with a truly *comparable grade* of our competitor's?

   Example: If our tire is being advertised as longer wearing than a competitor's, are we comparing our top of the line tire to our competitor's bottom of the line tire?

4. Can the consumer tell what is meant by the *descriptions* in the advertising?

   Example: If we compare the price of our automobile on the basis of specified "extras," do we ignore the fact that our competitor may have other equally desirable, but different, extras included in his price?

5. If we are using a *comparative demonstration,* is it fair in the way it is presented?

   Example: If two polishes are being demonstrated side by side, are they both being applied according to label directions? Are the lighting conditions for both identical in the camera's eye?

6. Does our message avoid *exaggerating* the consumer benefit in the comparison?

   Example: If our diet soft drink has two calories and our competitor's has four, can we say "50 percent fewer calories," and present meaningful, useful information to the consumer?

7. If comparative claims are made on the basis of *testing,* do the test results support all claims made or implied?

   Example: If our pet food is found to contain more protein than our competitor's in laboratory tests, are we reporting this fact only, or are we implying overall nutritional superiority on the basis of the tests?

8. Will the test results be achievable by most people *in actual use* of the product?

   Example: If our product, a floor wax, shows a better shine when demonstrated against a competitor's, is there a special preparatory action that has to be taken before applying our polish, but which is not mentioned in the ad or commercial?

9. In selecting media for comparative advertising, are we allowing *enough time or space* to tell the story adequately? Is there a chance of consumers being misled by getting only part of the message in a thirty-second commercial or a small print ad when more time or space is required to present the comparison properly?

10. In doing comparative advertising, are we truly helping the consumer make a *better informed choice* by presenting comparison facts that are significant, understandable, and useful? Or are we simply knocking the competitor's product without making a genuine claim to superiority in respects that are important to the consumer?

5

Comparison Advertising: Fair or Unfair?

Comparative advertising is not against the law. Nor should it be. But to practice it as we do today makes a mockery of pretensions to culture and refinement and decent corporate behavior.[1]

THIS STATEMENT by A.G. Kershaw, Chairman of Ogilvy & Mather and one prominent U.S. opponent of comparison advertising, reveals that non-legal factors bear on appreciating the appropriateness of this practice.

Feasibility

Is a fair comparative advertisement possible at all? A complete one that truthfully presents all the advantages and disadvantages of a product is in principle possible. However, it is unrealistic to expect it in the case of complex products because advertisements are by nature elliptic in order to obtain and retain attention and persuasion. After all, they are not consumer reports. On the other hand, a comparison *limited to essential attributes* may generate different opinions as to what is essential and regarding the accuracy of the general impression conveyed. A *grossly incomplete* one would, of course, be misleading and unfair.

Some argue that fairness only requires that advertisements contain nothing misleading, that any claim be substantiable, and that the appropriate disclaimers be used (e.g., to indicate that the ad applies only to one type of usage). Others, however, are not convinced that this is enough. This is a real problem, but it is not limited to comparisons, as is well evidenced by the

[1] "For and Against Comparative Advertising," *Advertising Age* (5 July 1976), p. 26.

complaints and suits about all kinds of advertisements—even in countries where direct comparisons are not allowed or used.[2]

Cultural Factors

Laws, codes, and informal rules reflect shared cultural values about what is "fair" in business behavior. Competition, of course, implies expressing and gaining advantages over rivals, but some means have generally been considered as "unfair." Defaming the person of a competitor, unnecessarily disparaging his products or services, or capitalizing on his hard-earned reputation ("My product is as good as his!") have been thought to amount to "dirty pool" in most places and at most times. As Jack Hinton, CBS Director of Broadcast Standards, put it: "No one names his competitor with any good in mind!"

Besides frowning upon the unfair, some cultures reject aggressive behavior. Thus, in such Oriental countries as Japan and South Korea, traditional values discourage direct confrontations, stressing instead decorum in business rivalry as well as gentle moods in advertising. United States advertisers, on the other hand, are more willing to square off with the competition, and to use dramatic means and strong contrasts such as "before and after" and "my products vs. theirs" commercials.[3]

The IAA conferences on comparison advertising that were held in Western Europe in October, 1977, revealed some additional cultural patterns during the presentations and discussions. In *Switzerland,* the reluctance to use direct comparisons (which are legal) reflects the feeling that audiences take advertising claims very seriously so that faulty comparisons are likely to be immediately challenged. However, Swiss businessmen feel that in such a small country they should remain united against their opponents, and therefore avoid fighting each other through comparative advertisements. They are also reluctant to spend the greater resources required by comparisons, what with few companies and agencies having the necessary legal expertise.

In *Italy,* the fear was expressed that, in less sophisticated countries, where the role and limitations of advertising are not well understood, comparisons can more readily lead to excesses. Thus, at least 20 percent of the decisions handled by the Italian self-regulatory body have recently dealt with indirect competitive comparisons (e.g., "ABC is better than all other detergents!").

British practitioners retain a gentlemanly aversion against "knocking copy." They are also opposed to the overuse of facts in advertising, stressing instead the evocation of hopes and pleasant moods: "The world is full of facts

[2] "All advertisements inevitably omit more than they include, and could therefore be said to give a false impression or arouse unsatisfied expectations in somebody, even though they are valid and helpful for the great majority of people." European Association of Advertising Agencies, "Memorandum on the Preliminary Draft Directive Concerning Misleading and Unfair Advertising" (Brussels, 7 October 1977), p. 2 of "Enclosure."

[3] Satoshi Mukai, "Japan–U.S. Contrast in Advertising Expressions," *Dentsu's Japan Marketing Advertising* (January 1977), pp. 54–56. It also appears that Japanese consumers do not recall product-oriented points very much. Hence, advertisers stress moods and nuances rather than facts. J.R. Thomson, "How Coca Cola's Hi-C Scored Success in Japan," *Advertising Age* (29 November 1976), p. 44.

but short of dreams!'' Disaffection with the comparative claims of rival parties and politicians could also spread to advertising: ''They all lie!''

Beyond the cultural differences, it is hard to determine the extent to which these reactions are a function of *novelty*—of the shock received when viewing the first comparative ads that name names. It may be that they will decline as audiences become accustomed to them, as they have with other advertising techniques.

In any case, cultural values often change. Increasingly, the question has been raised: *fair to whom?* Fairness has historically been defined in terms of other business firms, but are ''honest practices'' to refer only to their interests? What about also being ''fair'' to customers and the public at large? Here, the consumerist movement, which is fast spreading in developed countries, has helped refocus the issue. Comparison advertising may be ''dirty pool'' as far as competitors are concerned, but this technique may also give a ''fairer'' shake to consumers.

Even within business, the restrictions—formal and informal—against comparisons may be unfair to the firm that has a definite advantage to tout in a comparative format. And are these restrictions fair vis-à-vis creative people who would like to use their talents in a novel and (hopefully) more effective way, but are prevented from doing so by mandatory laws or voluntary regulations?

Hence, the regulatory trend in a number of countries has been toward providing a better balance between: (1) the traditional interests of businessmen for fair (and somewhat restrained) competition, and (2) the newly recognized rights of consumers and the public at large for more objective information and more active competition.

Recent Danish and Swedish market-practices laws, German court decisions, and Belgian government bills have already translated this trend into greater tolerance of comparison advertising. It has also come to be supported by the Council of Europe, the European Parliament, and the EEC Commission, and reflected in more tolerating advertising codes.[4]

The New ICC Code

A major leader in this respect has been the International Chamber of Commerce (ICC) whose revised (1973) Advertising Code now tolerates comparative advertisements that are done fairly. It has National Committees in nearly fifty countries and is represented in over thirty others; and its codes have been adopted by many organizations and countries, including some thirty advertising associations.[5] It also prides itself on having influenced legislation and court decisions in a number of countries.

---

[4] While this study did not cover company policies, such firms as IBM and Western Electric have formal written guidelines barring the criticism of competitors. Others such as General Motors and General Electric leave it to the judgment of their employees. Deborah Rankin, ''Competitive Zeal: How Far?'' *New York Times* (8 July 1977), p. D10.

[5] International Chamber of Commerce, *International Codes of Marketing Practice*, No. 275 (Paris, 1974). This compendium includes the advertising code last revised in 1973, which has been adopted even in some countries that ban comparisons (e.g., Belgium).

The ICC Advertising Code has been revised several times since its inception in 1937. It has increasingly come to blend its concern about "fair" relationships among competitors with that of safeguarding the legitimate interests of the public as consumers. Its "Basic Principles" also stress that: "All advertising should be legal, decent, honest, and truthful . . . should conform to the principles of fair competition as generally accepted in business . . . [and should not] impair public confidence in advertising" (p. 43).

More specifically, the 1973 ICC Code (pp. 45–46) lists the following "Rules" bearing on comparative advertisements:

Comparisons (Article 5): Advertisements containing comparisons should be so designed that the comparison itself is not likely to mislead, and should comply with the principles of fair competition. Points of comparison should be based on facts which can be substantiated and should not be unfairly selected.

Denigration (Article 7): Advertisements should not denigrate any firm or product directly or by implication, whether by bringing it into contempt or ridicule, or in any other way.

Exploitation of Goodwill (Article 9): (1) Advertisements should not make unjustifiable use of the name or initials of any firm, company or institution. (2) Advertisements should not take unfair advantage of the goodwill attached to the trade name and symbol of another firm or product, or of the goodwill acquired by an advertising campaign.

Responsibility (Article 17): Descriptions, claims or illustrations should be capable of substantiation. Advertisers should be ready to produce evidence without delay to the self-disciplinary bodies responsible for the operation of the Code.

Complaints about advertising are referred to the ICC's International Council on Marketing Practice, which investigates them and tries to have eliminated or modified any advertisement found to be in violation of the Advertising Code.

The 1973 Code represents a definite shift in favor of comparisons. Still, the obligation to "comply with the principles of fair competition" is rather ambiguous since countries differ in terms of what they consider to be "fair" practices; "unjustifiable use" is an elusive concept; and Rule 7 against denigration through contempt, ridicule "or in any other way" also takes away much of the permission to use comparisons that are denigrating by definition.

The ICC, in this respect, mirrors the changing policy of many organizations, governments, and individuals toward *simultaneously* authorizing (and even encouraging) comparison advertising *and* severely restricting its use—possibly to the point of making comparisons very difficult.

Other Private International Organizations

At its 1969 Venice Congress, the *International Association for the Protection of Industrial Property* (AIPPI) voted that: "Comparative advertising containing true statements should be allowed in principle, provided such statements do not needlessly damage a competitor or are unfactual." [6]

The *International League Against Unfair Competition* has also evolved in favor of comparison advertising. It still stresses truth and fairness in advertising, and that "competitors must not be denigrated; and all misplaced references to them should be avoided." However, a 1972 resolution now states that: "Comparisons with the products or services of a competitor are allowed when they are objective, and when they can be justified either by the public's need for information or by the need to defend oneself against forbidden comparisons." [7]

At its 1973 Salzburg conference, the *International Union of Young Lawyers* came out in favor of comparison advertising because it can improve consumer information.

National Self-Regulatory Codes

Voluntary codes of advertising practice exist in a number of countries. [8] They are sponsored by the advertising industry or are limited to some segment such as advertising agencies, advertisers, all or some of the media (print and audio-visual are usually handled separately), and even particular industries (typically, pharmaceuticals).

The major clout of voluntary regulations rests on the media's refusal of comparative advertisements that do not meet their own standards, or those that are being formally investigated and criticized by an advertising-standards board.

The codes' positions vis-à-vis comparison advertising range from very positive (e.g., the British Code of Advertising Practice states that: "Comparisons are permissible in the interest of vigorous competition and public information") to very negative (e.g., in Italy, and in Venezuela where comparisons are said to be "contrary to the principles of truth, morality, and lawfulness"). The Philippine advertising community has recently adopted an indefinite ban against comparative advertisements, following a Pepsi-type "challenge" to the orange drink manufactured by a powerful local firm. Other codes are silent or simply mention that local laws must be obeyed (e.g., in Belgium); but some countries subscribe to the favorable ICC guidelines although local law prohibits comparisons (e.g., Belgium and Austria).

The advertising industry often remains divided between: (1) agencies that favor greater freedom, (2) advertisers, only some of whom care to engage in comparative battles, and (3) the media, which do not welcome the additional

---

[6] Quoted in Janssen, *op. cit.*, p. 494.

[7] Resolution voted on the occasion of the 1972 Geneva Convention of the Ligue Internationale Contre la Concurrence Déloyale (LICCD). The 1978 meeting of the League will discuss this topic further.

[8] A.B. Stridsberg, *Effective Advertising Self-Regulation* (New York: International Advertising Association, 1974). Various examples of national codes are given in: Werner Janssen, Jr., "Some Foreign Law Aspects of Comparative Advertising," *The Trademark Reporter*, Vol. 64 (1974), pp. 454–57.

tasks of screening tricky comparative advertisements and complaints. The threat of government regulation, consumerist pressures, and/or some crisis are thus frequently needed to effect a change in self-regulation.

National codes serve the useful purpose of keeping current the notion of what is "fair" and "unfair" even though they cannot quite escape the elusive nature of these concepts. In countries where the law authorizes comparisons, the codes tend to restrict the use of comparisons since they spell out in greater detail what is legally off limits, some even going beyond what the law prohibits. For example, most voluntary guidelines oppose "disparagement," but assign to the term the broader meaning of "lowering the estimation of something;" while the legal concept may also require the element of falsity and ill-will.

Many national codes not only reflect the influence of the International Chamber of Commerce, but also that of some "pilot" countries. Thus, a pattern is evident in British-Commonwealth countries such as Australia, Hong Kong, and South Africa, which have identical wordings to discourage the use of true comparisons that name names, but which allow "competitive claims inviting comparisons . . . with other products in the same field." It will probably take a major increase in United Kingdom practice before these countries revise their stand and align themselves with their "pilot" country.

Some *industries and media* have their own rules about comparison advertising. Thus, stricter standards usually apply to tobacco and health-related products, with comparisons often banned for pharmaceuticals. The Swiss Advertising Association (SRV) allows comparisons, but the Swiss retailing, chocolate, and car trades urge their members against them; and the TV network and major newspapers do not accept price comparisons. Public television networks tend to be more negative or demanding because of their monopoly position in many countries and of the limited time devoted to commercials. This element is bound to limit the spread of comparison advertising.

In general, *industry codes* are more restrictive than national ones because of the "cartel" attitudes of many trade associations, which tend to dampen aggressive competition. This situation has led the U.S. Federal Trade Commission to wonder why there are not more comparative advertisements, and to investigate restrictions imposed by various industries, the government (e.g., the U.S. Internal Revenue Service prohibits references to calorie contents in beer ads), and the media (for example, is the rate of rejection higher for comparative advertisements, and is that rejection based on arbitrary grounds in fear of antagonizing other advertisers?).[9]

Besides, great pressure is exerted to keep deliberations secret in countries where comparison advertising is considered "unfair" to competitors—with the reverse situation existing in countries where comparisons have been advocated by advertisers and consumerists for being fair and useful. Since the general trend appears to be toward increased disclosure of self-regulatory deliberations

[9] "Widespread FTC Probe Will Seek Codes That Hinder Comparative Ads," *Advertising Age* (23 February 1976), pp. 1ff..

wherever consumerist pressures run high, this reinforces the possibility of using comparative advertising methods.

Regarding *regional associations*, the European Association of Advertising Agencies is in favor of comparison advertising being allowed, but it is not exhorting its members to use it—partly on account of the difficulties connected with its use.[10]

U.S. SELF-REGULATORY GUIDELINES

Due to limited U.S. government regulation, the practice of comparison advertising comes mainly under the purview of self-regulating organizations. The uncertainty and complexity of the issues involved in comparison advertising have been reflected by frequent guideline revisions, modifications, and additions.

The American Association of Advertising Agencies (AAAA)

The first comprehensive statement concerning comparative advertising was introduced in 1962 by the AAAA in its Creative Code, which condemned "comparisons which unfairly disparage a competitive product or service."[11] This code was further expanded and detailed in 1966, by adding tht the AAAA did not believe in "advertising that uses another product's trademark or brand name in an effort to trade on the reputation which the competitive brand had built through advertising and public acceptance."[12] This code confined the application of comparison advertising to cases where the competition had agreed to the use of its name or trademark—an unlikely occurrence.

As a result of FTC pressure and of the subsequent increase in usage by various media, the AAAA provided new 1974 guidelines for comparison advertising, acknowledging that its fair usage provides the consumer with needed and useful information, but urging that "extreme caution should be utilized."[13] (See Figure 1)

The Networks

Until the end of 1971, NBC Television was the only network to accept comparative commercials. At the encouragement of the FTC in 1971–1972, ABC and CBS started to accept them too, but there were no formal guidelines until January 1974, when NBC introduced written ones about comparison advertising:

[10] Interview with Nils Faernert, Secretary General of the EAAA (Brussels, 28 November 1976).

[11] It is well to realize that the *legal* concept of "disparagement" often incorporates the element of falsity, while marketers tend to give it a broader meaning of "lowering the estimation of a product," whether by false or truthful statements.

[12] American Association of Advertising Agencies, "Preserving the Right to Compete While Enhancing Public Confidence in Advertising" (New York, 1967).

[13] American Association of Advertising Agencies, "Policy Statement and Guidelines for Comparative Advertising" (New York, 1974). These revised guidelines deleted the required permission of the named competition. The NARB guidelines are very similar, and are listed below.

FIGURE 1

AMERICAN ASSOCIATION OF ADVERTISING AGENCIES

POLICY STATEMENT AND
GUIDELINES FOR COMPARATIVE ADVERTISING
(APRIL 1974)

The Board of Directors of the American Association of Advertising Agencies recognizes that when used truthfully and fairly, comparative advertising provides the consumer with needed and useful information.

However, extreme caution should be exercised. The use of comparative advertising, by its very nature, can distort facts and, by implication, convey to the consumer information that misrepresents the truth.

Therefore, the Board believes that comparative advertising should follow certain guidelines:

1. The intent and connotation of the ad should be to inform and never to discredit or unfairly attack competitors, competing products or services.
2. When a competitive product is named, it should be one that exists in the marketplace as significant competition.
3. The competition should be fairly and properly identified but never in a manner or tone of voice that degrades the competitive product or service.
4. The advertising should compare related or similar properties or ingredients of the product, dimension to dimension, feature to feature.
5. The identification should be for honest comparison purposes and not simply to upgrade by association.
6. If a competitive test is conducted, it should be done by an objective testing source, preferably an independent one, so that there will be no doubt as to the veracity of the test.
7. In all cases, the test should be supportive of all claims made in the advertising that are based on the test.
8. The advertising should never use partial results or stress insignificant differences to cause the consumer to draw an improper conclusion.
9. The property being compared should be significant in terms of value or usefulness of the product to the consumer.
10. Comparatives delivered through the use of testimonials should not imply that the testimonial is more than one individual's thought unless that individual represents a sample of the majority viewpoint.

1. Products identified in the advertising must actually be in competition with one another.
2. Competitors shall be fairly and properly identified.
3. Advertisers shall refrain from discrediting, disparaging, or unfair attacks.
4. The identification must be for comparison purposes and not simply to upgrade by association.
5. Advertising should compare related or similar properties or ingredients of the product, dimension to dimension, feature to feature, wherever possible by a side-by-side demonstration.
6. The property being compared must be significant in terms of value or usefulness of the product to the consumer.
7. The difference in properties must be measurable and significant.[14]

Subsequent ABC "Principles for Comparative Advertising" included most of the above points but went beyond them by emphasizing the accuracy and scientific nature of the product-test procedures. They also specified that the "net impression" made by the commercial should not be misleading, deceptive, vague, equivocal or disparaging—a reflection of the controversy over the testing used by Schick in creating its electric-razor advertisements.[15]

Following the Datril-Tylenol comparative-price battle (see case in Part III), NBC further widened its rules in 1975 by restricting the usage of price-differential and market-position claims (such as sales position Number 1) exclusively to those areas and time periods where and when the claim is valid.[16] ABC Guidelines soon followed:

> Because retail price is subject to constant change as well as fluctuation from outlet to outlet, comparisons of retail prices shall not be utilized in comparative advertising unless:
>
> (1) The compared prices accurately, fairly, and substantially reflect the actual prices of the products at the retail level during the period the commercial is broadcast and within the entire geographical area in which the advertising is broadcast; and
>
> (2) The copy discloses that the consumer should expect some variation from outlet to outlet.[17]

The National Association of Broadcasters (NAB)

The 1974–1975 revisions of the NAB Codes (one each for television and radio), which has been adopted by most of the independent television and radio

[14] Maurine Christopher, "NBC Spells Out New Formal Guides for Comparative Spots," *Advertising Age* (28 January 1974), p. 1; and National Broadcasting Company, Department of Broadcast Standards, *Comparative Advertising Guidelines* (New York, revised as of 2 September 1975).

[15] Maurine Christopher, "ABC Comparative Rules Stress Test Procedures," *Advertising Age* (18 March 1974), p. 1; and American Broadcasting Company, Department of Broadcast Standards and Practices, *Principles for Comparative Advertising* (New York, 18 March 1974).

[16] "NBC Widens Comparative Price Ad Rules," *Advertising Age* (1 September 1975), p. 1.

[17] "ABC Price Comparison Guides Out; NBC Formulates Similar Procedures," *Advertising Age* (25 August 1975), p. 2.

stations, include special provisions for the regulation of comparison advertising by stating that: ''Any identification or comparison of a competitive product or service, by name, or other means, should be confined to specific facts rather than generalized statements or conclusions, unless such statements or conclusions are not derogatory in nature.''[18] These guidelines deal in detail with claim substantiation, and with the use of comparative tests and of claims based on consumer or professional preferences or on sales data. They also stress that such advertising must deal with aspects that are significant and meaningful to the overall performance of the product. (CBS follows these guidelines rather than developing its own.)

Print Media

The American Newspaper Publishers Association, The Newspaper Advertising Bureau, and the Magazine Publishers Association have not issued guidelines about comparison advertising. Periodicals have, of course, had a hard time justifying the rejection of comparative ads in view of their frequent use of media comparisons.

The Proprietary Association

Its Code of Advertising Practices was amended in April 1976 to accommodate comparison advertising of proprietary medicines, in view of the fact that specific mention of competitors' products is common in this industry. Clause 18 states that: ''Comparisons with competing products, if used, should be based on differences which are perceptible to the consumer in actual use or which can be supported scientifically.''

THE U.S. SELF-REGULATORY SYSTEM IN ACTION

This system plays a major role in case of disputes about comparative advertisements.

The National Advertising Review Board (NARB)

This advertising self-regulatory body was established in 1971, mainly as a reaction to increasing consumer complaints against advertising during the late 1960s. It provides the industry with guidelines and standards for fair advertising as an alternative to government regulation, and it attempts to settle disputes among advertisers before recourse is taken to the legal route.

As the investigating arm of NARB, the National Advertising Division (NAD) of the Council of Better Business Bureaus[19] was also set up in 1971,

---

[18] National Association of Broadcasters, *Radio Code* (Washington, D.C., January 1974). See also ''Review Board Sets Guides on Comparisons,'' *Advertising Age* (7 October 1974), p. 8.

[19] Until 1973, the Council of Better Business Bureaus had definitely opposed ''knocking copy.'' It then stated that: ''Truthful comparisons with factual information are helpful to making informed buying decisions [but] advertising which improperly or falsely disparages either a competitor or his products should not be used.'' W.H. Tankersley, President of the CBBB, has recently

and it has been handling claims since then (NARB acts as the appeal board for complaints that cannot be settled within NAB). NAD maintains and operates a sophisticated videotape recording system that takes commercials off the air for later review by the staff. Print advertising in newspapers and magazines is also continuously monitored.

The NARB has addressed itself to the issue of comparison advertising through cases adjudicated in conjunction with NAD. Thus, in 1975, NARB served notice that the use of comparative advertising can impose an added burden of substantiation on its practitioners in cases where multiple attributes and characteristics are significant to the consumer: "It is insufficient to establish proof of one characteristic in such a way that the consumer can be led to conclude overall superiority" (first Behold case). In a 1977 decision about Planters peanut butter, NAD concluded that to say a brand is "better than the leading peanut butter," it must have superiority in virtually all the product's qualities—not just in the taste and spreadability advantages detected by tests. Besides substantiation, NAD is more generally concerned with truth and accuracy in such matters as misleading language and data, inaccurate comparison, and improper use of illustrative materials (see caselets below).[20]

Two special consultative panels were appointed by the NARB to address the issue of comparison advertising. The first one in 1975–1976 was essentially unfavorable, and its report was not accepted by the NARB's Steering Committee for fear of running afoul of FTC strictures against professional bans against comparison advertising.

The second panel issued a report in mid-1977 to clarify the chief issues and to present information and guidance.[21] After tracing the factors and controversies that have accompanied the growth of comparisons, the 1977 report stated that: "It is not possible to find a solid, objective base for concluding that comparative advertising since 1972 [date of the FTC support] has done more good than harm or more harm than good." This neutral statement really represents a mild expression of support for comparisons.

For that matter, this report does not present formal guidelines. Instead, it quotes the substance of various NAD/NARB case decisions, reprints major codes (AAAA, NAB, ABC, NBC), and raises "some questions for advertisers" in the way of providing guidance. This attitude reflects recent FTC warnings against trade, industry, and professional associations restricting competitive practices (see above).

---

taken a strong position against comparison advertising. He claimed that it has not produced the hoped-for consumer benefits, but has damaged the credibility of advertising and "the mores of civilized business behavior." "Comparative Ads Graded 'F' by CBBB President," *Advertising Age* (17 October 1977), p. 1.

[20] In a non-comparative case, NAD objected to a Cracker Jack ad stressing that it is "all natural ingredients [with no] stabilizers and preservatives." NAD's principal concern was that it might imply to consumers that all stabilizers and preservatives are, by their very nature, undesirable. The advertiser, while disagreeing with this interpretation, agreed, in a spirit of cooperation, to discontinue the ad in question.

[21] National Advertising Review Board, *Identifying Competitors in Advertising: A Report on Comparative Advertising* (New York, July 1977).

Grievance Procedures

When the manufacturer of a compared competitive product elects to challenge a television advertisement, he can do one of two things:

a. Present his challenge and supporting data to the media, with the challenged advertiser having then the opportunity to respond directly to the challenger.

   For example, according to NBC's Comparative Advertising Procedure, in cases "where NBC personnel do not have the expertise to make a judgment on technical issues raised by a challenge, NBC will take whatever steps are necessary to assist the advertiser and challenger to resolve their differences on their own, including cooperating with them in obtaining a determination from an agency which is better equipped to make the necessary judgments." [22]

   At the time of the challenge by the named competitor, NBC does not withdraw the advertising from broadcasting unless: (1) it is directed to do so by the advertiser; (2) the advertiser refuses to submit the controversy to a review agency; (3) a decision is rendered by such reviewing agency against the advertiser; and/or (4) the challenged advertiser, when requested, refuses to cooperate in some other substantial area.

b. The alternative approach which a challenged company can take—and this same avenue is open to any organization, consumer group, or individual—is to file a complaint with the NAD. The step-by-step procedure of NAD is outlined in the flowchart prepared by NARB (Figure 2).

Rules of the self-regulatory system do not allow it to adjudicate conflicts involving the private interests of advertisers claiming to have been wrongfully damaged by the competition. Instead, NAD/NARB decisions only deal with questions of truth and accuracy, while other matters must be settled through negotiation or litigation between the parties.

It is interesting to observe that while the FTC had accepted that Schick's absolute claim of closer shaving capability had been adequately substantiated, the NARB—following its self-initiated investigation of the Schick print and television advertisements originally accepted by the networks—concluded that they were "false in some details and misleading overall."

As Tanner points out, this landmark decision provides a stricter interpretation of the FTC advertising standards, and has created new standards for reporting test data in comparison-advertising cases. Besides, the NARB released information about this case instead of keeping the identity of voluntary compliers from public attention. Finally, by initiating this investigation, the NARB proved that advertising abuses will be self-regulated; while Schick's acceptance of the Board's recommendation reveals a growing acceptance of this concept by the advertising industry. [23]

[22] NBC, *Comparative Advertising Procedure* (1 February 1975); and "NBC Sets Guidelines for Comparative Ad Plaints," *Advertising Age* (7 October 1974), p. 8.
[23] Tanner, *op. cit.*, pp. 186–87 and 208–9.

FIGURE 2

ADVERTISING SELF-REGULATORY PROCEDURES,
STEP BY STEP

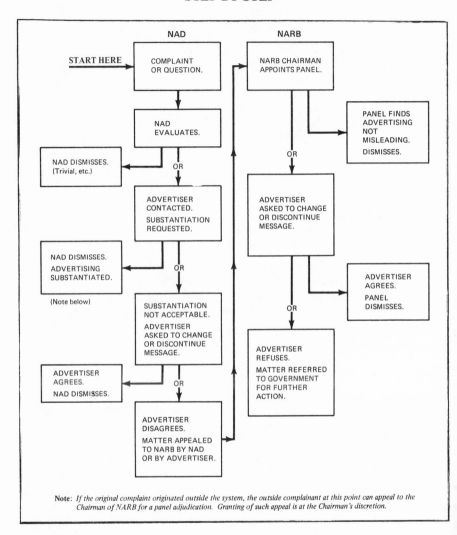

Note: *If the original complaint originated outside the system, the outside complainant at this point can appeal to the Chairman of NARB for a panel adjudication. Granting of such appeal is at the Chairman's discretion.*

Complaints

An indication of the fairness problems connected with comparison advertising and magnified by its increased volume is provided by the number of complaints addressed by the challenged competitors to the regulatory agencies and to the media.

In the case of NAD/NARB, Ronald Campbell, NAD's Senior Vice President, mentioned that over its first five years of existence (1971–1976), the proportion of complaints involving comparisons (*broadly defined, and thus including ads that do not explicitly "name names"*) jumped to 38 percent. A further area of concern expressed by Campbell was the dramatic increase of complaints filed by competitors (rather than by consumers) from the 8 percent level in 1971 to 27 percent in 1975, 25 percent in 1976, and 18 percent in January–May 1977. He gave as the major reason for this high rate of complaints that even if the advertiser does have an adequate substantiation for *his* brand, he generally falls short of providing proper substantiation for the *competitor's* brand.[24]

The 1977 NARB special report on comparison advertising provides a somewhat different picture:

> In 1976, 25% of the advertisements (broadcast and print) reviewed by the self-regulatory mechanism [NAD/NARB] actually identified competitors. Four years earlier, the total was only 11%. The majority of complaints concerning comparative advertisements . . . were those submitted by companies whose products had been identified by competitors. A smaller number came from consumers. Actually, the reasons for complaints differed little from those in non-comparative advertising.

The following NAD/NARB caselets reveal major disputed matters of truth and accuracy:[25]

Case #1. A television commercial for a toilet bowl cleaner claimed that it "disinfects and deodorizes better" than a named competitive toilet bowl cleaner. A probe of the substantiation proved the advertiser's superiority was actually limited only to deodorizing.

The NAD ruled that juxtaposing the words "disinfects and deodorizes" caused the consumer to believe that the advertiser's product was superior in *both* attributes—a case of *misleading language*.

Case #3. A credit card claimed that it was honored in more stores and restaurants than a well-known competitive credit card.

The NAD investigation showed that the advertiser compared its recently updated directory versus an outdated directory for its competitor. If equally current data had been used for both, the competitor's credit card would have demonstrated substantially more listings. This was ruled an *inaccurate comparison*.

[24] "Comparative Ads on Upswing, so Are Complaints," *Broadcasting* (10 May 1976), p. 27. Mr. Campbell's statistics (including updates) apply to all sorts of competitive ads, not just those that explicitly name a competitor (letter to the authors from Kathleen S. McGowan, Advertising Review Specialist, National Advertising Division, Council of Better Business Bureaus, 6 July 1977). Norman Gottlieb, President of the Council of Better Business Bureaus claimed that [the plethora of comparative ads] has so loaded our advertising division's complaint log that the NAD/NARB mechanism last year [1976] almost reached the breaking point." "Comparative Ads Graded 'F' by CBBB President," *op. cit.*, p. 1.

[25] NARB, *Identifying Competitors in Advertising, op. cit.*

Case #4. A television commercial for a furniture polish demonstrated its superiority in removing a waxy grease mark as compared to a competitive product.

The NAD probe showed that removal of waxy grease marks is but one of many attributes consumers expect from furniture polish—and that the competitive brand was superior in other desired benefits. (For example, the competitor's product was more effective in removing water-based stains.) The NAD ruled that the consumer was misled to believe *implied overall superiority based upon a single attribute.* This case was later adjudicated by NARB, which substantiated NAD's decision.

Case #5. A tire company advertisement compared tread wear versus a competitor's tire, showing clear-cut superiority.

The NAD review revealed that the advertiser was comparing its *bias belted* tire versus competitor's *bias ply* tire—an assured win for the advertiser. NAD ruled that this comparison could mislead consumers by *comparing dissimilar components and features.*

Case #6. An advertiser's housepaint headlines said, "Sorry, competitive paints A, B, C and D . . . advertiser wins!"

The NAD investigation revealed that the advertiser had ranked first in only one of the five separate tests of housepaint performance. The advertiser's "win" was a composite score of the five attributes surveyed—based on an averaging technique. The NAD ruled that the *statistical data were set forth in a misleading manner.*

Case #7. A drain cleaner claimed overall superiority versus a competitive drain cleaner because it contained a special ingredient which dissolved hair.

The NAD probe confirmed that the advertised product actually did dissolve hair better than the competitor's, but discounted the drain cleaning demonstration used because the clog was not representative of typical problems encountered in the home. The consumer might be misled because the *product was demonstrated in an uncommon usage situation.*

Case #8. A print advertisement for a little-known pantyhose claimed a lower price than a well-known pantyhose. The ad featured one picture—the well-known pantyhose.

Consumer perception research confirmed that some consumers believed that the ad was featuring the well-known pantyhose at an especially low price. The NAD ruled that the consumer might be misled by *improper use of illustrative material.*

Case #9. A print ad for a compact automobile claimed the advertised car "goes farther on a tank of gas than any other car." Advertising included a chart comparing the featured model to two other leading competitors on various characteristics, including price, engine size, EPA miles-per-gallon rating, and gas tank size.

NAD found that the advertising claim was based, not on superior gas mileage, but on the advertised car's larger tank size. Since the comparative statistics were not as prominent as the headline, NAD ruled that the *advertising comparison was misleading* in that consumers could be led readily to believe that the advertised automobile averaged more miles per gallon.

Case #10. A leading domestic car manufacturer, in print advertising, compared one of its compacts with a leading import on the basis of extra equipment and price. The headline said, "How come that $3330 (car) costs most people $4100? They've got you by the extras!" The advertising listed six items which come as standard equipment on the advertised car, but not on the import. However, the advertiser ignored listing "extras" included at no additional charge on the import that were not included in the advertised price of the domestic cars.

Without listing such complete information, it was NAD's opinion that the *advertising comparison was misleading* and the consumer was at a disadvantage in making a judgment between the two automobiles.

In the following seven cases the advertising was deemed *proper:*

Case #12. A pain reliever claimed superiority over a competitive product because it also reduced temporary water-weight gain often associated with a woman's menstrual cycle.

The NAD probe revealed that the advertiser's product did contain a special ingredient not found in the competitive product, which demonstrably reduced excess water retention. The NAD ruled that the advertiser's claim was *properly substantiated.*

Case #13. A paper towel claimed superior wet-strength versus a competitive paper towel—demonstrating its ability to support the weight of a full coffee cup even while wet. The competitive paper towel fell apart under the same stress.

The NAD investigation showed that the advertiser had pre-tested its wet tensile strengths under a variety of circumstances, and had subsequently conducted its coffee cup demonstration under conditions most unfavorable to itself, where its paper towel would be weakest. The NAD ruled that the advertising was *properly substantiated.*

Case #14. A television commercial for a mouthwash claimed that it kept breath fresh twice as long as a competitive mouthwash.

The NAD probe showed that the advertiser had established a reasonable criterion for measuring breath freshness, and had tested a representative and sufficiently large group of people. Test results showed that, on an average, the advertiser's product kept breath fresh for 105 minutes, while the competitive product's effect lasted an average of 45 minutes. The NAD ruled that the twice-as-long claim was *properly substantiated.*

Case #15. A television commercial for a refrigerator emphasized an energy-conservation theme, claiming that the refrigerator used ⅓ less electricity than well-known competitive products.

The NAD investigation revealed that the advertiser's refrigerator was a more efficient unit than the three comparable competitive models mentioned and did, on average, consume ⅓ less electricity in normal usage situations. The NAD ruled that the advertiser's claim was *properly substantiated.*

Case #16. A coffee creamer compared its cost-per-use versus a competitor's coffee creamer, claiming that dollar for dollar, the consumer would get enough of the advertiser's coffee creamer for twenty-five extra cups of coffee.

The NAD probe compared average retail prices, quantities, and usage instructions for both products. Under normal usage situations, the advertised product did, in fact, provide enough creamer to represent twenty-five more uses for the same total cost to the consumer. The NAD ruled that advertiser's claim was *properly substantiated.*

Case #17. Advertising for a hair spray claimed it dried "cleaner" than a competitive spray, and demonstrated its superiority on a bathroom mirror. The competitive spray left a visible film, while the advertised product did not.

The NAD probe revealed that the advertiser had substantiated the claim of superior clarity by using scientifically accepted measurement techniques. Further, the mirror demonstration was an appropriate way to illustrate greater clarity. The NAD ruled that the claim was *properly substantiated.*

Case #18. Television advertising for a snack pack pudding claimed that, compared to a named competitor, it is "creamier, more chocolatey and better-tasting." Superimposed on the screen was the statement: "Based on consumer testing."

The advertiser submitted research results of blind, paired comparison, home-use tests that had been supervised by an independent testing lab. Testing was conducted in a large number of households in which any canned, single-serving pudding had been served during the previous four-week period, and in which at least one child (age 6–12) was living.

Tests measured consumer preferences specifically in regard to the three characteristics mentioned in the advertising claim. Results indicated that consumers preferred the advertised brand over the named competitor at a 99 percent confidence level. On the basis of these data, NAD found the advertising to be *substantiated.*[26]

Commenting on these caselets, the special 1977 NARB report made an important point:

> Departures from truth and accuracy do occur in non-comparative advertising, but in every one of the [above cases] *the violation arises out of the comparison rather than out of the advertiser's statement about his own product standing alone. . . .* The record supports the old assumption that comparative advertising poses unuual threats to truth and accuracy. On the other hand, the record is equally clear that [it] *need not be false or misleading.* Many comparative ads are not challenged. Of those that are . . . a substantial number are able to substantiate the comparison made.

Comparison advertising is thus a mixed bag, but the NARB panel believes that codes and guidelines can help advertisers avoid abuses, and that they represent a commonsense approach toward the maintenance of high standards in advertising. In conclusion, they end up supporting it:

> Advertisers must not be inhibited, by codes or otherwise, from competing in any legitimate and honest way. Truthful and significant differences in competitive products should be made known to the public; and comparative advertising is a proper technique to accomplish this purpose. However, improper comparative advertising, which misleads or deceives, is not acceptable even though offered under the umbrella of "free competition."

As for the media, Jack Hinton, Vice President of CBS Television Network's Commercial Clearance Department, said that in 1975 they reviewed 490 comparative commercials, of which 252 were approved, and 238 rejected or pending.[27] Another CBS count gave a 45.5 percent rejection rate for compara-

[26] *News from NAD* regularly releases information about cases that come before it and are resolved—with advertisers either withdrawing the contested ad or providing adequate substantiation for their claims. The fact that the advertising has been modified or discontinued is not taken as an admission of impropriety on any advertiser's part. In some cases, advertisers have voluntarily changed or discontinued advertising in cooperation with NAD's self-regulatory efforts. In others, advertisers have discontinued challenged advertising for their own reasons, and have agreed not to run it again without consulting NAD or furnishing appropriate substantiation, if not previously supplied.

[27] Cited in Tannenbaum, "Comparative Advertising," *op. cit.,* p. 12.

tive advertisements at first submission in 1976, although less than 1 percent of all ads were of that type.[28]

ABC Television's Standards and Practices Department has stated that "the rejection rate for comparative advertising is noticeably higher than for other spot commercials." Mr. Schneider, Vice President of ABC, expressed his concern by saying: "The area is giving great consideration to all networks and the NAB Code Authority, as complaints and challenges mount from those companies mentioned adversely in the rival's ad."[29] NBC's Standards Department also pointed to the "more work, more research, greater vigilance, and more negotiations needed to process comparison commercials"—both before and after airing them.

Regulatory and Self-Regulatory Shortcomings

According to some opponents of comparison advertising, the existing regulatory system can be criticized on two major points. First, *comparative ads do not follow the established guidelines.* Thus, Kershaw has stated that: "I have amused myself by examining them to see if the cases of comparative advertising I know about comply with our rules. Well, they don't. At least, I could not find any single one."[30] This statement is somewhat extreme in the light of the 1977 NARB conclusions quoted above.

Thus, there are demands for more stringent and specific regulations by the NARB to define, by example, the meaning of "disparagement," "fairness," and "substantial benefit to the consumer," and to assist the media in the judgmental area of comparative advertising. However, the 1977 NARB report does not move in that direction even though NAD/NARB case decisions are progressively clarifying what does and does not constitute "truth and accuracy."

The second and more immediate problem is that *there is no adequate, speedy process for the examination of complaints, and no adequate speedy retribution for offenders.* The extreme slowness of the retribution process is demonstrated by the sixteen-month dispute of Behold furniture polish versus S.C. Johnson & Sons' Lemon Pledge, and the lengthy Pepsi/Coke controversy about the use of consumer taste–tests of competing brands. Besides, while the final decision of the reviewing board is pending, the commercial continues to be broadcast, and this can result in substantial loss for the challenged competitor, in reduced advertising credibility, and in consumer misinformation. This situation led McNeil Laboratories (Tylenol) to challenge American Home Products (Anacin) in court and obtain a speedy cease-and-desist injunction rather than resort to the lengthier NARB process.

Additionally, self-regulatory bodies cannot subpoena substantiation data;

[28] Letter from Ron Manders, Manager of Administration Commercial Clearance (New York, 11 January 1977).

[29] "ABC Censor Raps Trend to Naming Rivals in Ads," *Advertising Age* (31 March 1975), p. 62. However, on page 10 of his "Comparative Advertising" (*op. cit.*), Tannenbaum quotes ABC-TV staffers as saying that the amount of *viewer* complaints is negligible.

[30] "Comparative Ads in Center Ring at AAAA Meeting," *Broadcasting* (17 May 1976), pp. 32–40.

and there are problems connected with conflicting methodologies used in substantiating claims, but these are not proper to comparison advertising.

Self-Discipline

According to some advertising practitioners, most problems associated with comparison advertising can only be solved by the use of self-control and self-discipline resting on higher ethical standards by the agencies and their clients *before* the advertisement is released.

In the case of advertising agencies, the desire to avoid broad FTC restrictions (through a cease-and-desist order) on the use of a certain deceptive practice or even fines for violating such orders may cause them to exert a moderating and restraining influence on overzealous clients.[31] Similarly, advertisers may be cautious in order to avoid FTC orders that broadly restrict their advertising practices (see the General Electric and Matsushita cases cited in the legal chapter, for examples of such FTC orders).

CONCLUSION

"Fairness" is an elusive concept that comparison advertising is putting to the test anew. It is being increasingly urged and accepted that ads must also be fair to consumers—not just to competitors—by providing them with meaningful information, whether in a comparative format or not.

The movement toward considering truthful comparisons as fair has benefited from the tolerance granted to this practice by various international organizations such as the ICC. Some national self-regulatory codes are following suit, although cultural differences about what is fair are bound to continue restricting the use of comparisons in various countries.

Still, comparisons are putting an additional burden on the screening and self-regulatory processes because they are more likely to be challenged. The fact that their record is as good as that of non-comparative ads as far as substantiation is concerned suggests, however, that they are neither less fair nor more unfair than the other kind.

---

[31] For an interesting discussion of agency liabilities, see: Leonard Orkin, "Lawsuits Arising out of Comparative Advertising: Can the Agency Protect Itself?" (Paper presented at the AAAA Eastern Annual Conference, New York, 29 November 1977).

6

Comparison Advertising: Beneficial or Not?

OTHER QUESTIONS about comparison advertising center around: (1) its real usefulness to consumers, particularly as far as information for decision-making is concerned; (2) its impact on competitive behavior; and (3) its effects on the image of advertising and business. A fourth dimension, that of its effectiveness as an advertising and marketing tool, is discussed in the next chapter. These divided views are found in all of the nations surveyed, even though too few "hard facts" are available on this score.

CONSUMERISM

President Kennedy contributed to the framework for the modern consumerist movement by defining the rights of consumers to safety, information, choice, voice, and redress.[1] Thus, consumer information has been one of the major concerns of consumerism since its inception, and these "rights" have been subscribed to by many nations and international organizations (e.g., the European Parliament).

Yet, due to product proliferation and complexity, consumers perceive an information gap between the available information and the amount and quality needed for good decision-making.[2] While commercial sources provide the bulk of product information, there is evidence that consumers are skeptical about

[1] Executive Office of the President, *Consumer Advisory Council: First Report* (Washington, D.C.: U.S. Government Printing Office, October 1963).
[2] Hans Thorelli, "Testing, Labeling, Certifying: A Perspective on Consumer Information," in D.A. Aaker and G.S. Day (eds.), *Consumerism* (New York: The Free Press, 1974), p. 12.

their usefulness and credibility. Thus, in a 1972 study, about 45 percent of U.S. respondents considered that "most advertising today tries to deceive people rather than inform them," and 70 percent stated that the U.S. government should provide product information because producers and distributors do not give all the essential information.[3] These data have been recently corroborated by the 1976 Sentry Insurance survey, with 46 percent of the respondents thinking that most or all of television advertising is misleading, and 28 percent holding similar views about the print media.[4]

A 1976 EEC survey revealed similar consumer attitudes towards information and advertising within the nine member countries.[5]

1. Only about one consumer in two considers himself/herself well informed—43 percent for big-ticket items, and 51 percent for common food purchases. Insufficient information is particularly a problem among younger consumers.
2. Only half of the public thinks that advertising contributes useful information to consumers. Younger, better heeled, and more educated people feel more negative on this point.
3. Eight out of ten respondents favor the creation or development of special television programs (on government-owned networks, except in Luxembourg and the United Kingdom) to provide objective information to consumers. (Newspapers are thought to be more reluctant to do so for fear of upsetting advertisers).
4. Except in the United Kingdom, the public is rather poorly informed about the existence of specialized publications aimed at consumer information; but respondents with more education and larger incomes are ahead on this score.
5. Comparative tests by independent organizations are better known than consumer associations—particularly in West Germany, the Netherlands, an Denmark. The great majority of people who had heard of such tests trusted the results—particularly among the better educated people and those with higher incomes; and slightly more than half of test-aware respondents said that their buying habits had been changed thereby.
6. Eight people in ten expressed a desire for wide or wider publication of the results of product comparison tests by the government, or for the es-

[3] Daniel Starch and Staff, Inc., *Current Opinion* (1 February 1973), pp. 8–9. For similar pessimistic data, see: Rena Bartos, "The Consumer View of Advertising" (New York: J. Walter Thompson, 1974); and Rena Bartos and Th. F. Dunn, *Advertising and Consumers* (New York: American Association of Advertising Agencies, 1975).

[4] Sentry Insurance, *Consumerism at the Crossroads* (Stevens Point, Wisc., 1977).

[5] Commission of the European Communities, *European Consumers* (Brussels: Document X/309/76–E, May 1976). For related data, see: S.W. Dunn and D.A. Yorke, "European Executives Look at Advertising," *Columbia Journal of World Business* (Winter 1974), pp. 54–60. Fairly similar proportions were found in British surveys, revealing also that disapproval of advertising is spreading (*Gallup Political Index* in 1973 and 1975). For a more general analysis, see: Françoise Civeyrel, "Advertising on Probation," *Vision* (December 1973), pp. 59–62; and S.W. Dunn "The Changing Legal Climate for Marketing and Advertising in Europe," *Columbia Journal of World Business* (Summer 1974), pp. 91–98.

tablishment of easily accessible centers where consumers could receive guidance and report complaints.[6]

Consequently, governments have recently enacted new legislations to improve the quantity and quality of the information available to consumers in a potentially comparative manner. In the United States, for example, the Fair Packaging and Labeling Act (since July 1967) requires that labels show the net quantity of content, and it prohibits misleading packages, thus facilitating price comparison by the consumer. To further assist consumer comparison across products, unit pricing was first introduced in 1970 in Massachusetts—an example followed by other states, and in 1973 by federal legislation. Similar developments are apparent in other countries.

In this context, the central question becomes: "Does comparison advertising contribute to consumer information and decision-making?"[7]

Arguments in Favor

Comparisons represent an inherent and inevitable part of the decision-making process of buyers—particularly at the evaluation stage. It can indeed be argued that consumers become informed *only* through the process of comparisons—either directly through personal experience in shopping and using products, or indirectly through comparative data obtained from trusted friends and acquaintances, from advertising, and from consumer reports. Since consumers associate brands with quality, the only meaningful way to compare is by referring to other trademarks.

Comparison advertising can help operationalize this process of consumer decision-making because one cannot simply say: "ABC washes clothes white," since all detergents are supposed to do so. If the ad says: "ABC washes your clothes whit*er*," what is the reference point? Other brands of course, but which ones? The consumer wants to know, and to receive adequate proof in the process. Hence, Stanley Tannenbaum, one of its foremost exponents, refers to the lack of consumer information to argue for more comparison advertising:

> There are innumerable marketing and advertising techniques to capitalize on the "show me" attitude which has developed among information-hungry consumers. One of the best ways, I feel, to provide the information consumers are searching for—and to keep in step with consumerism—is through the use of comparison advertising. . . . The consumer is looking for performance and value benchmarks. And what better benchmark for

[6] Such advertising associations as the European Association of Advertising Agencies, the International Union of Advertising Agencies, and the [British] Institute of Practitioners in Advertising have criticized this study—especially its interpretation by the EEC Information Service.

[7] For a general discussion, see: Yale Brozen (ed.), *Advertising and Society* (New York: New York University Press, 1974); and J.J. Lambin, *Advertising, Competition and Market Conduct* (Amsterdam: North Holland Publishing Co., 1975), and "What is the Real Impact of Advertising?" *Harvard Business Review* (May–June 1975), pp. 139–47.

comparison than the brand leader. He automatically becomes the comparative target.[8]

Besides, critics of traditional advertising have attacked non-comparative ads for containing little information, and because they say sweet nothings (e.g., "Things go better with Coke!") about a product—coupled with unspecific, unsupported claims of superiority, which do not allow direct verification by the consumer. In contrast, comparison advertising is informative, since it points out real advantages by contrasting the products side by side, thereby reflecting the real-life situation of a competitive, multiple-brand market situation.

This side-by-side comparison makes consumers aware of the product's features, and helps them in the "shopping" process, which is comparative in nature—an example being the American Motors campaign comparing car-warranty services across brands, thus saving the consumer the necessity of going through the fine print of several advertisements. Similarly, price comparisons are thought to be particularly helpful for low-ticket purchases, such as paper napkins, where the consumer does not have the time to compare prices across brands. In this way, comparative price advertising helps consumers make more efficient decisions.

Tannenbaum has also argued that it is the advertising industry's "own brand of consumerism" because:

- it makes the consumer more conscious of his/her responsibility to compare before buying
- it forces agency and client to work more closely together to ascertain what is important to the consumer
- it forces agency and client to keep the consumer informed and to run informative advertising and back-up claims with demonstrable proofs
- it forces the manufacturer to build consumer-wanted attributes into his products, because the only way to neutralize a competitor's comparative advertisement effectively is to produce a better product, which deprives him of his comparative demonstration.[9]

Finally, it is often said that consumers want more information, while advertisers complain that they do not use the information already available. Comparison advertising can help resolve this dilemma by providing better and more relevant data to assist consumer decision-making—as is achieved to a certain degree through comparative product testing by independent organizations.

[8] S.I. Tannenbaum, "Better Products Through Comparative Advertising" (Speech before the San Francisco Advertising Club, 6 October 1976), p. 11, and "Comparative Advertising: The New Opportunism . . . Frustrating Marketers Out of Step With Consumerism" (Speech before The American Marketing Association Midwest Research Conference, Chicago, Illinois, 10 November 1976), p. 8. See also his "Comparative Advertising: The Advertising Industry's Own Brand of Consumerism," *op. cit.* Mr. Tannenbaum is Chairman of Kenyon & Eckhardt Enterprises.

[9] Tannenbaum, "Better Products Through Comparative Advertising," *op. cit.,* pp. 30–34.

These checks are not free.

Conditions for Chase Manhattan "free" checking: Customer must keep $500 in a savings account. If savings account falls below $500, the account immediately reverts to a checking account with charges. Or the customer keeps $500 in a checking account as a minimum. No additional charges on the account unless checking balance falls below $500.

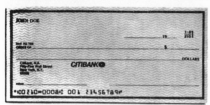

Conditions for Citibank "free" checking: Customer must keep an average monthly balance of $500 in a checking account. If average balance falls below $500, there are onetime-per-month charges. Or customer keeps an average monthly balance of $500 in a savings account. If average balance in both the savings and checking account falls below $500, the higher average in both accounts is determined and the account is charged on the basis of the higher balance.

Conditions for Chemical "free" checking: Regular Account: customer keeps $500 in a checking account. If checking account falls below $500 minimum, there are onetime-per-month charges of up to $4.00. Grand Account: customer keeps $500 in a savings account. If savings account dips below $500, the checking account reverts to a Regular Account.

Conditions for Manufacturers Hanover Trust "free" checking: Customer must keep $400 in either a savings or checking account. A onetime charge of $3.00 is made to the checking account during the month if the balance falls below $400.

This is.

Conditions for Bowery "free" checking: None.

Recently, we went to the commercial banks at the left and asked about their free checking accounts.

Spelled out under each check are the conditions and obligations exactly as they were given to us.

We have always thought the word "free" meant: Without conditions or obligations. Without strings. At no cost.

"Free," in the jargon of these commercial banks, seems to mean the opposite.

That's their problem, but it doesn't have to be yours.

At The Bowery, "free" means what the dictionary and common sense says it means. FREE.

Conditions for free Bowery checking: None

At The Bowery free checking means:
- No per-check charge.
- No monthly service charge.
- No minimum balance required in your checking account.
- No minimum balance required in your savings account.
- No savings account required if you don't want one.

But if you do want a savings account....

If, of your own *free* will, you do want a savings account, note that a Bowery regular or day of deposit-day of withdrawal savings account pays more than one at any commercial bank. At least ¼ percent more!

Can you still afford commercial banks?

If not, we invite you to open a free checking account, or a savings account, or both, at The Bowery. There's a branch minutes from where most of New York works or shops.

It pays to bank at

Member FDIC

THE BOWERY SAVINGS BANK: 110 E. 42nd St./Grand Central Sta./5th Ave. & 34th St./7th Ave. & 34th St./8th Ave. & 34th St./Penn Sta./B'way & 47th St. 6th Ave & 47th St. Lex Ave & 54th St. 3rd Ave & 60th St./130 Bowery & Grand St./145th St. & St. Nicholas Ave./Queens Blvd. & 62nd Dr.,Rego Pk.,Queens/947 Old Country Rd., Westbury, L.I./5100 Sunrise H'way, Massapequa Pk.. L.I. South Shore Mall. Bay Shore L.I

This award-winning ad, which meets all of the criteria of comparison advertising (names are named, the comparison is specific, and substantiation is provided), was prepared by Ogilvy & Mather (USA); they also used non-comparative versions of the same theme ("The myth of free checking at commercial banks"). This comparative ad achieved better recall, according to the Bowery Savings Bank of New York.

Arguments Against

Critics consider that the risk of consumer confusion and deception is great in comparison advertising. The use of non-representative product-test methods as well as the comparing of unimportant product attributes may make consumers more uncertain in their purchase decisions or resentful of the cognitive-dissonance effect of being told *after* a purchase that they acted foolishly.

Thus, Wilkie and Farris have argued that consumer confusion might occur if the advertisers of two or more competing brands make *substantiated but irreconcilable product claims,* as when all manufacturers of deodorants state that they provide better body-odor control and protection.[10] Additionally, consumer confusion may arise from the information overload resulting from *too much information* being presented in comparative claims and counterclaims. On the other hand, deception may result not only from false comparative claims but also from *incomplete comparisons,* and from those that leave the reader or viewer with an erroneous "net impression" by implying too much or the wrong thing. Thus, an ad may state correctly that a Duracell lasts three times as long as others, but fail to reveal that this battery costs two or three times more.

There are, of course, many ways in which an advertisement can *imply* a false claim. "Hedge words" weaken an assertion but can leave a strong implication (e.g., the statement that "ZAP pills *may* help relieve pain"). Imperatives may be juxtaposed to imply a causal relationship (e.g., "Get through the winter without colds. Take Eradicold!"). Asking a negative question is a useful device for implying an affirmative answer that may not be true (e.g., "Isn't quality the most important thing to consider in buying aspirin?"). Closer to comparison advertising is the reporting of piecemeal results to imply an unwarranted general conclusion ("The VW Rabbit has more front-seat headroom than a Datsun B-210; more backseat legroom than a Chevette; and a larger trunk than a Ford Pinto")—implying that the car has more interior room by all measures than the three competitors. There is evidence that advertising audiences do not discriminate well between such *implications* and clear *assertions of fact* ("Citibank has more branches in New York than Chase Manhattan").[11]

It remains to be seen, however, whether these dangers are any greater than in traditional advertising using a non-comparative format or relying on exaggeration or innuendo. Thus, the reports of various self-regulatory bodies (such as the Jury d'Ethique Publicitaire of Belgium, where direct comparisons are forbidden), reveal plenty of consumer and competitor complaints about false, exaggerated, misleading, or unacceptable claims in non-comparative advertisements.

Furthermore, even comparative tests by consumer associations can be criticized on the grounds of being incomplete, since they also choose the criteria for product comparison. If only the removal of food particles is stressed, then

[10] W.L. Wilkie and Paul Farris, *Comparison Advertising: Issues and Prospects* (Cambridge, Mass.: Marketing Science Institute, August 1974), p. 14.

[11] R.J. Harris, "Comprehension of Pragmatic Implications in Advertising," *Journal of Applied Psychology,* 62, 5 (1977), pp. 603–08.

vigorous brushing can be held to be equal or even superior to the average application of any toothpaste. But what if other criteria are chosen: abrasiveness (salt might do quite nicely), tooth-decay protection, pleasant taste, discoloration–removal, and so on?

At present, the arguments about lower advertising credibility (see below) as well as about consumer confusion and deception do not have any research substantiation on an aggregate scale. These phenomena are extremely difficult to measure and, as pointed out by the critics, some negative aspects of comparison advertising may only come about in the long run, when it reaches a certain volume that would seem a waste or an overload to society and to the consumer. (Supporters, of course, see consumers as becoming more accustomed and favorable to comparison advertising.)

On a more ideological level, it is obvious that the adversaries of advertising (e.g., some consumerists, jurists, regulators) do not believe that it serves *any* informative purpose, but only tries to convince, persuade, and cajole. For such critics, even the supplementary information provided by comparative advertisements is suspect and manipulative. It would, of course, be more correct to say that any form of consumer information—whether through advertising or through non-commercial forms—is manipulative since it is usually provided in the expectation that "better behavior" will follow!

Finally, the point has been made that some comparative ads or counter-ads have been justified more by the professional pride or pique of some advertising practitioners or product managers than by real concern for providing consumers with more meaningful information,[12] and companies with an effective advertising stragey:

> [Comparison advertising] will unquestionably tend to generate campaigns in which the efforts to name names may very well swamp the real product message. In other words, in order to make the name-calling possible, it may require a communication that overlooks the prime prospect's problem and its solution. Thus, we hope that naming names does not become a fad that swamps all other marketing considerations.[13]

Three U.S. Surveys

1. A 1974 telephone survey of 200 Dallas residents was rather negative:[14]

- 54 percent of aware respondents stated that they did not like comparative advertisements (38 percent in favor and 8 percent undecided, but singles were more favorable)
- 49 percent thought it was not truthful (42.5 percent were positive and 8.5 percent undecided)

[12] Emanuel Voisin, "Pour ou contre la publicité comparative," *Stratégies*, No. 129 (December 1976), pp. 76*ff*. The author comments that the battle between SOS and Brillo was an idle intellectual exercise that may have been "funny"—but did it sell more soap pads?

[13] "Comparative Ads in Center of Meeting at AAAA Meeting," *Broadcasting* (17 May 1976), p. 32.

[14] Quoted in: Th.E. Barry and R.L. Tremblay, "Comparative Advertising: Perspectives and Issues," *Journal of Advertising* IV, 4 (1975), p. 18.

- 74 percent had not changed their purchasing behavior (18 percent had and 8 percent were unsure)

2. Recent interviews by Oglivy & Mather[15] provided the following mixed findings among those aware of the practice of comparison advertising:

	April 1976	*September 1977*
More *useful* to consumers		24%
Less useful		27%
About as useful		49%
Approve of naming		
competitors	40%	39%
Disapprove	24%	29%
Neither approve nor		
disapprove	36%	32%

Those who approve say that comparison advertising "helps you know which is best to buy." To a lesser degree, they support it because it represents "free enterprise/competition." Some approve of comparison "if it is honest," while others observed that "they could not compare if it were not true."

Those who disapprove feel that comparisons "run down other brands," and that "advertisers should prove their own products" and "should let the public make up its own mind." Some consider them unethical if not dishonest.

Reaction to comparison advertising was not differentiated by medium, with almost 90 percent saying that they do not approve or disapprove of the practice any more in one medium than in another.

3. An October–November 1977 nationwide survey of 2,005 adults (eighteen years and over) conducted by Starch INRA Hooper for the International Advertising Association was rather favorable:[16]

Have seen comparative ads?

Total	71%
Female	74%
Male	69%

The highest proportions were found among the college-educated (82%), the 18–29 age group (78%); and the upper-income groups (78–83%).

[15] *The Listening Post* (Ogilvy & Mather Research), No. 31 (1977), p. 8. This survey was based on a national sample of 200 people.

[16] Through personal interviews, the respondents were asked the following three questions, with no example of a comparative ad being shown to them: "You may have seen ads in the press or on television that referred to competitive products by name. For example, an ad saying that Brand A is better than Brand B based on scientific tests. (A) Have you seen any ads in the last six months that referred to a competitive brand by name? (B) All other things being equal, which ads are more useful to you—those that name competitive brands for comparative purposes, or those that do not? (C) Do you think that ads which name a competitor are more believable, less believable, or about the same as ads which do not name a competitor?" Further details about this survey can be obtained from the International Advertising Association, 475 Fifth Avenue, New York 10017 (tel. 212/684-1583).

Which ads are more useful?

Comparative ads	34% (males, 35%; females, 32%)
Non-comparative ads	22% (males, 20%; females, 24%)
No difference	43%

Younger respondents were more positive than older ones:

18–29 years	43%	(20% con)
30–44	35%	(23% con)
45–59	28%	(25% con)
60+	23%	(23% con)

Blacks (42% pro, 16% con); blue-collar workers (39% pro, 19% con); executives and professionals (37% pro, 22% con); and college graduates (36% pro, 23% con) found comparisons definitely more useful than the average respondent.

Which ads are more believable?

Comparative ads are more believable	25% (males, 27%; females, 23%)
Comparative ads are less believable	18% (males, 16%; females, 20%)
About the same	55%

Comparisons are considered more believable by blacks (33%), young people (18–29 years old: 32%), blue-collar workers (31%), Catholics (31%), and singles (31%). They were least believable among older people (60 and over: 23%) and low-income (less than $7,000 of annual family income: 23%) respondents.

These figures are not out of line with statistics about overall attitudes toward advertising (see above); and the three series seem to indicate an improving reaction toward comparison advertising over time.

Two Unfavorable Canadian Surveys

1. More damning data comes from the Consumers' Association of Canada (CAC), which conducted a survey of its members in April 1977.[17] These CAC findings are completely opposite those advocated by supporters of the practice. They reveal that the majority of CAC members perceived that comparison advertising does not provide facts (61 percent negative); does not offer a useful evaluation (75 percent negative); and does not reduce the time required to shop for a product (76 percent negative).

In evaluating the methodology of comparative tests, the majority of consumers perceive them as unfair (61 percent negative) and invalid (64 percent negative), and they feel that they need more elaboration (75 percent).

[17] The assistance of Mrs. Jo-Ann Chrstian, National Research Chairman of the Consumers' Association of Canada, is gratefully acknowledged. One hundred and fifty questionnaires were mailed out to CAC members, with seventy-six usable responses. The CAC is in the process of extending this survey.

Besides, 72 percent of the respondents do not think that comparison advertising is useful to consumers. Based on the perceived quantity and quality of information that it provides, this survey suggests that comparisons have low social usefulness to the Canadian consumer.

A second similarly surprising finding is related to the perceived impact of comparison advertising on consumer decision-making. Based on these data, the frequently mentioned argument that comparative advertisements create more awareness and are more persuasive than their non-comparative counterparts has to be rejected. To the question: "Are you tempted by comparison advertising to try a brand other than your usual brand?," 53 percent responded negatively, and 28 percent gave neutral responses. Similarly, to the question: "Do you buy brands conducting comparative advertising, or do you go out of your way to avoid purchasing them?," close to a majority of the respondents had no feeling one way or another.

Of course, this finding on the perceived impact of comparison advertising on consumer decision-making has to be interpreted with a certain degree of skepticism. The influence of advertising is subtle, often subconscious, and seldom amenable to conscious personal evaluation of its effect on the decision-making process. More generally, the CAC survey cannot be considered to be representative of all Canadian consumers, since it comes from a small group of "concerned" members who tend to be more critical of advertising than the average consumer. Still, it raises disturbing questions about the favorable claims advanced by the supporters of comparison advertising, and it certainly suggests that such a survey be replicated on a more representative scale in a number of countries—as has been partially achieved by the 1977 International Advertising Association surveys in the United States and the United Kingdom (see above).

2. Equally unfavorable is a 1976 survey by McDougall, who had 225 females (eighteen years and older) interviewed in one Canadian city in order to determine consumer attitudes toward comparison advertising and reactions to various types of ads. Three tests (involving actual comparative claims as well as a hypothetical situation) were used to measure the perceived reliability and helpfulness of the claims made. Some of the ads made "direct" comparisons, naming two or more brands, while others were "indirect" (e.g., "Brand A lasts longer than other [unnamed] brands"). Some claims were "substantiated" (e.g., "*Tests* show that Brand A lasts longer than Brand B"), while others were "unsubstantiated" (e.g., simply stating that "Brand A lasts longer . . ."—without any reference to tests).

McDougall's findings are rather negative, though there are some important qualifications:[18]

[18] G.H.G. McDougall (Wilfrid Laurier University, Waterloo, Ont., Canada), "Comparative Advertising: Consumer Issues and Attitudes," in B.A. Greenberg and D.N. Bellenger (eds.), *Contemporary Marketing Thought* (Chicago, Ill.: American Marketing Association, 1977), pp. 287–91. See also his report: *A Study of Comparative Advertising in Canada* (Ottawa: Consumer Research Council Canada, 1976).

The average response to most of the statements was negative and few positive attitudes were held concerning comparative advertising. In general, the respondents felt that advertisers should not be allowed to name other brands in their ads; comparative ads did not provide the consumer with more useful information; they were not more believable than other types; and ads naming other brands did not help consumers in their buying decision. Still, the respondents felt that if an advertiser has a better product, he should say so in his ads. This apparent conflict may be reconciled by suggesting that respondents feel the advertiser should make superiority claims but not by directly naming the competing brands.

Respondents were skeptical of the test claims made in comparative ads. They felt, on the average, that tests were not fairly and reliably conducted, and that advertisers may not have the facts to back up their claims.

With two exceptions, the majority of respondents either agreed or disagreed with the statements rather than remaining neutral. The significance of the bimodal distribution is that a substantial minority of respondents held positive attitudes towards comparative advertising.

Attitudes towards comparative advertising were not significantly related to respondent demographics, suggesting that they are affected mainly by factors other than demographic characteristics, but also that the findings can be extrapolated to larger populations.

In most cases, substantiated claims were perceived as significantly more reliable and offering more helpful information to consumers than unsubstantiated claims. Respondents did not see direct claims (naming the competition) being more reliable or helpful than indirect claims (referring only to "other brands").

A substantial minority (one third or more) of respondents held favorable attitudes, feeling that comparative ads are useful, reliable and helpful. Unfortunately, those holding favorable views were not different on a demographic basis from people who held unfavorable views, which precludes identification for strategy or regulation purposes.

Clearly, these findings cannot be extrapolated to the whole of Canada or the rest of the world. Still, they are certainly unfavorable to direct comparisons—although one must keep in mind that other types of ads did not always do that well either (as was also true in other surveys).

Besides, it is not clear to what extent these negative reactions are a function of novelty. People are shocked at first by aggressive comparison advertising, but will they get accustomed to it and finally welcome such an approach? It is still too early to say after only six years of experience in the first country to use it, and minimal experience elsewhere.

A Favorable British Survey

A country where comparisons are relatively new and few is the United Kingdom, where most advertisers remain skeptical because of unfamiliarity, a cultural preference for gentlemanly behavior in competition, and some strong feelings that advertising should be built around images rather than cold facts.

Yet, a 1,762-respondent survey run in October of 1977 for the International Advertising Association by Starch INRA Hooper in Great Britain (England, Scotland, Wales) is rather favorable among the relatively few people familiar with comparison advertising.[19]

Have seen comparative ads?

Total	19% (only 332 out of 1762 respondents)
Males	22%
Females	17%

The proportions were higher among upper-income (24%) and younger respondents (24–22%).

Which ads are more useful?

Comparative ads	35%
Non-comparative ads	18%
No difference	35%
Don't know; no idea	13%

Again, upper-income (41%) and younger people (46–44%) were more favorable.

Which ads are more believable?

Comparative ads are more believable	21%
Comparative ads are less believable	17%
About the same	50%
Don't know	12%

Younger people believed them more (28–29%), while older respondents were less inclined to do so (19–24% of those over 35 years of age thought them less believable). The negative elements of novelty and cultural "shock" thus appear to be greater among older people—as could be expected.

This survey—based on a national sample—reveals that consumers do not feel as negative toward comparison advertising as many British advertisers and agencies.

The Position of Consumer Associations

Such bodies cannot quite oppose the use of comparisons, since a number of them sponsor comparative-product surveys. They have often reacted positively to the actual or potential legalization and spread of comparison advertising. Some observers, however, interpret this support to amount to demands

---

[19] The questions asked were similar to the U.S. ones (see above); copies of the results can also be obtained from the International Advertising Association in New York and London.

designed to embarrass business, since practice will reveal that many products have no comparative advantage, that most firms will be unwilling to compete aggressively on the basis of factual comparisons, or that advertising is unable to do as good a job of comparing as independent consumer reports can.

Still, the support is there as is revealed by various developments:

1. The authors of this study contacted sixty-five consumer associations by mail in the spring of 1977: twenty-five in the United States and forty in twenty other countries. Seventeen answers were received, and they revealed generally that they have a limited interest in comparison advertising but are in favor of it, while remaining suspicious of advertising in general.[20]

2. The Consumers Association of *Canada* has recently put comparison advertising on its agenda for discussion and evaluation. Due to its perceived potential of providing additional information to consumers and of making them more conscious of comparing products, the initial reaction of CAC representatives has been positive toward it. In April 1977, the CAC undertook a mail survey of its members to measure their attitudes toward comparisons. The results (discussed above) revealed strongly negative attitudes; but this Association is maintaining an overall positive attitude, provided the claims of advertisers can be substantiated and do reflect consumer-oriented issues (e.g., miles per gallon) rather than insignificant features.

3. Similar support and cautions were expressed by the *Australian Consumers' Association* and by *Canberra Consumers Incorporated;* by the *United Kingdom*'s Consumers Association; by the Consumers' Association of *Ireland;* and by various consumer-oriented public bodies in *Belgium, Denmark,* the *Netherlands,* and *Sweden.*

4. *New Zealand's* Consumer Council does not have a policy on comparison advertising, nor has it discussed its desirability. Mr. Smithies, Director of the Consumer's Institute, thinks that on the face of it, given that the information is accurate, comparison advertising gives more information to the consumer and looks to be a desirable development. However, he expressed a valid concern about the objectivity of comparisons:

> We know from our experience of comparative testing of products over seventeen years, how easy it is to produce inaccurate, unfair, or misleading comparisons. We also know how unreliable advertisements may be when they are seeking a competitive advantage. It happens that we are set up under an Act of Parliament which, among other things, prohibits the use of our name or findings for advertising purposes. On the relatively rare oc-

---

[20] The country synopses and analyses include additional information about consumer reactions (see below). According to Stridsberg, pressure groups concerned with consumer welfare tend to keep their distance from the self-regulatory process—either as complainants or as members of review boards. [A.B. Stridsberg, *Effective Advertising Self-Regulation* (New York: International Advertising Association, 1974), p. 29.] Thus, the Executive Director of the Consumer Federation of America stated in 1971 that this body "has no faith in industry self-regulation or voluntary agreements." (Quoted in Tanner, *op. cit.,* p. 208.)

casions where our findings are used illegally in an advertisement, we find very frequently that they are used misleadingly out of context—sometimes thoroughly distorted. I think from that experience we would have some doubt about the likely accuracy and fairness of comparison advertising.[21]

5. In *West Germany,* the Consumers Association (Arbeitsgemeinschaft der Verbraucher, AgV) accepts advertising as a necessary instrument of consumer information that helps render the market more transparent. However, the AgV's primary efforts are aimed at more effective measures to fight against misleading and unfair advertising by the courts' changing of the present interpretation of the Unfair Competition Act to require stricter standards of fairness and more objective information. In this context, they support greater usage of comparative advertising by manufacturers.[22]

6. Finally, the constituent (national) members of the *European Bureau of Consumers Unions* (BEUC) have supported comparison advertising, provided it is not misleading.[23]

COMPETITIVE EFFECTS

If we accept competitive advertising claims such as "King William fans used to drink more expensive Scotch—enjoy what made them switch!," why is there so much controversy about going a bit further and naming the competition?[24]

Arguments in Favor

Clearly, the proponents of comparison advertising believe that it benefits competition in ways that eclipse arguments about its "fairness" since it increases the chances of success for a small producer or a newcomer with a low advertising budget, thereby reducing oligopolistic market developments.

Furthermore, pointing out and identifying product superiority on specific product features acts as an incentive for the challenged manufacturer to improve his product, and this eventually contributes to higher product-quality standards. For example, one cooking spray attacked a competitor's product smell, but the latter reformulated his product in order to eliminate the offensive smell. Also, an analgesic improved its quality to parity level, and forced a competitor to cease his quality claims. Similarly, SOS—following its comparative-advertisement battle with Brillo—signed off by saying: "Thanks pink pads for keeping me on my toes: maybe I can do the same for you some time!" The

[21] Letter to the authors from R.J. Smithies, Director of the Consumers' Institute, Wellington, New Zealand (4 May 1977).

[22] Arbeitsgemeinschaft der Verbraucher, "AgV-Positionspapier Werbung," *Verbraucher-Politische Korrespondenz, Sonderbeilage,* Nr. 25a/1976 (22 Juni 1976).

[23] Letter from Claudine Van Lierde, Executive Secretary of the Bureau Européen des Unions de Consommateurs (Brussels, 23 February 1977). Its position was taken in reference to the EEC Commission proposal of a draft directive about misleading and unfair advertising (see above).

[24] R.E. Oliver (President, Canadian Advertising Advisory Board), "Comparative Advertising" (Address to the Association of Canadian Advertisers, Toronto, 6 May 1975), p. 2.

aggressive comparative approach used by companies such as Savin, Toshiba, and Addressograph-Multigraph forced Xerox to lower its prices three times in little more than one year; and APECO and Canon are now comparing themselves to both Xerox *and* Savin—a partial proof that comparison advertising has loosened Xerox' control of the photocopier market.[25]

Finally, some advertisers welcome comparison advertising as "a new method of communication which may well be the most vital new creative weapon to have come into our hands in many years," although Kershaw thinks that "naming names is a creative cop-out."[26]

Arguments Against

The negatives focus on the issue of unfair competition, which has been discussed previously, and which has been evidenced by the complaints associated with comparison advertising (see above). One additional question is relevant however:

> Would our sympathies for the newcomer [using a comparative advertisement against the brand leader] be equally great if that newcomer were an exceedingly powerful company extending its activities to a new field heretofore occupied by a smaller company whose success was confined to a single product?[27]

ADVERTISING'S AND BUSINESS' IMAGES

Arguments in Favor

Since consumer information and better competition are "good things," the proponents of comparison advertising take it for granted that its overall perception by the public is favorable. This view is of course supported by the definite relaxation of government regulations and of some voluntary rules against comparative ads, and by the positive (if grudging) approval of this practice by consumer associations in many countries (see above).

Moreover, in the mid-1976 *ANNY* survey of the usage of comparison advertising by 278 East Coast advertising agencies, the question: "Is comparative advertising good for business?" received "yes" answers outnumbering the "no" responses by two to one. A sizable number of the responding agencies, however, did not believe that an answer could be given in a simple "yes" or "no" fashion, because the correct answer would depend on *how* the comparison is made. Too, many of the agencies surveyed (including those who evaluated comparison advertising in a positive manner) expressed a concern that "it will lose its impact if it is used too often."[28]

[25] Jack Fever, "The Great Copier War," *Marketing Communications* (July–August 1977), pp. 28–29.

[26] Ph.H. Dougherty, "Advertising Comparison Issue," *New York Times* (14 November 1973), p. 61; and "For and Against Comparative Advertising," *op. cit.*, p. 26.

[27] "Introduction" to the special issue on comparative advertising of *The Trademark Reporter* (July–August 1977), p. 352.

[28] "Comparative Ads More 'Preached' than 'Practiced'," *ANNY* (13 August 1976), p. 1.

Comparisons may also have the potential of remedying some of advertising's widely acknowledged shortcomings. Thus, critics often argue that advertising tries to create psychological ("mood" or subjective) differentiations among brands when physical differences are hardly perceivable by the consumer. Here, comparative advertisements would reduce this criticized practice by stressing measurable, objective, and verifiable facts. Eventually, this would result in higher credibility for advertising.

Similarly, the use of "puffery" and of vague and unsubstantiated claims ("the best," "better than ever," "30 percent off") apparently irritates many audiences. Comparisons would limit this use of vagueness and exaggeration in advertising on account of the requirements of the media for supporting data, and of the fear of litigation, counterclaims, and complaints from competitors, consumers, and regulatory bodies.

Arguments Against

Even when the positive benefits of giving more specific information to the consumer are recognized, criticism is directed against the abuse of this technique, which could lead eventually to low credibility for all types of advertising and intensify the distrust in business firms. In this view, consumers could be shocked by the "knocking" of the competition, and this may further lower their estimation of business and its "savage" practices.

Thus, Jack Roberts of Ogilvy & Mather has argued that: "Naming competitors could turn the advertising business into a carnival brand-name shooting gallery—noisy, unproductive, and unprofessional." [29] While he does not reject the usage of all comparison advertising, he recommends more stringent self-regulation guidelines for the industry and faster handling of complaints. Andrew Kershaw, one of the strongest opponents of comparative advertising, quotes a consumer-opinion poll done by his firm to the effect that as many as 30 percent of the respondents end up disbelieving both the comparative advertiser and the named competitor. [30]

While one could readily agree that tough ads, such as Bayer's "Makers of Tylenol, shame on you!," or scary ones, such as "Our pressure cooker won't explode in your face," go too far in this respect, [31] there is no indication or measurement available as to the amount of comparison that would result in such negative attitudes against all advertising. Still, Kershaw has argued that its use be minimized in order to avoid this problem:

> The right to use comparative advertising should be absolute and un-challenged. But we who call ourselves principled professionals, and clients

[29] Don Grant, "Be Hard on Comparison Ads: Roberts to Four A's," *Advertising Age* 94 May 1974), p. 1.

[30] "For and Against Comparative Advertising," *op. cit.,* p. 26.

[31] Ernest Dichter supports Kershaw in this respect, stating that: "The more confusing and vicious the mutual attacks become, the more the respondent comes to the conclusion that he had better rely on his own judgment and not on what he is being told in the ad." *Marketing News* (7 October 1977), p. 8.

who are businessmen of honor and principle, should reject its use voluntarily, except in the very rarest of cases.[32]

An additional reservation was raised by a Swiss advertiser:

Should businessmen fight among themselves when—particularly in such a small country as Switzerland—they have so many enemies against whom they must stand united? Comparative advertisements can be very divisive on this count, and not worth the cost of disunity!

This attitude may well be prevalent in small countries, and in larger ones where business feels besieged by its adversaries. In the United States, however, the Federal Trade Commission and the Justice Department are delighted when competitors are mad at each other! Thus, the FTC's Deputy Director recently stated that if comparison "promotes a 'jungle morality' in the marketplace, this is fine . . . competition at times can be compared to warfare, and out of such combat 'maximum truth' emerges." [33]

[32] *Ibid*, p. 26.

[33] "Westen: Comparative Ads Spur Flow of Facts," *Advertising Age* (14 November 1977), p. 6. This same article mentions that the President of the Council of Better Business Bureaus had previously blasted comparisons as "damaging to ad credibility and a negative value in business conduct."

| 7

Comparison Advertising: Effective or Not?

SOME PEOPLE FEEL strongly that comparative ads "smell"—but do they "sell"? Various general arguments as well as some empirical evidence bear on the effectiveness of comparison advertising. Unfortunately, research data are still few and limited in coverage, and the problem is compounded by the relative paucity of knowledge we have of how *any kind* of advertising works.

GENERAL ARGUMENTS FOR AND AGAINST

Advertisers have expressed a growing concern about the declining influence of advertising and its growing cost so that it takes more dollars to accomplish a given communication objective than before. There is also the dilemma of consumers complaining about the lack of meaningful information, though advertisers retort that consumers do not use the available product information. In this context, comparisons provide a cost-effective way of focussing on the significant differences among similarly perceived products.

Besides, social-psychology research has shown that when a high-status object is associated with a low-status one, the former loses a little while the latter gains a little from the association. This, of course, is a rationale for riding the coattails of the brand leader. Even retaliation can help the underdog in such a case if only because the audience is likely to interpret the counterattack as an indication that the original attack was founded.

Other pro arguments have been advanced by Tannenbaum, who claims to have successfully used it since 1969:

Our research, over a seven-year period, shows that in employing the [proper guidelines], the effective comparative TV commercial produces a set of predictable reactions:

- **Gains a greater target audience** . . . by bringing a sensitive brand decision area into focus.

- **Incurs a degree of negative reaction.** This is to be expected. The comparative commercial challenges the brand user's judgment. You cannot switch them all.

- **Introduces a proper doubt.** Some may term this "confusion"—' "proper doubt" is a better term. A primary objective is to have the targeted brand-user question his present brand determination.

- **Moves consumer from rejection to willingness to consider** . . . by presenting a product attribute of such significant superiority that it invites trial.

- **Wins "half-hearteds" and "undecideds."** Pulls in consumers who have been sitting on the uncommitted sidelines by providing a product benchmark heretofore lacking.

- **Develops consumer climate for increased market share.** Provides any brand which has a significant and superior brand attribute the opportunity to gain market share literally overnight against entrenched competition.

Comparative advertising is most productive when it deals with truly important and easily demonstrated product attributes. There can be no weasels or disclaimers.

Our use of the comparative commercials has been effective simply because when two or more products are designed to do the same thing, the consumer benefits by learning which one does it better. And that is what we demonstrate. Not who says it funnier, or more tenderly, or with a more likeable spokesman.

Experience tells me that there are just not that many significant and demonstrable brand differences to warrant the current level of comparative commercial usage [on the air].[1]

As Tannenbaum's last point demonstrates, even its proponents acknowledge that the effectiveness of comparison advertising is limited. In the first place, it is only one of many execution *techniques* that should be considered in developing an advertising strategy.

Besides, there is the unresolved dispute between advertisers who believe in the power of facts and those who stress the importance of dreams—the eternal question of selling the "steak" or the "sizzle." Some people at home and abroad are shocked that Louis Sherry would try to sell its ice cream by prosaically comparing the number of its cherries or nuts with that in a Breyer's pint,

---

[1] "For and Against Comparative Advertising", *op. cit.,* p. 29. See also: "Should You Name Your Competitors in Advertising?" *BBDO Newsletter* (February, 1975), p. 1. The International Harvester letter included below, refers to "curious disbelief" instead of "proper doubt;" Fred Westen, current Deputy Director of the FTC's Bureau of Consumer Protection, feels in any case that "confusion is a higher state of knowledge than ignorance."

instead of evoking the pleasure or context of a fine dessert. Dichter, for one, has recently criticized "over-obviousness" in advertisements, as well as their overlooking the fact that consumers buy "the satisfaction of hopes and dreams, not only fulfillment of needs."[2] Here, too many comparative advertisements may deliver information but evoke no emotional response.

Another counter-argument centers on comparisons being easily duplicated by the competition. The barrage of comparative counter-claims about similar or different features can only generate disbelief on the part of consumers and ultimately hurt the market for the product—as happened during the "coffee war" of the 1950s, and may happen again with analgesics and colas (see the Pepsi-Coke and Datril-Tylenol cases in Part III).

Various negative theoretical arguments have also been advanced against comparative advertisements:

1. Since they are mainly based on cognitive-dissonance principles—telling users that they are in fact using the wrong product—, comparisons do not necessarily improve the position of the advertised brand but may well alienate consumers.
2. Since advertising's main role is "defensive" and aims at reinforcing feelings of satisfaction, comparisons fail in this very important respect.
3. If consumers attribute advertising claims to the characteristics of the products, the probability of purchase is higher than if they attribute them to the advertiser's desire to sell them the products. Comparative claims of superiority, in such a case, would not be very effective.[3]

In a more balanced manner, Wilkie and Farris, on the basis of their review of behavioral-science concepts, have tentatively concluded that:[4]

1. Comparative advertisements may attract more *initial attention* because of: (a) their relative novelty and (b) their greater relevance for the users of the brands compared. This would result in a larger "net audience" for comparison advertising. (But misidentification and giving undue attention to the competing brand must be avoided.)
2. Comparisons may be more effective in communicating a *clearer image and a more focussed perception* of the brand's rating along the advertised attributes, thus resulting in better brand comprehension vis-à-vis competitors either through differentiation or by association with the leader.
3. However, the possible superiority of comparison advertising is less obvious as far as *persuasion based on credibility* is concerned. On the one

---

[2] Quoted in *Marketing News* (7 October 1977), p. 8.

[3] Th. E. Barry and R.L. Tremblay, "Comparative Advertising: Perspectives and Issues," *Journal of Advertising* IV, 4 (1975). pp. 15–20. This article also provides a useful review of the history of comparison advertising, and cites many lesser known sources.

[4] W.L. Wilkie and Paul Farris, *Comparison Advertising: Issues and Prospects* (Cambridge, Mass.: Marketing Science Institute 1974), pp. 21–35, and *passim;* and "Comparison Advertising: Problems and Potential," *Journal of Marketing* (October 1975), pp. 7–15. See also their *Consumer Information Processing: Perspectives and Implications for Advertising* (Cambridge, Mass.: Marketing Science Institute, 1976), which refines their analysis of comparison advertising.

hand, its potential for specificity is useful for product positioning and target-segment selection. Particularly for brand-differentiation strategies, comparisons can help isolate and stress "determinant" attributes; and "association" is helpful for attributes on which consumers perceive the sponsored brand to be weaker, when in fact it is at parity or better. On the other hand:

> "Credibility" is seen to be a function of both the specific claims and the image of the source. In general, we expect that comparison ads would offer an advantage in these respects. But consumer cognitive responses hold the key to effectiveness; and it is here that we are most uncertain because of off-setting influences. It does seem clear that users of competing brands employed for comparison would tend to increase their counter-arguing activities, while users of the sponsoring brand would tend to engage in support arguments. Whether counter-arguments are necessarily bad, however, is not clear. If negative, these could obviate most or all of the earlier advantages for comparison advertising by polarizing consumer attitudes and thus reducing probabilities of purchase.[5]

Since "broad generalizations concerning the net effectiveness of comparison advertising are, at this point, impossible," Wilkie and Farris have urged that more research can be conducted on: (1) the *fundamental dimensions* of audience awareness, knowledge, and message acceptance and (2) the more *tactical problems* of the number and selection of particular brands and attributes to compare, the specificity and range of the claims to be made, the use of test results, the choice of media, the avoidance of confusion in copy, and many other topics (see below).

EMPIRICAL RESEARCH

What we have in the way of hard data is still scanty, but it provides relatively little support to comparison advertising. A first *Ogilvy and Mather* study measured the effectiveness of comparison versus non-comparison advertising for eight brands of five different products.[6] One hundred and five *female* heads of households were exposed to comparison and non-comparisons advertisements (thirty-second TV commercials) for the same brand. Subsequent measuring of the effectiveness of these ads led to the following conclusions:

- The comparative commercials created greater negative attitudes toward advertising because of greater confusion and lesser believability.

- The comparative commercials did not create higher awareness of the sponsor brands.

---

[5] Wilkie and Farris, *Comparison Advertising, op. cit.*, p. 35.

[6] Philip Levine, "Commercials That Name Competing Brands," *Journal of Advertising Research*, XVI (6 December 1976), pp. 1–14. There were three different brands of a health and beauty-aid product; two brands of a drug product; and one brand each of a second health and beauty-aid product, of a household product, and of a beverage.

- The comparative commercials generated greater sponsor misidentification, to the advantage of the named competitors.

- Despite its novelty, the only comparative commercial among eight (in a test series) did not increase *awareness*.

- The comparative commercials created more skepticism toward commercial claims, and more miscommunication—primarily sponsor misidentification. In particular, the data suggest that the more direct and potentially threatening the comparison is, the greater danger there is of creating negative reactions.

- In most cases, the comparative commercials were no more persuasive than the non-comparative versions.

- However, when only one comparative commercial was seen among a group of non-comparative commercials, it was found to be significantly more persuasive, suggesting a positive effect on *persuasion* (rather than awareness) due to the "novelty" factor.

According to Levine, this study has several implications. For the *consumer,* comparative ads seem more confusing. If these commercials had been more informative, it should have been reflected in differences in persuasion. However, the non-comparative ads were just as persuasive as those that named competing brands. The *sponsoring advertiser* is hurt by increased awareness for his competitor's named brand, by miscommunication and skepticism toward his claims, and by no benefits in persuasion (except possibly when the sponsor is the only advertiser naming competitive brands). The *named competitor* benefits through increased awareness of his brand; at the same time, the *advertising industry* is hurt through a decrease in the believability of advertising.

A second Ogilvy & Mather study (April, 1977) extended the scope of the initial research to *men* for two brands of a consumer service (air transportation), three brands of durable goods (cars), and two brands of packaged goods (soft drinks).[7] The findings are equally negative for comparison advertising:

- Comparative commercials are less believable (but not so much in the case of cars).

- They are not less confusing (but not so much in the case of cars).

- There does not appear to be any clear-cut advantage in using comparative advertising to differentiate between brands. (Still, in air transportation, it strengthened men's belief that one airline is substantially different from another).

[7] Ogilvy & Mather Research, "A Further Investigation into the Effects of Comparative Television Advertising That Names Competing Brands" (New York, 1977). Further details were provided by Andrew Kershaw at the IREP conference in Paris (May, 1977).

- Comparative commercials are not demonstrably superior in creating higher identification of the sponsor brand.

- They created greater sponsor misidentification among airlines and cars.

- In one of the seven cases (actually, the only one with a significant difference), a comparative commercial proved more persuasive than the non-comparative version.

This is of course damning evidence regarding the effectiveness of comparison advertising, although these findings must be qualified in a number of ways. First, the Ogilvy & Mather findings should not be automatically extended to products and services with significantly different characteristics.

Second, they should not automatically be applied to other media such as print and radio, since they are based on thirty-second TV commercials—a medium which is considered by Krugman to be less "involving" and less "rational" than others.[8] Even Kershaw has acknowledged that it may fare better in print, since this medium lends itself to fair, full, and thoughtful comparison, while the short commercial does not.

However, a third O & M study dealing with *print* advertising is somewhat negative. Involving both men and women, and a dozen brands, it concluded that: (1) comparative ads are about as believable; (2) are neither more nor less confusing; and (3) are equal in creating the feeling that there are important differences among brands. On the other hand, non-comparative ads: (1) did better in terms of correct identification of the sponsor brand, with the named competitor often benefiting from sponsor misidentification; and (2) are often more persuasive than their comparative counterparts. In terms of persuasiveness, non-comparative ads had an advantage in some environments in the case of women, but it was a toss-up as far as men are concerned.[9]

Third, the Ogilvy & Mather findings are not as bad as they sound, because in many cases either the comparative commercials received fairly high ratings or both types of ads got mediocre results. For example, in answer to the question: "Do you feel that the commercials are confusing?," 77 percent of the respondents disagreed for the comparative ads, and 90 percent did likewise for the non-comparative ones in one product case. In another category, the scores for *both* types of ads were in the 56 to 59 percent range for consumers agreeing that "there are important differences among products advertised." Though comparative advertisements fared poorly, it does not mean they did not perform well at all or that non-comparative ads always did better.

Fourth, the implications of these findings are not necessarily obvious. In support of the Ogilvy & Mather study, Rockey has observed that: "Further

    [8]For a discussion of "high and low involvement," see: H.E. Krugman, "The Impact of Television Advertising," *Public Opinion Quarterly* (Fall 1965), pp. 349–56.

    [9]Ogilvy & Mather Research, "An Investigation into the Effects of Comparative Print Advertising That Names Competing Brands" (New York, March 1978).

compounding the potential sponsor's confusion and fear is the concern that the [comparative] approach may engender increased counter-arguing by comparative-brand users. Thus, if it helps increase attention by comparing oneself to a brand leader, that advantage may be lost by an increased hostility among that larger audience."[10] Tannenbaum, however, counters that a degree of negative reaction is to be expected: "The comparative commercial challenges the brand user's judgment. You cannot switch them all." He also disputes the use of the term "confusion," arguing instead that a "proper doubt" is a better term, since a primary objective is to have the targeted brand-user *question* his/her present brand determination.[11] Rocky adds that if price is the major argument used, confusion is not harmful if the shopper seeks out the product category and compares prices.[12]

A more extensive replication was done in mid-1976 by Ogilvy, Benson & Mather (OBM), the U.K. subsidiary of the U.S. advertising agency. The occasion was the launching of the Ford Fiesta through unilateral advertising, which was countered by a VW–Polo comparative-advertising campaign.[13] OBM reached the following conclusions about the communication effectiveness of three Polo *print* ads (one non-comparative and two comparative) shown to 333 small-car owners likely to be involved in the choice of a new car within the next three years:

- *Confusion about sponsorship* was significant, since only about one-half of the respondents correctly identified Polo as the sponsor. The evidence suggests that the more aggressive the ad, the greater the confusion.
- Regarding the quality of *communicating important points,* the non-comparative ad and one of the two comparative ads did a good job, but the second comparative one did not do so well: "On communication, then, the lesson is clear: there is no superiority of style . . . just good ads and bad ads."
- *Attitudes toward advertising style:* the non-comparative ads were considered more "honest, believable, telling the whole story, not misleading, fair." Besides, the non-comparative ad was thought to be more informative, helpful, easy to understand, and interesting, although one of the two comparative ads was a good second best.

In rebuttal, VW–Polo's advertising agency argued that the campaign worked out well in terms of large sales and market-share increases—and that

[10] E.A. Rockey, "Comparative Advertising Fair or Unfair? Effective or Ineffective?" (Paper presented at the ANA Television Network, New York City, 24 February 1976), p. 6.

[11] Tannenbaum, "Better Products Through Comparative Advertising." (Presentation before the San Francisco Advertising Club, 6 October 1976), pp. 21–22.

[12] Rockey, *op. cit.,* p. 7.

[13] This section is based on: Neville Darby (OBM Research Director), "Shall I Compare Thee to a Ford Fiesta?" *Campaign* (25 November 1977), p. 38; and on the counter-article by Keith Shingfield (Accounts Manager for the U.K. subsidiary of Doyle, Dane, Bernbach, Inc., VW–Polo's advertising agency), *"The Argument with a Hole in It?" Campaign* (2 December 1977), p. 29.

this was the main point anyway: "Now, if we had researched the campaign prior to insertion, as a number of clients demand, this advertising may not have run, and the industry would have been deprived of one of the best automotive campaigns of the decade—so far." [14]

VW–Polo's ad agency also commented on OBM's methodology:

> However, we must be fair to the research findings. They probably do reflect the mass-market opinion—but they ignore the existence of market segments. We know that the car market—like most markets—is made up of segments. We know that some people think Ford is tinny; we know that some people think Ford is workmanlike. We also know that there are some people who think VW are "expensive/foreign;" others who think VW are well-made quality cars.
>
> We aimed to tap the latent goodwill for VW and exploit the perceived disadvantages of Ford. If we could get one in ten Fiesta buyers to switch, this would give Polo a 34 percent sales increase at the expense of 5 percent to Ford.
>
> A close examination of the research will almost certainly confirm the "hostility" referred to came from the committed Ford consumer. Surprise, surprise! One might even find that the reverse applies to the other segment! . . .
>
> In conclusion, as anybody knows, it's pretty easy to create ads that ring research bells. It's another matter to create ads that ring sales-till bells!

A *Gallup–Robinson* study covered ninety-seven television commercials, contrasting each different comparative commercial against all other executions for the same brand (other controls were used for commercial's length, sex, time of day, and year).[15] Three out of ten comparative commercials produced negative results or were ineffective in terms of brand registration (recall). The other 70 percent enjoyed varying degrees of effectiveness—some modest, some of outstanding proportion, but averaging a 22 percent premium over non-comparative advertisements (this increase from 14 to 17 percent is really statistically insignificant due to the small sample size). However, the Gallup–Robinson scores showed no significant differences between comparison and non-comparison commercials in terms of persuasion and motivation.

On the basis of 499 commercials, the *Burke Research Company* did not find any significant difference in the "day-after recall" scores between comparative and non-comparative ads. The research agency *McCollum/Spielman* analyzed 864 commercials using a demonstration in the copy, with 139 of them identifying the competitor. There was no significant differences in either persuasion or recall between commercials with or without competitive identifica-

---

[14] In connection with this campaign, some fifty Polo dealers actually bought a Fiesta and displayed it on their forecourts under a banner saying: "Test drive a [Ford] Fiesta before you buy a [VW] Polo." In every single instance, the dealer got a marked uplift in Polo sales. Shingfield, *op. cit.*

[15] Rockey, *op. cit.*, pp. 7–10. He gives details about several brands (Datril, Reading Beer, Schmidt's Beer) in this presentation.

tion.[16] These findings are somewhat limited because they are based on large numbers of unrelated commercials rather than on contrasting a comparative with a non-comparative format for the same ad.

Prasad's experimental-laboratory research indicated that message-recall effectiveness of *print* comparative ads can be somewhat higher than for non-comparative ones. On the other hand, comparative-ad claims achieved lower consumer credibility than their non-comparative counterparts (this finding is consistent with the Ogilvy & Mather results, which indicated a 14 percent drop in the credibility of comparative ads).[17] In particular, credibility of the claims made in the comparative ads was lower among consumers who preferred the competitor's brand—possibly due to cognitive dissonance. Prasad points out that this may be a serious problem for advertisers using comparative ads, since consumers who prefer or use the competitor's brand chosen for the comparison generally constitute an important segment of the intended audience. He suggests that credibility may be increased by citing tests conducted by independent and trustworthy sources and by disclaiming superiority in some product features.

It is well to realize that Prasad's study dealt with a single product category (movie cameras) and that 90 percent of the respondents were "not confident at all" or "slightly confident" in judging these cameras. An actual target group can be expected to be more informed, and might react quite differently to comparative ads concerning products important to them. Prasad said that future areas for research should include experimenting with repeated exposures (the study included only one), working with different product categories, and examining product-involvement questions such as brand preferences and purchase intentions.

Etgar and Goodwin,[18] in the most ambitious research design to date, tested 180 business students in the Spring of 1977. Two types of *products* (a fictional cold remedy with high "functional utility" and a fictional beer with high "social" utility),[19] three different numbers of *product attributes* (two,

---

[16] Quoted in: "For and Against Comparative Advertising," *op. cit.,* pp. 25–26.

[17] V. Kanti Prasad, "Communication-Effectiveness of Comparative Advertising: A Laboratory Analysis," *Journal of Marketing Research* (May 1976), pp. 128–37.

[18] Michael Etgar and Stephen Goodwin, "An Experimental Investigation of Comparative Advertising: Impact of Message Appeal, Information Load, and Utility of Product Class" (Working Paper No. 334; School of Management, State University of New York at Buffalo, November 1977). Their study differed from previous work in this area along the following dimensions: (1) it strived to explore simultaneously the effect of the relative effectiveness of comparative advertising vis-à-vis supportive and "Brand X" ads; (2) it compared the effectiveness of using supportive, "Brand X," and comparative advertising in products that provide functional and tangible versus social/psychological non-tangible benefits; (3) it incorporated different amounts of attribute information, all dimensions having been discovered through pretests to be salient to the subjects used in the study; (4) it controlled for the potential effects of personality variables and prior usage history; (5) it measured the communication effectiveness of comparative ads in terms of both ad and brand-related measures; and (6) it used manipulation checks to ensure the validity of the measures used in the experiment.

[19] "Functional" refers to products with primarily utilitarian and easy-to-compare benefits, while "social" ones have more elusive qualities that are hard to compare (e.g., status, pleasure).

five, and seven), and three types of *print* advertisements (supportive [unilateral or non-comparative], Brand X, and comparative) were included in the eighteen ads shown to the students. Etgar and Goodwin also controlled for the potential effects of personality variables (dogmatism, tolerance for uncertainty, arousal-seeking tendency, and cognitive clarity), prior-usage history, and brand loyalty. They reached the following still-tentative conclusions:

> *For all six product/brand-related criterion measures, the "Brand X" treatment reveals its superiority.* Quality assessment is highest; the promoted brand is perceived as a better buy; knowledge is felt to be enhanced the most; overall affect [favorable disposition] toward the brand promoted is highest; the intention to buy the promoted brand is highest; and the perception of the risk for buying the brand promoted is lowest (p. 19).

> [In the case of responses to the *advertisement* itself]: If cognitive [awareness] response dimensions are of primary concern to the advertiser, it appears that such responses are generally improved by use of a "Brand X" message appeal. On the other hand, if affective [emotional] dimensions are of utmost concern . . . it appears that such responses [to the *ad*] are generally improved by the use of a comparative message appeal (p. 24).

> Overall, the results seem to suggest that comparative advertising is a *much less powerful tool than is expected.* It may be only marginally advantageous in improving consumers' feelings toward the *ad* presented. However, it performs relatively worse in improving respondents' feelings toward the promoted *brand.* As advertisers are eventually interested more in the latter than in the former, the advantage of using comparative advertising is small (p. 26) . . . [Brand X appeals] may be more effective in generating positive feelings toward the promoted brand. Supportive [unilateral] message appeals did not emerge as superior in any case (p. 26).[20]

In trying to explain these differences, Etgar and Goodwin hypothesize that comparative ads that attack leading brands explicitly and that extol the relative virtues of relatively unknown brands are disbelieved due to the inherent strength of belief in the former. On the other hand, a Brand-X approach may provide anchor points for comparison with the new brand without, at the same time, requiring people to alter their beliefs about specific brands.

They qualify these conclusions, however, by pointing to: (1) the lack of a large number of statistically significant results, (2) the exclusive use of convenience products in the tests (shopping and specialty goods may differ), and (3) the use of a single exposure to the ads: "It is possible that because comparative ads are relatively new and complex, consumers need several exposures before they can get used to this type of message appeal and start utilizing the pertinent information" (p. 27).

---

[20] They also observed that individual usage experience and psychological differences do not substantially affect reactions to different modes of advertising (p. 25). The results also suggest that advertising managers may make decisions about: (1) type of advertisement (unilateral, comparative, Brand X); (2) amount of information in the ad; and (3) type of product—*independently of each other* (p. 25).

This CARLTON cigarette ad heralds a modified use of the "Brand X" approach, since the other brands can be readily identified by their initials. While the FTC does not like this approach, the research by Etgar and Goodwin suggests that it is more effective than direct comparisons that "name names."

Golden[21] investigated the relative influence of comparative and non-comparative ads upon the purchase intentions of 594 college undergraduates. The test involved both mock and real ads and products (a deodorant). The advertiser's market position, claim substantiation, and theme were considered, while brand loyalty was controlled. Golden found that comparative ads appear to be no more effective than non-comparative ads, except when copy theme is considered:

> However, in conjunction with specific themes, a comparative advertisement may have a relatively stronger influence upon purchase intentions than a non-comparative advertisement. Thus, the choice of an advertising strategy should be mediated by the specific themes under consideration.
> . . . An advertiser should consider his market position as unique, and use

[21] L.L. Golden, "Consumer Reactions to Comparative Advertising," in B.B. Anderson (ed.), *Advances in Consumer Research*, Vol. III (Atlanta, Ga.: Association for Consumer Research, 1976), pp. 63–67.

the theme which most favorably affects the impact of his competitive position upon consumer response.

Golden also commented that the naming of a substantiating agency could have made the claims more believable, although consumers have by now been exposed to so many claim substantiations that they may be inoculated to them. Repeated exposure, too, could have produced results different than were achieved in the test. She concluded that there is no simple way of determining the effectiveness of comparative advertisements because many other variables which require further study bear on the problem.

Pride, Lamb and Pletcher[22] studied the perceived informativeness and product-feature awareness of seven mock ads (six comparative and one non-comparative). They differed in terms of: (1) whether similarities or differences were stressed (*directionality of ad*) and (2) whether the ads provided a casual mention of the existence of a competitive brand (Texas Instrument SR–11), an intermediate, or a very high-level, point-by-point comparison of the sponsored (fictional) and competitive (TI SR–11) brands (*intensity scale*). The test was administered to 210 students, the majority of whom owned a TI calculator. The researchers concluded that:

> Relative to non-comparative messages, comparative advertisements are, in general, no more or no less informative for either owners or non-owners of the competing brand mentioned in the advertisement. Even though comparative advertisements are not more informative than non-comparative ones, the fact that they appear to be no less informative may be important for advertisers, because by knowing that comparative messages are no less informative, advertisers have a broader range of approaches to use when developing advertisements. [This is, of course, a circuitous form of reasoning!]

> Directionality does not appear to influence the informativeness of comparative messages for either owners or non-owners of the [other] brand. This finding suggests that an advertiser has the freedom to use either associative or differentiative messages, since neither format is more informative than the other.

> With respect to variations in intensity, owners of the competing brand respond differently from non-owners. For non-owners, variations in the intensity of comparison have very little impact on the informativeness of comparative messages. One exception to this general finding is that low-intensity advertisements were perceived to be less informative than moderate-intensity ones. However, for the owners of the competing brand shown in the advertisement, variations in intensity seem to have significant effects on informativeness of the advertisements. The objective of many comparative advertisements is to attract and appeal to the owners of the competing brand mentioned in the advertisement, because often that brand is the

[22] W.M. Pride, C.W. Lamb, and B.A. Pletcher, "Are Comparative Advertisements More Informative for Owners of the Mentioned Competing Brand than for Non-Owners?," in B.A. Greenberg and D.N. Bellenger (eds.), *Contemporary American Thought* (Chicago, Ill.: American Marketing Association, 1977), pp. 298–301.

market leader. If this is a primary goal, the findings suggest that the advertiser should avoid the use of high-intensity comparisons and should attempt to achieve a moderate intensity of comparison in order to maximize the informativeness of the advertisement.[23]

Wilson[24] had eighty undergraduate students evaluate eight comparative and eight non-comparative advertising messages for eight different products (only typed headline and copy were shown). Seven different response dimensions were elicited: the *advertisement's* informativeness, believability, offensiveness, and interest produced; attitude change toward the *product* and its perceived quality; and trustworthiness of the *sponsoring company*.

Although the results seem to be specific to the products and ads included in the study, Wilson concluded that:

> In cases where brand comparisons provide little or no factual information, comparative advertising offers no advantage. In fact, on the dimensions of believability and offensiveness (and to a lesser extent for informative value and interest produced), the two-product comparative ads are evaluated more negatively than single-product advertisements.

These various experimental findings do not reveal any simple, clear-cut advantage to using comparison advertising. In fact, some of them are downright negative toward this practice. However, it is well to keep in mind that similar ambiguities exist about the effectiveness of all forms of advertising. Only the accumulation of further research data will help clarify these issues.

NEEDED RESEARCH[25]

What is the effect of exposure frequency on comparison advertising?

Tests have usually been limited to one exposure, with recall measurements made right after it; and the number and sequencing of ads presented have not been controlled in most cases. This situation raises serious questions about the realism of such experiments when compared to the normal conditions under which audiences are exposed to comparative advertisements.

Since a comparative message seems to be more complex and confusing

---

[23] In "high-intensity" ads, the competing brand: (1) is identified by name, (2) is illustrated if the sponsored brand is illustrated, and (3) the two brands are compared in a high-frequency point-by-point manner. A "moderate-intensity" comparative message is one where the competing brand(s) is identified by name but is not shown, and there is not a high-frequency, point-by-point comparison.

[24] R.D. Wilson, "An Empirical Evaluation of Comparative Advertising Messages: Subjects' Responses on Perceptual Dimensions," in B.B. Anderson (ed.), *Advances in Consumer Research,* Vol. III (Atlanta, Ga.: Association for Consumer Research, 1976), pp. 53–57.

[25] This section borrows from Stephen Copulsky, "Comparative Advertising of Consumer Products" (unpublished MBA thesis: Graduate School of Business Administration, New York University, May 1977); and Michael Etgar and S.A. Goodwin, "Comparative Advertising: Issues and Problems," in K. Hunt (ed.), *Advances in Consumer Research,* Vol. V (Atlanta, Ga.: Association for Consumer Research, forthcoming). The latter analyzed the previously mentioned Ogilvy & Mather, Prasad, Mazis, McDougall, Golden, and Wilson studies. See also Wilkie and Farris (*op. cit.*) for further research suggestions.

than most non-comparative ones, it seems logical that repeated exposure might be necessary before such an advertisement is clearly understood and recalled by consumers. But then, the need for higher frequency might be one of the costs of comparison advertising, although it is possible that effectiveness for comparative ads increases at a greater rate than for non-comparative ones as frequency of exposure increases. In other words, the comparative message may take longer to sink in, but may be more effective when it does so.

This observation seems especially important for short television commercials. Even if a consumer is interested in a specific comparative ad and inclined to accept the claims made in it, a single thirty-second exposure may be ineffective. In print, on the other hand, a consumer who is attracted by a comparative ad has time to involve himself in the explanatory body copy and to reflect on the claims made.

One problem, however, with increasing the frequency of comparative ads is that if many advertisers choose to do so, consumer confusion may result, with frequent misidentification of the sponsor and a lack of credibility for comparative claims.

How much of a comparative advantage must be claimed?

Is it sufficient to claim superiority in a single major product function or trait or must overall superiority be claimed? If a single area is chosen, viewers of a comparative ad might assume that claims could not be made in other areas. In any case, are the product advantages that are contrasted in the ad the ones really considered salient by the consumer?

Conversely, does disclaiming superiority in some areas and/or pointing out one's own shortcomings increase believability? However, taking time to do this—especially in a thirty-second TV commercial—may result in even greater consumer confusion! A related question is: should one start with one's advantages or disadvantages?

How effective are comparative ads that cite test results or show demonstrations of the products being used?

It is possible that citing test results or showing demonstrations may tend to be confusing. Also, consumer skepticism—due to the ease with which tests and demonstrations can be manipulated—may make these procedures dangerous even if independent and trustworthy sources conduct the testing.

Too, how much substantiation should be provided to improve credibility, and how can it be provided when the superior attributes are more subjective than objective and/or rest more on psychological and social rather than functional attributes (e.g., how do you prove that a Peugeot has more "class" or "comfort" than a Volvo?).

How many competitors should be named in a comparative ad?

If only one competitor is named, consumers may feel that other products in the category also have comparative advantages. This may be less of a problem if the ad attacks a well-known market leader with a reputation for being one of the best products on the market. Attacking several products at once may make for a stronger claim, but it may also increase confusion and reduce awareness for the sponsoring advertiser. Besides, when and where in the ad do you mention or show the competitive brand(s)—and with what prominence?

What effect does the market position of a product have on comparative advertising?

Do comparisons work well for established products that are facing competitors with slightly larger market shares, or are they more suited for products with very small market shares as compared to their competitors? In any case, experimental tests have not sufficiently manipulated the market position of the promoted and the compared-to brands. Yet, it may make quite a difference to compare Number 10 to Number 1 rather than Number 2.

Is comparison advertising better for products aimed at highly segmented target markets?

For such products, purchase decisions may be based on a single key factor. If an advertiser has a comparative advantage along this line, it may be worthwhile to let this be known. For products aimed at broader markets, however, purchase decisions may be based on many factors, with a comparative advantage in one area carrying only minor weight.

How important is brand loyalty in comparison advertising?

A comparative ad may be more effective than a non-comparative ad in awakening brand-loyal customers to the benefits of the sponsoring advertiser. However, such consumers may reject comparative ads against their products due to cognitive dissonance. Much depends on the reasons for brand loyalty. If brand-loyal consumers buy merely by habit, they may be swayed by a comparative ad. If their brand loyalty is based on benefits that they believe exist in their product, comparative ads may be rejected unless they are extremely clear and convincing. Thus, comparisons may be much more effective in attracting non-brand-loyal, undecided consumers. In this context, Etgar and Goodwin (*op. cit.*) did not find that product usage substantially affected reaction to the type of advertising used.

Can there still be a "novelty" effect for comparison advertising?

The Ogilvy & Mather study found such an effect for a comparative commercial when it was the only such ad shown in a group of non-comparative commercials (the benefit was for increased persuasion, not increased awareness). With the large number of comparative ads in existence, such a novelty effect should be short-lived. However, a novelty effect may still exist if there is only one comparative ad in a particular product category.

Can comparison advertising be successful if the real goal of the sponsoring advertiser is to "upgrade by association" rather than to really compare products along specific features?

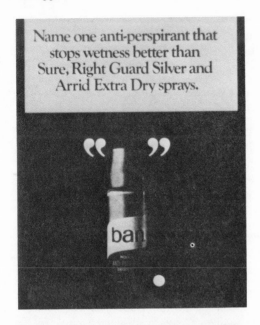

Three largely unresolved problems in the execution of comparison advertising are: (1) *How many* competitive products should be involved in the comparison? (2) Should they be *shown* or simply *mentioned*? (3) How much *prominence* should be given to the competition in the comparative presentation?

These four Ban comparative advertisements show a variety of treatments but provide no answers to these questions.

Prasad did not find any upgrading by association in his study, but the aim of the ad in his study was to show comparative superiority. If the actual goal is to upgrade by association ("My copier is as good as Xerox!"), this kind of message may work.

Is comparative advertising successful on radio?

Studies to date have dealt with television and print. Since visual aid may be important in order to avoid brand confusion, comparisons on the radio may be limited to a supporting role for comparative campaigns in other media. In any case, experimental research has typically been restricted to one medium, with limited testing of the claim that comparisons work better in print.[26]

Is it fair to experimentally compare new or fictitious brands to well-known and entrenched ones that have benefited from numerous messages and/or prolonged consumer experience?

Should more sophisticated distinctions be made in choosing the product categories to use in comparison-advertising research?

Comparisons may be more applicable to products primarily bought on account of objective "functional" attributes that are related to performance under measurable dimensions (e.g., "eighteen miles per gallon"); it may be less effective when social or psychological benefits matter most (e.g., "satisfies more" or "gives you more status")—only Etgar and Goodwin (*op. cit.*) have incorporated that dimension in their research. Besides, research has not as yet clarified the effect of comparing different sub-groups of a product category— for example, luxury vs. economy vs. sports cars. Does it make a difference if you compare a Volkswagen rather than a Peugeot to a Mercedes on some specific feature?

Have the people tested been the most appropriate ones in terms of product knowledge, purchase interest, and usage frequency?

How brand-loyal are the respondents? Were they checked for relevant personality traits? For example, comparisons may appeal more to curiosity, novelty, and information seekers. Experimental research to date has seldom bothered to manipulate these and other variables, besides failing to pretest their operationalization and discriminating character (Etgar and Goodwin were much more careful in this respect).

Clearly, our research-based knowledge of comparison advertising is very imperfect, and any progress is bound to be complex, time-consuming, and expensive. In this context, it is well to observe that it is difficult to find many commercials suitable for testing—that is, comparative ads with non-comparative variations that are basically equivalent in all aspects, except naming the competition. Unfortunately, this can make it impossible to test certain comparative ads that may appear to be particularly effective. Their absolute effectiveness can be determined, but their relative effectiveness vis-à-vis a similar non-comparative ad cannot be known unless both have been created and tested against each other. This is an important limitation for this type of research.

OPERATIONAL EVIDENCE

One can, of course, question whether this kind of research considerations really interest most advertisers and advertising agencies. As the following letter from International Harvester as well as cases in Part III indicate, very few com-

[26] The third Ogilvy & Mather study (*op. cit.*) reached somewhat negative conclusions about print comparisons.

panies have any measurement or estimate of the impact of their comparative advertisements in terms of awareness, recall, and/or interest. In terms of increased sales, practically all said that they thought it had helped, and they referred to favorable reaction from salesmen, dealers, and customers; but they could not definitely say how or how much, because so many other factors affect sales. A typical comment came from a United Kingdom firm about the effectiveness of its comparative advertisement of golf balls: "Unfortunately (but typically), neither agency nor client seem to have research on the effectiveness of this campaign."

Moreover, the caselets in Part III reveal in many cases a good or at least a plausible rationale for choosing a comparative format: the need to position a totally different cigarette (More in Sweden); the opportunity to capitalize on a current auto show, and offering its equivalent in the ad (Chevrolet dealers in Brazil); providing dealers with talking points (VW–Polo in the United Kingdom, and Continental Insurance Stores in the United States)—and so on.

Other "reasonable" uses include: (1) handling misperceptions, as when Goodrich tried to clear its perennial confusion with Goodyear—which is much better known because of its blimp balloon; and (2) drawing the attention of professional investors and financial analysts who are more familiar with competing companies. Thus, a Great Northern Nekoosa ad stated: "We're among the six largest papermakers in the United States. We have more capacity than Mead, Union Camp, Westvaco, Potlatch, Boise Cascade and many other fine and familiar names. But, a lot of the bankers, investment advisers, brokers, and market analysts we are just beginning to reach thought of us until recently as the company we used to be."

One can definitely question the lack of scientific rigor of such comparative campaigns, but this kind of complaint can be addressed to non-comparative ones as well. Besides, a number of comparison users were obviously pleased with the results, even though only the successful ones cared to discuss this subject ("Victory has a thousand fathers, but defeat is an orphan!"), and we will never know if a comparative format would have done better.

SALES RESULTS

The primary basis for marketers' interest in comparison advertising is its potential for increasing sales and market share. Little published data is available on this question, but Schick's controversial comparative campaign for its Fleximatic electric shaver was credited with a market share that increased from 8 to 24 percent, and with a gain of $28 million in sales. A somewhat modest claim of 6 percent increase in market share was reported by Doulton china since it started its comparative advertisements using the brand-leader's name Lenox.[27] A top credit-card firm tripled its sales by advertising that its card

---

[27] "Schick, Inc. Teeters on the Razor's Edge," *Business Week* (5 May 1975), p. 38; "Doulton Credits 6% Share Gain to Ad Comparing Its China with Lenox Line," *Advertising Age* (5 February 1973), pp. 4–6; Tannenbaum, "Better Products Through Comparative Advertising," *op. cit.,* p. 24; Rockey, *op. cit., passim;* and Tanner *op. cit.,* p. 210.

INTERNATIONAL HARVESTER

October 13, 1977

Dear Professor Boddewyn:

Our overall strategy for selecting comparative product advertising was based on the fact that our awareness levels for Scout were below that of Jeep and Chevrolet Blazer. Our market share indicates that we are in the third position in the Sports/Utility industry. We have approximately 13 percent of the market while Blazer and Jeep enjoy shares of 32 percent and 33 percent respectively.

As you can well imagine, the name Jeep is synonymous with four-wheel drive. Thus, we felt we had "nothing to lose" by comparing ourselves to the industry leader. If we could arouse <u>curious disbelief</u> then we would have achieved the first step towards serious purchase consideration.

Four-wheel drive owners are very much oriented toward product facts. We tried to blend product facts with additional advertising copy to present a logical alternative purchase decision. This strategy was chosen over generic brand advertising.

The results of the campaign were that people became much more aware of Scout and International Harvester as a manufacturer of four-wheel drive vehicles. Our corporate reputation combined with our product advantages caused many people to ask questions when they came into the dealer showrooms. This indicated that the advertising was having an impact. In terms of effectiveness, we cannot determine that until the results of our annual Tracking Study which becomes available next February.

If you would like further details on this information, please contact me and I will be happy to provide them to you.

Sincerely,

Jerry Juska [signed]
Planning Coordinator
Light Line Trucks

A fairly typical rationale for using comparison advertising.

could be used to obtain cash, while the recognized leader's card (American Express) could not. Schmidt's Beer and Life Savers CareFree Sugarless Gum have made similar claims that comparison advertising has *contributed* to their growth and success.

INTERNATIONAL HARVESTER

SCOUT® II
30-Second Television Commercial

From the ground up, the International Scout II is designed for rugged

four wheel-drive performance.

Smaller and

narrower than a

Chevy Blazer on the outside.
(SFX: BONK!)

But inside,

Scout gives you

almost half a foot more cargo length

behind the rear seat.

And six hundred pounds more payload than Blazer.

Test drive the incredible International Harvester Scout today.

LOCAL ANNOUNCER: (Live-5 Sec)
(MUSIC: "SCOUT" THEME UNDER

INTERNATIONAL HARVESTER

GREY ADVERTISING INC.

CLIENT: B. F. GOODRICH
PRODUCT: TIRES
TITLE: "B. F. GOODRICH **LENGTH:** 60 SECONDS
PRESIDENT'S COMMERCIAL" (REV. 2)

DATE: 11/14/73
CODE NO.: GRPT3136

PATRICK ROSS: I'm Patrick Ross, President of the B. F. Goodrich Tire Company.

2. Not Goodyear. Goodrich.

3. As if our names weren't confusing enough,

4. Goodyear advertises more than we do.

So I'm not too surprised a lot of people

6. forget Goodrich and remember Goodyear.

7. Maybe even go to Goodyear for Goodrich tires.

8. But you can't get Goodrich steel radials at Goodyear.

You see, we introduced the first American-made radial tire in 1965.

10. The radial was, and is, the biggest tire innovation in nearly a quarter century.

11. For five years, nationally, we've advertised nothing else.

12. Not because everybody wants radials -

But because no conventional tire we've ever made, none,

14. Stops as fast, corners as well,

15. and lasts as long as our Lifesaver Steel Radial.

16. Now without a dobut, doubt, you'll see Goodyear advertising a steel radial too.

Along with all their other tires.

18. But don't get confused.

19. Lifesaver Steel Radials.

20. If you want Goodrich, you'll just have to remember Goodrich.

Using a comparative ad to clear up confusion.

Other success stories[28] include that of Borden's Wise Potato Chips, which were compared to Procter & Gamble's Pringles. They claimed that they thereby maintained their market share for Wise and increased it in New York, even though in some markets they were being outspent five to one. Vivatar challenged Kodak's Instamatic pocket camera on television and gained a 10 percent market share, and Pepsi increased its share from 8 to 18 percent in Dallas as a result of TV ads showing taste tests of Coke drinkers. Helene Curtis price-comparison TV spots have helped quintuple sales in the last four years.In the United Kingdom, VW–Polo claimed that its comparative campaign helped it increase sales and market share significantly against Ford's Fiesta and other competitors (see above).

On the other hand, it appears that Tylenol, which had done little advertising, benefited from the comparative ads run by Datril and aspirin makers, so that by mid-1977 it had become the top-selling pain reliever, with more than 20 percent of the market, while Datril's share never climbed much above 2 percent.

Still, it is not entirely clear due to the lack of proper test controls, whether these increases in sales and market share were attributable to an increased advertising budget or whether the same results could have been achieved with advertising of a non-comparative nature. In the Pepsi "taste-test" challenge to Coca-Cola, there were also price reductions and other promotional activities that masked the effects of the comparative advertisements; thus, Pepsi does not seem to have made such a dent in the national market after all.[29]

WHEN TO USE COMPARISONS

Keeping in mind negative findings and gaps in our knowledge, proponents of comparison advertising believe that it is particularly effective when:

1. *The brand has a small market share or is a newcomer.* Then, comparison with the leader rapidly creates high attention for the brand as well as a positive image through a "halo effect" or "upgrading by association" with the leader. Thus, Datril went after Tylenol in a comparative fashion because it was an upstart, and as a non-aspirin analgesic, it could not attack aspirin products since the parent company also sold Bufferin and Excedrin.

2. *The brand has a built-in advantage and the claimed superiority is meaningful, demonstrable, and verifiable by the consumer.* Conversely, phony or insignificant comparisons will be recognized as such by the consumer; they will lower the credibility of the brand and even of all ad-

---

[28] Letter from Barbara Wolfson (Needham, Harper & Steers International; New York, 25 March 1977); Niles Howard, "Battle Over Comparative Ads," *Dun's Review* (November 1977), p. 60; and Keith Shingfield, "The Argument with a Hole in It," *Campaign* (2 December 1977), p. 29; A.L. Morner, "It Pays to Knock Your Competitors," *Fortune* (13 February 1978), pp. 104–11.

[29] Nancy Giges, "Coca-Cola—Reluctant Entrant into Comparative Ad Warfare," *Advertising Age* (3 January 1977), p. 2ff. See the Pepsi–Coke case in Part III of this study.

vertising; and should thus be avoided. This suggests that comparisons are best used in "verbal" media such as print, that generate greater consumer "involvement" than television.

3. *The specific market or target audience does not have well-established preferences* and there is a significant segment of "undecideds" with a low degree of brand commitment, who are consequently open to new information.

4. *"When your advertising budget is much less than [the competitor's]*—especially where the bulk of your prospects are already customers of his. Your first problem may be to crack his image, to shatter their loyalty, before you can rechannel their desire around to you." [30]

5. Comparisons can be used *defensively* to neutralize the competitor's comparative claims with comparative counterclaims. Also, the competitor's testing methods can be challenged or ridiculed. Thus, Coca-Cola's experience in countering Pepsi's "taste-test challenge" suggests that a counterattack can be based on the technique used by the original comparative advertiser: "We felt like we weren't really knocking Pepsi, which we didn't want to do, but we were knocking the technique an advertiser was using—and that advertiser just happened to be our competitor, Pepsi." [31] In this case, Coca-Cola challenged and made fun of the tests used by Pepsi without, however, pursuing the matter for too long.

In the same vein, disclaimers made by other comparative advertisers can be put to good use. Thus, Volkswagen has quoted Opel ads that acknowledged that the VW Rabbit was superior to it: "General Motors names Rabbit best of five economy cars tested. . . . It takes a very big company to admit publicly that our car is better than their car!" (A picture of the original Opel ad was shown in the background).

The defensive use of comparisons need not be directed to the same target nor use the same media. Thus Lenox was challenged ("Royal Doulton, the china of Stoke-on-Trent, England, vs. Lenox, the china of Pomona, New Jersey"). It responded to the *trade* press with a humorous ad showing a Lenox interoffice memorandum superimposed on a copy of Doulton's, with the notation: "Remember what happened the last time [the British] attacked a Trenton headquarters [where Lenox is based]!" It also prepared materials for the personnel of china stores and departments that answered or refuted the Doulton claims about color, translucency, strength, resonance, design, and quality. (This was linked to a contest that encouraged salespeople to read this documentation.)

6. When a comparative advertisement represents a *novelty* in a particular product category.

---

[30] Eugene Schwartz, *Break-Through Advertising: How to Write Ads that Shatter Traditions and Sales Records* (Englewood Cliffs, N.J.: Prentice Hall, 1966), pp. 176–77.

[31] "Underdog Advertising Wins in 'Naming Names'," *Advertising Age* (10 March 1975), p. 61; and Nancy Giges, "Coca-Cola—Reluctant Entrant into Comparative Ad Warfare," *Advertising Age* (3 January 1977), pp. 2, 35.

Opel makes news.

The results of the Buick Opel 5-Car Showdown are in! Opel finishes...uh...2nd.

GM

A lot of car makers compare their car to other cars.

We compare our car *with* other cars.

In a daring, fender-to-fender competition called The Buick Opel 5-Car Showdown. In it, we pitted our Opel against four better known competitors in point-by-point, side-by-side, independently supervised tests of acceleration, cornering flatness, parking-lot maneuverability, pulling power, gradability, and a few other areas. In short, some of the things you'd like to know when you go out to shop for a car.

It was a bold move. After all, what if we didn't win?

Well, to make a long story short—we didn't. When all the tests were completed and all the figures tallied up, Opel finished second, right behind VW Rabbit. You can imagine how thrilled we were. But look at it this way: in order to finish second overall, we had to beat Toyota Corolla, Datsun B-210, and Subaru DL in a number of instances. (And in some areas, we beat VW, too, as you'll see.)

Which is a victory. And not just a moral one.

You see, we know Opel is a little dynamo of a car. But apparently no one else did. Because it seemed that whenever anyone went out looking for a practical little import, they looked real hard at the other cars in the Showdown. But hardly ever at ours.

So we wanted to show that Opel could hold its own against its famous competitors. That it should definitely be considered when you wander out to shop.

In other words, we were confident Opel was good enough to take on this competition.

Opel announces 4-doors.

Then we went one step further. And made Opel good enough to take on your family. By offering you our new, just-introduced-in-this-country Opel 4-door Sedan.

After all, if you've got a family (or maybe some friends you like taking along on spirited spins around the countryside), you need to carefully examine a car's ins and outs. So we gave you two more.

Easy come. Easy go.

Final Test Results	VW Rabbit	Buick Opel	Toyota Corolla	Subaru DL	Datsun B-210
	(Showdown Point Summary)				
Interior Noise	5	5	5	5	5
EPA Interior Room Estimates	5	3	4	2	1
EPA Trunk Capacity Estimates	5	3	2	4	1
Pulling Power	3	5	4	2	1
(30mph 3rd gear)					
(55mph 4th gear)					
Parking Lot Maneuverability	3	5	4	2	1
EPA Mileage Estimates	3	2	4	4	5
Estimated Range	2	3	5	5	4
Maintenance Stops*	5	3	4	2	4
(Recommended)					
Acceleration	5	4	3	2	1
(0-55mph, 20-35mph)					
(30-70mph)					
Gradability***	5	4	3	3	2
(30mph 3rd gear)					
(55mph 4th gear)					
Cornering Flatness**	4	5	3	4	5
Steering Quickness	5	5	5	4	5
Grand Total	**50**	**47**	**46**	**39**	**35**

*The less frequent the number of visits over 37,500 miles of normal driving, the higher the score. The number and type of inspections, adjustments and replacements would vary by visit.

**Based upon opinion that less lean is preferable to more lean.

***Includes vehicle weight.

In California, Opel placed second on an overall basis. Individual test results vary from those shown above.

See your Buick Opel dealer for complete details.

A self-derogatory ad of the ''We're Number 2'' type, which was picked up by Volkswagen.†

†For further details about this Opel campaign and its subsequent use by Volkswagen, see: A.L. Morner, ''It Pays to Knock Your Competitor,'' *Fortune* (13 February 1978), p. 106.

7. *When the market is static* and comparison may be the ultimate weapon in order to get a bigger share of it.

8. *When non-comparative methods have ceased to be effective*—as when Pepsi concluded that its unilateral slogans were not sufficient to make a significant dent in Coca-Cola's share of certain markets. Still, it is well to remember that: "Naming names is not a strategy. It is an execution."[32] If necessary, in order to provide a demonstration (the strongest form of proof), comparison should be used, but means should not be confused with ends.

Even as a tactic, the comparative approach should be well aimed. The objective is not necessarily to take business away from a stronger competitor, but to use its position to establish one's own:

> "Avis is Number 2 in rent-a-cars. So why go with us? We try harder." Avis didn't take business away from Hertz. The numbers show that Avis took business away from the other car-rental firms.

> And what about 7-Up's "Uncola" program? In a three-year period, sales went up 58 percent. Again, 7-Up didn't take business away from Coke and Pepsi. It took business away from ginger ale, root beer, and the other soft drinks.

> The most effective positioning programs are never what they seem to be. "My parking ticket said Cadillac. But my car is a Ford Granada." The objective of Ford is not to take business away from the Cadillac Seville. The objective of Ford is to take business away from Chevrolet by positioning Granada as the car with the high-price look.[33]

9. *Comparative demonstrations are more effective when both video and audio are used,* with side-by-side demonstrations of the competitive products (as compared to simply mentioning the competitive brand without showing it), because visual elements tend to dominate a viewer's perception (video-cum-audio usually predominates in a comparative TV commercial).[34]

10. Comparative commercials that do not emphasize a price-economy argument but tell *why* the product or service is superior, produce significantly higher registration (recall) results.

11. *Showing several competitive brands* appears to be advantageous because it increases the involvement potential: the more brands shown, the more people in the exposed audience will be directly involved in the "targeted" sense.

[32] "Should You Name Your Competitors in Advertising?" *BBDO Research Newsletter* (February 1975), p. 1.

[33] Al Ries, "Clausewitz on Market Positioning," *Campaign* (10 June 1977), p. 8.

[34] S.I. Tannenbaum makes the same point in "Comparative Advertising: The Advertising Industry's Own Brand of Consumerism" (Paper presented at the AAAA Convention, Greenbrier, W.Va., 15 May 1976), p. 5.

WHEN NOT TO USE COMPARISONS

1. When a good product can be successfully *communicated on its own merits,* without any reference to others.
2. *When the advertiser dominates the market* and has no need to attract attention to its challengers. Even counterclaims are dangerous, because consumers may assume that there was an original justification for the claim.
3. *When products are not amenable to comparison* because there are no meaningful scientifically measurable product differences. Thus, for many food and clothing items, consumer preferences are formed on more subjective evaluative criteria such as taste and style. Differences in product features in these categories are purposefully directed to different consumer needs, which thus precludes meaningful comparisons.
4. When the likelihood of *valid counterclaims by the challenged competitor* cannot be ignored.
5. *When production costs* for comparative commercials (including tests running up to $100,000) and the probability of litigation *are high.*
6. When regulatory and self-regulatory bodies might respond to the increasing volume of complaints by advertisers and the media through *more restrictive rules and guidelines* (the Philippine case is very illuminating in this respect).
7. *When the appeals are more emotional* ("Things go better with Coke!") *than rational,* and when there is no objective argument to support a claim of superiority (as has been said of all cosmetics and perfumes: "The main ingredient is hope!"). This also suggests that it may be better to use fewer comparisons on television, which is not the "medium of reason," and normally elicits a "low involvement" and lower rates of recall among viewers (*cf.* Krugman).
8. When comparisons generate either *too much confusion* because of irreconcilable claims or "information overload" because of specifying too many product attributes, both of which can lead consumers to "tune out."
9. When the *attack on the competitor is too vicious or self-serving* and makes the audience rally to the underdog or curse all forms of advertising.
10. Last but not least, *when the product has no significant comparative advantage.* It is sobering to observe that there are now on the U.S. market some 58 deodorants, 75 shampoos, 85 soaps and detergents, 132 domestic and foreign models of cars, and 138 cigarette brands.[35] Clearly, they cannot all be superior.

[35] H.D. Maneloveg, "Comparative Advertising: A Position in Favor" (Paper presented at the IREP conference in Paris, 26 May 1977). He is Senior Vice-President of Kenyon & Eckardt, whose chairman is Stanley Tannenbaum. He also commented that some of the opposition to comparison advertising comes from brand leaders and their agencies.

Tom Scott, Vice-President of Foster Advertising (Canada) has brought up points to consider *even if* there are advantages to using comparison advertising:

> Good comparison advertising is hard to do, to recommend, and to approve, and it is usually very expensive because much information is required about one's product and all the other products in the category. Besides, a series of subsidiary questions must be answered.
>
> 1. Is our product sufficiently superior to make its difference significant to the consumer in a direct side-by-side presentation?
> 2. How much time and money is it going to take in order to find out?
> 3. If there are good comparative points, how much more time and money will it cost to produce the legally required documentation?
> 4. How long can we expect to be able to support our story before the competition introduces changes and nullifies the validity of the comparison?
> 5. Will a comparative execution be as persuasive as a solo presentation with no comparison or reference to the existence of a competitive product?
> 6. Is it appropriate to use comparisons which are very *rational* by nature, when emotional appeals might be more effective?
> 7. Will the agency and client people really *cooperate* if they do not consider comparative executions (and the required documentation) to be very "creative," "decent," and/or "sportsmanlike?"[36]

[36] Tom Scott, "Comparative Advertising: Why Is There so Little of It?" (Address to the Association of Canadian Advertisers, Toronto, 6 May 1975). This is a condensation of his remarks.

[handwritten notes:]
Expensive => Kraft shouldn't
Acquire reputation for being embroiled
in litigation
Is it sustainable
"Real" admits possibility of fakeness
perhaps consumers used to
fakeness

8

Comparison Advertising: Where Do We Go from Here?

EVIDENCE ABOUT the fairness, benefits, and effectiveness of comparison advertising is mixed—very much as it is with any other form of advertising (see Figure 3). There is one major difference, however, namely that the matter is more serious because the reputation and goodwill of other firms are at stake. Besides, consumer confusion is an important issue, and the cost of making comparisons is not negligible. The dilemma presented by comparative advertisements is thus a real one:

> Does comparison advertising constitute a simple problem whose apparent difficulties simply result from the fact that it raises a maximum number of questions which are already raised about other types of advertising? Or does it exhibit its own complexity and ambiguity so that any solution would be imperfect if not dangerous?[1]

Our answer leans more toward the first view: comparison advertising is desirable and works well under certain conditions, and it can be made to function better. These and the following views, however, are only those of the main authors of this report, and they should not be interpreted to represent the position of the International Advertising Association, its National Chapters, and/or its Sustaining and Organizational Members, who sponsored and financed this study.

[1] Ligue Internationale Contre la Concurrence Déloyale, Report of the *Journées d'Etudes d'Edimbourg* (18–21 September 1977), p. 3.

FIGURE 3

THE PROS AND CONS OF COMPARISON ADVERTISING

A. Potential Positive Impacts:

For the Consumer:

1. Provides *clearer brand perception* by pointing out meaningful differences.
2. Helps *evaluate* the performance of brands by providing significant criteria.

For the Marketplace:

1. Stimulates *product improvement* through increased competitiveness.
2. Helps smaller brands and new ones which compare themselves to betterknown ones, thereby *weakening monopolistic positions*.

For the Advertiser and Business:

1. Provides *higher effectiveness* by: (a) creating increased *attention* (at least due to the novelty of comparison advertising), and (b) generating *more persuasion* since consumers believe that the comparative ad would not be run if it were not true.
2. Proves that advertising can be most *informative* rather than merely manipulative.

B. Potential Negative Impacts:

For the Consumer

1. Creates consumer confusion by: (a) presenting *irreconcilable claims*, (b) *overloading* them with information, and (c) conveying misleading information as a result of selecting *nonrepresentative* consumer endorsements and product tests, and/or *unimportant* product featuers.

For the Marketplace

1. Augments the volume of *ineffective* advertising because of unbelieved comparative claims and counterclaims.
2. Raises the *cost of advertising* on account of the additional research and clearances required, and because of the complaints and litigation that must be handled.

For the Advertiser and Business:

1. Harms a firm's goodwill because of *disparagement,* or *unfairly* capitalizes on the brand name of the leader.
2. Creates *divisiveness* within the industry.
3. Damages advertising's *credibility*.

C. *Application and Research Problems:*

1. *Difficulty of interpreting* such guidelines as "unfair," "significant product attribute," "net impression," "not deceptive," and so on.

2. *Difficulty of observing* effects on the marketplace because questions concerning the effectiveness of comparison advertising remain largely unanswered: (a) various communication hypotheses need further empirical validation, (b) tentative research findings cannot be generalized to all brands and market conditions, and (c) there is no large-scale representative study available on consumer behavior, following their exposure to comparison advertising.

SOME INTERIM CONCLUSIONS

1. *Comparison advertising is here to stay in many countries, and signs of its increasing usage and acceptance are unmistakable.* There are more comparative advertisements around the world; consumer associations welcome them to a degree; the International Chamber of Commerce's Advertising Code now allows them, as do a growing number of voluntary codes; courts are proving more lenient in various countries (e.g., West Germany); and laws are likely to be revised to accommodate comparisons even in such negative nations as France and Belgium.

The use of comparisons already accounts for between 1 and 10 percent of advertisements and/or advertising expenditures in some developed countries. Admittedly, this range is low, and it probably represents a maximum because comparative advertising only suits certain marketing situations. There are also the problems of saturation and declining novelty that cause diminishing returns after a while. In the long run, consumer reactions may not be that favorable, and there will be increasing regulatory and self-regulatory restrictions. Hence, its practice will remain negligible in many countries and quickly reach an upper limit (5 to 10 percent) in others.

In any case, countries can no longer isolate themselves from comparative advertisements. Such international magazines as *Reader's Digest, Vision,* and *International Management* as well as radio and television stations with a multinational reach bring them to countries where they are forbidden. Even if Swiss watchmakers do not want to use comparisons, what will they do if Bulova or Seiko attack their products through comparative ads?

2. *Comparisons properly belong to the arsenal of advertising techniques because they are effective under certain conditions,* as even people like Andrew Kershaw—a leading opponent of comparison advertising—admit. Like other techniques (sex, humor, testimonials, imagery), comparisons have their uses in good advertising.

Comparison advertising is of course not a panacea—but what is? There are alternative or complementary sources of comparative information such as consumer reports, informative labeling, unit pricing, fact-loaded unilateral ads, and the like. Some or even much of it is poorly conceived and executed, but this is true of all advertising. The distinction then—as Tannenbaum has repeatedly argued—is really between "good" and "bad" rather than between "comparative" and "unilateral" advertising.

Comparison advertising is not an inexpensive technique to use, and it is true that it creates jobs for those lawyers needed to pre-check ads or to litigate complaints. But, as Pierre Lemonnier put it:

> Even if firms will need more lawyers, it is not such a nuisance after all. It beats any conspiracy to remain silent because the better brand should win. This is the best benefit we can offer to consumers. . . . Comparisons should not be left exclusively to consumer associations.[2]

3. *Most of the problems associated with comparisons really lie with advertising in general.* One cannot fail to observe: (1) the persistent anti-advertising attitudes of elites, regulators, and consumerists in many countries, even those with no comparison advertising, (2) the growing influence of the latter in legislative chambers, regulatory bodies, and consultative[3] assemblies, (3) the rather mediocre ratings given advertising by recent consumer surveys (see previous setions), and (4) the increasingly strict provisions of recent advertising legislation or regulation (whether only proposed or already enacted) as a reflection of the above.

The general criticisms of advertising remain the perennial ones: that it is uninformative, overpersuasive, manipulative, degrading, materialistic, wasteful, and oligopolistic. An outcome of this state of dissatisfction with advertising is the regulatory trend toward requiring that: (1) all claims—*whether comparative or unilateral*—be scientifically substantiated *before* they are advertised, not after the fact,[4] and (2) the *overall impression* communicated by the advertisement be truthful—not just the specific facts mentioned in the ad—or that disclaimers be used for other significant data.

This regulatory development will certainly require more sophisticated and objective testing and consumer-research facilities under the aegis of truly independent bodies: in-house research will not be sufficient any longer. Governments are also likely to provide more of the information used in advertising claims (see cigarette and automobile ads), and to monitor and/or supervise

[2] Quoted in: Emmanuel Voisin "Pour ou contre la publicité comparative," *Stratégies*, No. 129 (December 1976), p. 55.

[3] Many European countries have legally appointed bodies such as the Consumers Council in Belgium, where consumer representatives must be heard on the impact of proposed legislation on the consuming public.

[4] This requirement is often combined with reversal of the burden of proof—that is, the advertiser will (or would) have to prove that his ad is not false or misleading, rather than the plaintiff having to do it. See, for example, the Belgian bill and the EEC draft directive on misleading and unfair advertising, which also provide for speedier and easier adjudication, stiffer penalization, and corrective advertisements.

Este es
el conocido amarillo.

No es ningún secreto . . .
Caterpillar® es el gigante de la
industria de equipos pesados . . . e indu-
dablemente merece su gran prestigio.
    Para que TEREX adquiera
igual renombre, también
ha de ganarlo.
    Comparada con
Caterpillar, nuestra
Compañía es relativa-
mente "un recién
llegado" a este campo.
    Sin embargo,

sabemos que hemos alcanzado
"la mayor edad" y nos proponemos
convencerlo.
    ¿Cómo? Mediante una
"nueva generación"
de mototraíllas,
camiones, cargadores
y tractores de orugas
TEREX, que por sí
mismos están
forjando una
sólida
reputación . . .

Example of a comparative ad run in an international magazine (*Progreso–La Revista Economica Interamericana*) reaching a number of Latin-American countries with a variety of regulations and industry guidelines.

TEREX DIVISION, GENERAL MOTORS OVERSEAS
DISTRIBUTORS CORPORATION, HUDSON, OHIO 44236, U.S.A.

more closely this kind of research since different techniques can lead to different results and thus create a danger of fraud.[5]

More generally, *there is demand for more "meaningful" information in ads*. Consumerists and government officials[6] in many countries are really pressing for the type of promotional advertising (*réclame* in French and other continental European languages) that makes a definite informative point—pos-

[5] For U.S. developments along these lines, see: W.L. Wilkie and P.W. Farris, *Consumer Information Processing: Perspectives and Implications for Advertising* (Cambridge, Mass.: Marketing Science Institute, 1976), particularly the Appendix on "Public Policy Perspectives," pp. 117–38. See also the General Electric consent order with the U.S. Federal Trade Commission, which imposes various "evidence" requirements in future GE advertisements (Docket #9049, 19 April 1976).

[6] The U.S. Federal Trade Commission is planning an assault on promotional campaigns that—even without misrepresentation—encourage shoppers to make "unwise" buying decisions. "The FTC Broadens Its Attacks on Ads," *Business Week* (20 June 1977), p. 27. For similar demands in France, see Voisin, *op. cit.*

Ahora le presentamos una excelente alternativa.

. . . Mediante una red de Distribuidores tan eficaz como bien organizada . . .
. . . Mediante un renovado sistema auxiliar para suministrar repuestos y prestar un excelente servicio de mantenimiento, a fin de conservar sus máquinas en actividad . . .
. . . Y con un criterio de asistencia a los clientes no aventajado por nadie. Sabemos qué tan buenos son nuestros competidores.
Ahora estamos empeñados en probarle qué tan buenos somos nosotros. Nos damos cuenta de que no va a ser fácil . . . porque tenemos que alcanzar y perpetuar la misma fama extraordinaria del otro.

TEREX- GENERAL MOTORS. Nos empeñamos en cambiar sus costumbres de selección y compra.

sibly or preferably in a comparative format: "Now 49¢ instead of 69¢" or "ABC batteries last twice as long as DEF batteries, for the same price"). On the other hand, they want fewer "image" or "mood" advertisements, which build up a brand in terms of a number of subtle differentiations and subjective appreciations.

Most modern advertising has, of course, been of the latter type in the historical process of setting XYZ salt apart from the undifferentiated salt that used to be bought out of a barrel. This often results in minor quality differences among brands, or to a sum of real but very subtle or subjective distinctions that are hard to pin down and measure. In either case, this type of "non-objective" advertising does not lend itself well to comparisons. The dispute about the informative content of advertising is thus not likely to abate, even if comparisons become authorized and/or more widely used.

Still more disturbing is the comment occasionally heard that "there are few new products, and many old ones have no real comparative advantages to convey." Even Tannenbaum has acknowledged it: "Experience tells me there are not that many significant and demonstrable brand differences to warrant the

Guess which is the world's fastest growing airline?

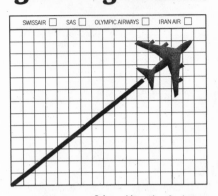

SWISSAIR ☐   SAS ☐   OLYMPIC AIRWAYS ☐   IRAN AIR ☐

Which of these airlines operates the longest non-stop scheduled flight?

BRITISH AIRWAYS ☐   IRAN AIR ☐   LUFTHANSA ☐   TWA ☐

Only one of these airlines flies to London, New York, Moscow, Peking and Tokyo. Which is it?

Only one of these airlines flies the most comfortable plane in the sky, the new 747SP, on regular schedule between London and New York. Which one?

BRITISH AIRWAYS ☐   PAN AM ☐
AIR INDIA ☐   IRAN AIR ☐

PAN AM ☐   LUFTHANSA ☐   BRITISH AIRWAYS ☐   IRAN AIR ☐

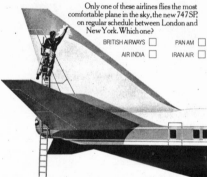

There's only one airline in the world that will fly you to four continents in the same plane on the same day. Which is it?

QANTAS ☐   TWA ☐
KLM ☐   IRAN AIR ☐

The world's fastest growing airline, believe it or not, is Iran Air. It really is.

For instance, every year for the past five years we've bought more new planes. (This year, we take delivery of our new 747-200Bs. The very latest Jumbo.)

And every year for the last five years we've flown more passengers to more destinations.

So that today you can fly Iran Air to any one of twenty seven major cities throughout the world. (Including, by the way, London, New York, Moscow, Peking, and Tokyo.)

If the flight takes your fancy, Iran Air can also fly you to four different continents, in the same plane on the same day. (Tehran to Cairo, on to Paris, finishing up in New York.)

Quite a hop.

Do it in reverse though, New York to Tehran, and you'll experience one of the longest non-stop scheduled flights ever.

Over 6,200 miles.

A distance covered with ease by Iran Air's new 747SP.

The 'Special Performer' Jumbo.

It flies a mile above normal air routes. A mile above the bad weather.

Making it the most comfortable plane in the air.

And that's not pie in the sky. It's a fact. Like everything else on this page.

IRAN AIR
The world's fastest growing airline.

THE IRAN AIR ALL BOEING FLEET FLIES TO: NEW YORK, LONDON, PARIS, FRANKFURT, VIENNA, GENEVA, ZURICH, ROME, MOSCOW, ATHENS, ISTANBUL, CAIRO, TEHRAN, ABADAN, BAGHDAD, KUWAIT, JEDDAH, BAHRAIN, ABU DHABI, DHAHRAN, DOHA, MUSCAT, KABUL, KARACHI, BOMBAY, PEKING, TOKYO. ALSO SALES OFFIES IN GLASGOW, MILAN, HAMBURG, DUSSELDORF, MUNICH, LOS ANGELES AND HOUSTON.

Another comparative ad run in an international-circulation medium (*International Management*)

current level of comparative commercial usage.'' [7] If this is true—and the large number of similar products on the market would tend to support this contention—it bodes ill for the fate of advertising and of business in general.

The real danger here is that the enemies of advertising will seize upon this confession to stress the sham of business competition, the surfeit of products, and the pointlessness of many ads. Besides, if comparative advertisements (which are supposed to be informative) turn out to mislead consumers, these opponents will argue that all advertising is either a lie or a futile exercise. Their present support of comparison advertising could even amount to a nasty plot to prove even more strongly that advertising really has nothing valuable to communicate, but is condemned to remain misleading and/or to generate pleasant moods to nobody's real benefit—apart from that of its practitioners.

This serious challenge should be met by proving that advertising has meaningful information to transmit in a truthful and useful manner. A comparative format can definitely help convey that impression in a number of cases.

4. *The use of comparisons must definitely be "controlled"* because of the dangers they pose. The question is "how"—that is, what mixture of regulations, voluntary codes, media supervision, and self-discipline will prove appropriate. Clearly, the answers will vary from country to country, due to different traditions and experiences. Also, time will be needed to refine this "control" as more is learned about the benefits and limitations of this practice as well as about the controls' effectiveness.

Should the *law and government regulations* be altered? Definitely so in countries that forbid or restrict it unduly, and where the status of comparison advertising is ambiguous (in many statutory-law countries, what is not permitted is often forbidden). This can be achieved in successive stages—for example, by enlarging the number of exceptions and/or by allowing it first for certain types of products only.

The problem here is how ponderous and inflexible the new regulations will turn out to be, since this exercise could very easily result in greater shackling of *all* forms of advertising—all the way to forbidding "non-informative" advertisements, and to requiring prior bureaucratic clearance of all ads on the basis of various criteria (this has been proposed in several European countries).

Undoubtedly the trend is toward requiring prior substantiation of all advertising claims and forbidding the use of false, unfair, and misleading advertising—however nebulous the latter concepts will remain. The crunch, however, will really lie around the perennial problem of defining "denigration."

There are two options here: (1) the Anglo-Saxon approach of considering all *truthful comparisons as non-denigrating in nature,* or (2) the position of the second EEC draft directive on misleading and unfair competition: ''Denigration means the practice of casting discredit, *either by false allegations or, without justifiable reason, by true statements,* on the commercial reputation of another

[7] S.I. Tannenbaum, "Better Products Through Comparative Advertising" (Speech before the San Francisco Advertising Club, 6 October 1976), p. 20.

person . . . (Art. 5.2.)." [8] A similar position is found in German jurisprudence, where comparisons are now allowed if they are sufficiently justified, if the data are correct, and if these data—in terms of their nature and scope—remain within what is necessary for discussing the product (see country synopsis).

What about the *courts?* Legal decisions are slow and sometimes contradictory or evasive. However, West Germans seem generally satisfied with their flexible and evolving approach; existing legislation is being put to greater use in the United States; and Scandinavian countries are developing the role of the Consumer (or Market) Ombudsman who provides greater consumerist input but still allows for appeal to regular courts. Other nations, unfortunately, are less imaginative in this respect.

Voluntary self-regulation through industry, media, and advertising codes provides an obvious alternative or complementary approach. The signs are very encouraging in a number of nations and through the efforts of the International Chamber of Commerce. The proposed EEC draft directive on misleading and unfair advertising also encourages self-regulation, though only as an alternative or complement. [9]

Such voluntary guidelines have increasingly evolved in the direction of allowing comparisons (indirect or direct) and of setting up fairly specific criteria for their acceptance. Clearly, practitioner and media codes will have to be refined and broadly shared around the world under the recognized leadership of the International Chamber of Commerce and of international advertising bodies. Undoubtedly the spread and longevity of comparison advertising will largely depend on how well the advertising community develops and applies such new rules and voluntary guidelines and submits to the decisions of its self-regulatory bodies. Some countries, however, will continue to refuse to relax their practices and codes because of strong cultural factors such as, for example, non-aggressive patterns in the Orient and notions of fair-play ("anti-knocking") in some British Commonwealth nations. Others will reverse their earlier positive stand as in the recent Philippine case (see country synopsis).

While the self-regulatory approach is flexible and close to where the action is, its perennial curse has been to favor "mild" competition in order to protect the weak, the laggard, and those that have already succeeded. It appears, however, that consumerist pressures and regulatory threats are eliminating some of that complacency and are injecting greater public-interest considerations in self-regulation. The U.S. Federal Trade Commission, for one, has strongly warned industry against such restrictions of comparison advertising.

---

[8] The third draft (September 1977) has dropped this definition, which remains useful, however.

[9] Article 8 of the June 1977 draft provided that: "Where Member States permit or recognize the operation of controls exercised by voluntary bodies on misleading or unfair advertising, persons entitled to a right of action by virtue of Article 7 shall be entitled to exercise that right as an alternative, or in addition, to recourse to such controls."

Still, one can expect consumer associations to oppose leaving all rule-making to trade organizations.[10] They will demand regulations, possibly insist on being represented on self-regulatory boards, and/or require that a more impartial consumer ombudsman be set up. Clearly, self-regulation is important, but it cannot carry the whole burden, nor will it be allowed to.

Self-discipline by advertisers, agencies, and the media will also play a crucial role because this is where the action starts. Mistakes and excesses are inevitable, and nobody should try to ban foolishness.[11] Fortunately, growing experience with comparison advertising is helping the industry obtain a better understanding about when and how much to use it. This is a good argument for allowing comparative advertisements, because practitioners will soon find their limits; and excesses will be largely taken care of by regulation and self-regulation or by the threat or reality of litigation.

SOME POSSIBLE RESTRICTIONS

1. *Should the thirty-second (or shorter) comparative television commercial be banned* on the ground that it cannot possibly provide a meaningful and truthful comparison in such a short time—not to mention the preliminary research findings that it is not particularly effective (see above)? This approach would, of course, relegate most comparative ads to the printed form which is a more rational medium anyway (*cf.* Krugman).[12] It would also probably reduce the overall use of comparisons, thereby satisfying those who claim that comparisons are already overused on the air.

One definitely hesitates to urge such a drastic step, hoping instead that self-discipline, the fear of litigation, and screening by the television networks on the basis of more rigorous guidelines will suffice to significantly reduce the volume of broadcasted comparative commercials.

2. *Should price comparisons be banned* because: (1) there is usually a range of prices practiced for the same product—depending on the locale or the channel of distribution—so that it is often impossible to definitely say (without some sort of disclaimer) that product A is cheaper than B, and (2) price cuts can quickly be matched by competitors so that such a claim is more likely to have a very short life as compared to product differences?

Some countries (e.g., Belgium) are already limiting price comparisons to *one's own previous prices* (e.g., "$10 instead of $12 during the month of

---

[10] Thus, the Bureau of European Consumers Unions (BEUC) accepts self-regulation only to the extent that it goes beyond what the law requires, but not for adjudication purpose.

[11] "Consumer naming in commercials nearly always is telling the consumer something factual about the difference between products. In my view, the differences cited are often frivolous or *trivial*. However, the reasons for brand selection are often trivial, and I am not sure consumers should be *protected* from making decisions on a trivial basis." Quoted in Tannenbaum, "Comparative Advertising," *op. cit.*, pp. 6–7.

[12] Yet, one must realize that printed comparisons survive forever in old publications, while the broadcast is transient—although not without lasting effects.

July'') in order to prevent contrasts with meaningless "list" or "regular" prices or with vaguely defined prices established by the competition. The example of ABC Television Network, which has already severely restricted price comparisons (see above), suggests that this problem can be handled through media and voluntary guidelines; but the latter could easily be turned into a mandatory regulation.[13]

3. *Should mere association ("coattail-riding") with brand leaders* be prohibited on the grounds that it is parasitic and not particularly informative (e.g., "Kodak instant pictures are as good as Polaroid's")? If one accepts the principle of naming others, it does not quite matter if this is done by stressing the superiority of one's product or their equality with that of others. Many valid comparisons can be made that way (e.g., "ABC cars get twenty miles to the gallon, but so does the new XYZ sedan!"), and it helps position products in a meaningful manner. Thus, it seems that requiring—through regulations and/or guidelines—that comparisons always be material along specific and measurable attributes would suffice.

4. *Should negative features of the advertised product also be mentioned in comparative ads* in order to avoid consumer deception through implied claims of overall superiority? Definitely so in some cases. Guidelines as well as regulation (e.g., in Sweden and the United States) are already moving in that direction by: (1) stressing the importance of the "net impression" created in judging whether an ad is unfair or misleading, and (2) requiring disclaimers and warnings when the claim is too general. Some recent ads are quite frank in this respect; and such an approach may well increase the credibility granted to advertising by consumer audiences and the public at large. In this context, one could force advertisers to compare themselves to a broad array of competitors rather than to inferior brands with marginal market shares.

5. *Should comparative advertising be limited to certain types of products?* Industrial products and commercial services (e.g., media) may be bought more rationally by professional buyers so that comparisons may thus be very appropriate for this kind of audience who can send for more information and double-check with salesmen. The same argument may be applied to consumer durables that are "shopping goods." Seeking such, the buyers typically visits several stores to "comparison shop," discusses the item with sales clerks, and may even, consult independent comparative reports. On the other hand, convenience items as well as those in which fashion and taste are critical factors, may be too susceptible to superficial and ultimately deceptive comparative advertisements,

---

[13] It is interesting to observe that the New York State Board of Regents in authorizing physicians, dentists, and other professionals to advertise their services also banned *price* advertising on radio and television (but not in print) because "prices were most closely identified with the problem of hucksterism . . . and the possibility of abuse seemed to be greater in the electronic media then in the printed media." R.J. Meislin, "New York Regents Vote to Allow Doctors and Dentists to Advertise," *New York Times* (29 July 1977), pp. A1, B2.

Rockwell Sabreliner® 65, a unique aircraft.

Too much business jet can cost you hundreds of thousands each year. Too little can mean cramped quarters that tire your executives and reduce their efficiency. Consider, then, the new Sabreliner 65, designed to fit between those two extremes.

Sabre 65 offers a unique combination of advantages. It has true transcontinental range — enough to fly from New York to L.A. against prevailing winds, with IFR fuel reserves. It will accommodate six passengers very comfortably. And Sabre 65 does all this at a price that's well under $4 million. No other business jet offers you so much for so little so soon.

Alternatives?

Yes, but you'll have to pay $5 to $6 million and you'll probably wind up with too much aircraft, or settle for not enough. (The only transcontinental business jet that costs less than a Sabreliner is smaller and has only two reclining seats. Sabreliner has six.) The chart shows just how well the Sabre 65 stacks up against the competition when it comes to comfort.

Cabin volume per passenger

The first American business jet to offer fanjets and a supercritical wing.

Fuel-efficient Garrett fanjet engines and supercritical wing team up to give Sabreliner 65 true transcontinental capability — all without losing Sabre's traditionally pleasing handling characteristics.

 Member of GAMA

Maximum range (stat. miles) ISA 4 pass., NBAA VFR reserves zero wind

Sabreliner 65	3324 miles
Lear 36A	3341 miles
Lear 35A	2836 miles
Westwind 1124	2829 miles
Falcon 10A	2195 miles

Save time, save fuel.

You can expect greater takeoff thrust, lower engine noise, and 29% better specific fuel consumption than the Sabre 60. What's more, Sabre 65 will climb to 39,000 ft. at a maximum weight of 23,800 lbs. in under 24 minutes.

JFK to Los Angeles — 6 pass., IFR reserves, long-range cruise speed against the average winds (85% probability –75 mph)

	Nonstop?	Carry Six nonstop in separate seats?	Fuel used (gals)
Sabreliner 65	Yes	Yes	1161
Lear 36A	Yes	No	991
Lear 35A	No	No	1000
Falcon 10A	No	No	1168
Westwind 1124	No	No	1397

We'd like to tell you more.

Call our Vice President of Marketing, Jud Brandreth, (314) 731-2260. We invite inquiries about our Sabreliner 60 and 75A as well. Sabreliner 65 certification is anticipated for early 1979 with delivery of the first production model planned for April 1979. Sabreliner Division, Rockwell International, 6161 Aviation Drive, St. Louis, Missouri 63134.

The Sabreliner 65 information is preliminary and subject to change prior to certification. Data for other aircraft have been computed from appropriate manufacturers' current published operating data.

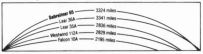

Rockwell International

...where science gets down to business

Neatly positioned between too much business jet and too little.

Sabreliner 65.
A new option in business jets.

This comparative ad includes some unfavorable data (maximum range and fuel consumption) about the sponsored product. Honesty of this sort is likely to become more common—whether required or not.

with no adequate opportunity for double-checking the impressions thus conveyed.

This distinction is valid to a point. Still, there are innovations in the latter category that deserve being stressed in a comparative manner and that are quite amenable to meaningful comparison. It is probably better to handle such specific problems through voluntary guidelines—as is already done in a number of advertising codes that have special sections on health products, alcoholic beverages, toys, and so on. Mandatory regulations would seem to be unavoidable in this area though, because governments are likely to either restrict or ban the advertising of such products.

6. *Does comparison advertising require stricter standards of truthfulness?* Definitely so, because the stakes are higher than in the cases of unilateral advertisements, of "puffery," and of ads where the competition is not named nor readily identifiable. Not only may the dangers of consumer deception be greater, but the precious reputation of other firms is at stake even when the comparisons are truthful.

Hence, comparative advertisements should be even more carefully, precisely, and fully substantiated by objective tests. If absolute documentation is impossible, they should contain qualifying language. Such requirements are essential to mollify the opposition against this form of advertisement. Fortunately, voluntary guidelines and regulations are moving in exactly this direction in the United States and various other countries.

It is not clear what the ultimate impact of comparisons will be on the image of advertising. One can argue that considering the various pros and cons, it will not make that much difference—particularly if its usage remains limited (as is likely to be the case) and if it is properly legislated and self-regulated.

7. Obviously, there are still other problems, but many apply to all forms of advertising and do not require special treatment as far as comparisons are concerned. The use of *testimonials* is one of them: "This Coke drinker says he prefers Pepsi"—but how representative is he/she? Clearly, we are back to the general problem of what constitutes misleading advertising. The need to protect the *privacy of respondents* in tests, as shown in the recent Mirinda case in the Philippines (see country synopsis), is another problem. The frequent *confidentiality of self-regulatory* bodies' deliberations—especially where the industry considers comparisons as unfair—presents the additional danger of secret deals and/or gentlemen's agreements not to compete that way.[14] Requiring disclosure of *all* complaints and of their mode of settlement would probably result in greater use of comparisons. Finally, the possibility of *advertisers withholding their business from media that accept comparative advertisements* directed against the former cannot be gainsaid. Vigilance against such practices

---

[14] A.B. Stridsberg, *Executive Advertising Self-Regulation* (New York: International Advertising Association, 1974), pp. 32–33. The low proportion of published complaints about comparative advertisements in some countries (e.g., the United Kingdom) probably reflects such behind-the-scene settling of disputes.

by bodies of the FTC-type is clearly indicated in the context of pro-competition legislation.

EPILOGUE

Gone are the days when "name-naming" could simply be equated with "name-calling." [15] Clearly, comparison advertising is no panacea for all that ails advertising today, but neither should the issues it raises be handled as if it were a plague when it represents merely a touchstone of today's advertising problems.

The pros and cons of comparison advertising are fairly obvious by now, and they can be disputed endlessly—particularly if one chooses to discuss them on the basis of such elusive concepts and ideals as fairness, consumerism, and advertising's image. However, as often happens in human affairs, its fate will only be *prepared* by such discussions.

Ultimately, some unexpected push will be necessary to get it going or to stop it: another version of the Pepsi challenge, perhaps, that makes too much of flimsy consumer opinions and leads to an indefinite ban on comparisons (as in the Philippines), *or* conversely, an imaginative comparative claim for a smart economy car that pushes it ahead of other compacts on the basis of important and incontrovertible facts, and swings opinion in its favor, *or* a Consumer-Affairs Minister in need of popular support, who trial-balloons or proscribes it. This is often what it takes to make or unmake comparison advertising.

The final word then can only be "caveat promotor," who—as in the famous Avis quasi-comparative advertisement—will have to "try hard*er*" to justify this mixed-blessing addition to our repertory of advertising technology.

[15] This point was already made in 1966 in "Naming Competitors in Ads: Forthright, Fair? Foolish?" *Printers Ink* (28 January 1966), p. 32.

Part Two

COUNTRY STUDIES

Comparison Advertising: Country Studies

THIS SECOND PART includes three types of treatments. The *country synopses* provide one-page summaries of the major legal and self-regulatory features of comparison advertising in a particular nation, together with indications about its present and future use in the light of various developments such as consumerist and other pressure groups. Questionnaires filled in by IAA Chapters were particularly helpful here, but they were supplemented by correspondence with legal experts [1] and advertising practitioners, whose help was invaluable.

The *country notes* offer shorter glimpses gleaned from the literature [2] and from correspondents around the world. They apply mostly to countries about which little information could be obtained—often because comparison advertising is hardly used there or is even forbidden.

The *country analyses* provide longer treatments of countries where comparison advertising is rather widely practiced (United States [3] and Canada), where it is definitely emerging (United Kingdom, Denmark, and even West Germany), and where special circumstances make it impossible for legal (Belgium), cultural (Japan), or self-regulatory (Philippines) reasons. IAA Chapters and various correspondents helped immeasurably in this respect.

The following list summarizes the impact of legislation, self-regulation, and cultural attitudes in a score of countries:

[1] As was mentioned in a previous chapter, Werner Janssen, Jr. (New York), Bernard Francq (Belgium), Maurizio Fusi (Italy), and K.H. Troxler (Switzerland) were particularly helpful in this regard.

[2] Particularly: Werner Janssen, Jr., "Some Foreign Law Aspects of Comparative Advertising," *The Trademark Reporter*, Vol. 64, No. 6 (November–December 1974), pp. 451–97 (Copyright © 1974, The United States Trademark Association, and reprinted with permission of the copyright owner); and Bernard Francq, "La publicité comparative," *Bulletin de l'Institut International de Concurrence Commerciale* (Bruxelles, Belgium: April 1977), pp. 25–78.

[3] The United States is analyzed in a separate section of each one of the previous Chapters in Part I.

A. *Essentially Legal with Minor Restrictions—and Used*

Australia	Sweden
Canada	United Kingdom
Denmark	United States

B. *Essentially Legal with Major Restrictions (Abuse Principle)—Minor Use*

Netherlands	Greece
West Germany	

C. *Essentially Legal but Banned or Restricted by Self-Regulation*

Hong Kong	Philippines (ban)
New Zealand	South Africa

D. *Essentially Legal but Restricted by Cultural Attitudes or Gentlemen's Agreements*

Brazil	South Korea
Japan	Switzerland

E. *Essentially Illegal*

Austria	Italy
Belgium	Luxembourg
France	Spain

COUNTRY SYNOPSES

AUSTRALIA

Special Legislation: None.

Interpretation: As in the United Kingdom, truthful comparisons are allowed under common law; so is the use of scientific comparative test results. Puffery is tolerated.

Major Restrictions: In a set of Guidelines to the Trade Practices Act, the Trade Practices Commission warns advertisers that they should only compare "like with like," and must be able to substantiate their claims.

Self-Regulation: The Code of Advertising Standards of the Australian Association of National Advertisers states as one of its "recommendations" under *Article 10—Disparagement:* "Advertisements shall not contain disparaging references to products and services of other advertisers. However, substantiated competitive claims inviting comparison with a group of products or with other products in the same field shall not necessarily be regarded as disparaging." More generally, "knocking copy" has been considered by most advertisers as ungentlemanly.

The Advertising Code of Ethics of the Media Council of Australia (MCA) states: "Advertisements shall not disparage identifiable products, services or advertisers." However, in 1975, the Australian Media Accreditation Authority (a division of MCA) has removed its prohibition of "name naming," while providing various "advices" resembling U.S. guidelines.

The Australian Media Accreditation Authority (AMAA), which accredits all advertising agencies, long outlawed comparisons. However, it has followed the MCA in removing this ban. Its Disparaging Copy Committee handles complaints, and has recently intervened in the Slazenger–Spalding dispute.

Practice: Minor—mostly for motor vehicles (Leyland, Volvo) and accessories, building materials, foods, liquors, golf balls, cosmetics, and toiletries—both in print and on television. See the Slazenger-Dunlop and Triumph examples in Part III.

Prospects: No changes are being contemplated, and the Australian Consumer Association definitely favors comparison advertising.

AUSTRIA

Basic Legislation: Section 1 of the Unfair Competition Law (26 September 1973) states: "Whoever undertakes immoral actions in commerce and for competitive purposes may be served with an injunction and sued for damages." Direct comparisons are considered "immoral" in this context.

> *Interpretation:* Indirect comparisons are permissible only if not derogatory of others, and if a specific competitor or his product/service is not named or otherwise identifiable. Truthfulness and the lack of criticism *per se* are irrelevant. Parasitical use of another's reputation is also forbidden ("My products are as good as his!").

Major Exceptions:
Answers to criticism.
Answering a specific request from a customer.
Explaining a technical improvement.
Laudatory or superlative advertisements, unless
    they may seem worthy of belief.
Comparisons of systems (with no names mentioned).

Self-Regulation: Austrian advertising agencies and the media subscribe to the ICC Advertising Code, which authorizes the fair use of comparison advertising.

Practice: Nil.

Prospects: The Ministry of Justice and the trade unions are favoring relaxing this ban, provided the burden of proof that the advertisement is truthful and fair lies with the advertiser rather than with the plaintiff.

BELGIUM†

Basic Legislation: Commercial Practices Law (14 July 1971), Article 20.2.

Interpretation: This article specifically forbids any advertising using comparisons that are misleading or denigrating, or which make it "unnecessarily" possible to identify one or more businessmen (not only competitors).

Major Exceptions:
Self-defense.
Comparison of systems and presentation of technical progress, if it is done objectively and without referring to any specific competitor or group of them.

Self-Regulation: The Advertising Code makes no reference to comparisons, although the Advertising Council (Conseil de la Publicité) subscribes to the ICC Code, which tolerates them.

Practice: Nil.

Prospects: Several proposals to revise the 1971 law as well as the proposed EEC directive would liberalize the use of fair comparisons, but they also would increase the obligations and liabilities of advertisers. Consumer associations cautiously support this liberalization, but business remains very divided about it—including the Advertising Council.

Still, Article 13.A.2 of the Benelux Uniform Law on Trademarks (1969) allows the owner to oppose any use of this registered trademark, which without a valid reason ("just motive") would cause him damage. This provision could definitely restrict the use of comparison advertising.

BRAZIL

Basic Legislation: The general clause of the unfair-competition statute (Art. 178 of the 1945 code) gives one the "right to recover losses and damages caused by other acts of unfair competition, which are not foreseen in this article, tending to prejudice another's reputation or business." (This article may be omitted, however, in the revised Penal Code).

References that "detract" from competitive products are forbidden in the case of pharmaceutical and medicinal preparations (Art. 5.XI of Decree-law No. 4113 of 14 February 1942).

Article 17.I.e. of Decree No. 57690 of 1 February 1966 (which regulates the Brazilian advertising profession) provides that advertisements shall not "attribute defects or faults to competing merchandise, products or services."

† See also country analysis of Belgium below.

Interpretation: Recent use of comparative advertisements seems to indicate that these restrictions are not prohibitive when the comparison is not unnecessarily derogatory.

Self-Regulation: A voluntary code does not exist yet, but is being developed.

Practice: Minor but growing for cars (Volkswagen Beetle vs. Fiat 147; and Ford–Willys vs. VW Kombi), soft drinks (Pepsi vs. Coke), cigarettes, whisky, and tomato paste (Cica vs. Peixe). See the Chevrolet comparative ad in Part III.

Prospects: While comparisons are gaining ground, most advertisers and agencies remain opposed or dubious.

CANADA†

Special Legislation: None

Interpretation: The federal Department of Consumer and Corporate Affairs definitely supports the fair use of comparison advertising.

The courts appear to have taken a lenient view of comparison advertising in applying the relevant statutes.

Major Restrictions:

The Combines Investigation Act (Competition Act) is applicable in cases of false and misleading statements and in cases of claims not based on adequate and proper testing.

The Trade Marks Act forbids the use of someone else's registered trademark on products or packages—but not of a trade name.

There are also provincial Business Practice Acts that restrict the use of comparisons.

The Food and Drugs Act limits the use of comparisons in nutritional claims, and it forbids their use as far as drugs and proprietary medicines are concerned.

Self-Regulation: The Manual of General Guidelines for Advertising of the Canadian Advertising Advisory Board (CAAB) allows comparison advertising but insists that rules be applied in such matters as dangling comparisons, superlatives, visual representations, testing, and surveying.

Trade associations are tolerant too, but some major dailies effectively refuse comparative advertisements that cannot be substantiated.

Practice: Comparisons already represent up to 5 percent of national advertising expenditures. All media are used and the major users are automobiles, personal-care and household products, and soft drinks.

Prospects: Opinion remains divided on the subject. Thus, the Canadian Bar Association has opposed it, but the Consumers Association of Canada generally supports it. Still, it appears likely that comparison advertising will at least maintain its present share of national advertising expenditures.

† See Country analysis of Canada below.

DENMARK†

Basic Legislation: Marketing Practices Act (No. 297 of 14 June 1974).

Interpretation: This Act does not include any reference to comparisons, but they are allowed, provided they are not false, misleading, unreasonably incomplete, or unfair ("improper") toward other tradesmen or consumers on account of form or reference to "irrelevant matters" (Article 2). Besides, comparisons must agree with "fair [proper] marketing practices" (Article 1).

Major Restrictions: The unauthorized use of someone else's registered trademark constitutes an infringement under the Trade Marks Act (11 June 1959) and of Article 5 of the 1974 Marketing Practices Act. However, such use is tolerated when intended to assist consumers rather than to simply further one's commercial position in a parasitic way.

Implementation: The Consumer Ombudsman supervises the implementation of this Act and "uses his best endeavors by negotiation" to insure compliance with it. Otherwise, unfair marketing practices are brought before commercial courts which use the ICC codes as guidelines.

Self-Regulation: The ICC Code prevails; and the former Danish Advertising Board (Dansk Reklamenaevn) used to support completely truthful, relevant, and fair comparison. This board has been dissolved, so that businessmen now use the Ombudsman and/or the courts.

Practice: Recent and growing use (1.7 percent of ads in a 1976 survey), mostly in print—by the automobile, consumer-electronics, and insurance trades as well as by the media.

Prospects: No further changes are presently contemplated although most businessmen appear reluctant to use comparative advertisements. Consumer associations support this practice, but excesses could well lead to the issuance of guidelines by the Consumer Ombudsman.

FRANCE‡

Basic Legislation: Article 1382 and 1383 (tort law) of the Civil Code prohibit acts that unnecessarily harm others. Comparisons are held to constitute such acts committed with a view toward creating confusion or casting discredit. In fact, what is forbidden is as much the act of denigration as comparison for the sake of gaining a comparative advantage in an unfair manner.

†See Country Analysis of Denmark below.

‡The assistance of Messrs. Claude Chauvet (President, French IAA Chapter) and Laurent Templier (Director, Association des Agences Conseils en Publicité) and of Ms. Hélène Ploix (Sécrétariat d'Etat à la Consommation) is gratefully acknowledged.

Interpretation: Comparison, even if truthful, amounts to criticism and thereby depreciates others and their products. Even advertisements that favorably compare one's products with those of others in general and without singling anyone of them out constitute a form of "collective denigration," and are therefore unlawful.

Using the results of scientific comparative tests prepared by others is forbidden in advertisements that name others.

Article 422.2 of the Penal Code forbids the commercial use of someone else's registered trademark without his permission.

Major Exceptions:

Comparative data requested by customers.

Defensive comparisons in answer to criticism or provocation (this right is limited).

Comparisons of systems and methods that are objective and moderate.

Superlative ("So much better!") and very general statements that aim at no particular specific competitor.

Implementation: Very strict, with cease-and-desist orders, penalties, and damages imposed on the guilty party, although no proof of damage is required. The advertising agency and the medium can be jointly penalized.

Self-Regulation: Not applicable since comparisons are unlawful, although the self-regulatory body BVP (Bureau de Vérification de la Publicité—similar to the U.S. NAD/NARB)—has screened advertisements with comparative overtones in the fields of car radios, encyclopedias, and appliances, and has suggested modifications in them because superlatives are frowned upon.

Practice: None

Prospects:

The Economic and Finance Ministry and its Under-Secretary for Consumer Affairs (Sécrétaire d'Etat à la Consommation) are in favor of comparison advertising because it would increase competition and improve consumer information. The VII Plan recommended it on the advice of its Consumer Affairs Commission, and various official advisory bodies (e.g., the Comité National de la Consommation) are studying the matter—with the EEC draft directive on advertising providing additional impetus and support.

Advertising agencies rather favor it if the revised law includes various restrictions, and if self-discipline and self-regulation can be improved and reinforced.

Advertisers rather oppose comparisons for being conducive to "savage competition" and increased litigation.

The self-regulatory body (BVP) is rather reticent on account of the difficulty of making fair comparisons, but would accept it under strict standards.

Consumer associations are divided on the subject, but the head of the Institut National de la Consommation—as the main spokesman for consumers—is rather against comparisons if only because they consider *all* advertising to be persuasive rather than informative.

The media also express various reserves in view of the difficulties connected with screening comparative ads.

Judges are opposed to any relaxation of the present ban, but younger and more consumer minded lawyers favor it.

La Lamborghini Countach consomme entre 14 et 25 litres aux 100.
La Matra-Simca Bagheera S consomme entre 6,2 et 10,1 litres aux 100.
La Lamborghini Countach possède une suspension à 4 roues indépendantes.
La Matra-Simca Bagheera S possède une suspension à 4 roues indépendantes.
La Lamborghini Countach dispose d'un coffre d'une capacité totale de 175 litres.
La Matra-Simca Bagheera S dispose d'un coffre d'une capacité totale de 350 litres.
La Lamborghini Countach bénéficie de l'assistance d'un réseau de 20 concessionnaires en France.
La Matra-Simca Bagheera S bénéficie de l'assistance d'un réseau de 300 concessionnaires en France.
La Lamborghini Countach est livrée avec glaces teintées, intérieur cuir.
La Matra-Simca Bagheera S est livrée avec glaces teintées, vitres électriques, intérieur tweed.
La Lamborghini Countach coûte 235 000 F.
La Matra-Simca Bagheera S coûte 41 610 F.
La Matra-Simca Bagheera S démontre brillamment la supériorité de son rapport qualité-prix.
Toutefois, si vous doutez encore, achetez une Lamborghini Countach.

QUE CHOISIR :
LA FABULEUSE LAMBORGHINI COUNTACH
OU LA SURPRENANTE BAGHEERA S?

La Lamborghini Countach emporte deux personnes à des vitesses parfaitement indécentes.
La Matra-Simca Bagheera S emporte trois personnes à des vitesses parfaitement illégales.
La Lamborghini Countach est propulsée par un moteur central arrière développant 375 ch.
La Matra-Simca Bagheera S est propulsée par un moteur central arrière développant 90 ch.
La Lamborghini Countach avoue 23 CV fiscaux.
La Matra-Simca Bagheera S avoue 8 CV fiscaux.

MATRA SIMCA BAGHEERA
Bienvenue à bord

A curiosity item: A *French* comparative ad—done with the permission of Lamborghini!

GREECE

Basic Legislation: Law 146 (1914) on unfair competition prohibits any competitive act that is contrary to good morals (Art. 1).

Interpretation: Whether advertising that specifically mentions competitors or their products is lawful or not depends upon the particular circumstances of the case—with a bias toward considering such a practice as illicit, especially if unnecessarily offensive.

Major Exceptions:

Self-laudatory and superlative advertising.

Uncritical comparative advertising equating one's quality with that of another may be permissible.

Self-Regulation: The Greek Advertising Agencies Association (EDEE)'s revised Advertising Code allows comparison advertising when truthful, not misleading, and fair (Article 5).

Practice: Practically nil.

Prospects: Some increase appears likely as the use of advertising grows in Greece.

HONG KONG

Special Legislation: None.

> *Interpretation:* As in the United Kingdom, truthful comparisons are allowed under common law, and so is the use of scientific comparative test results. Puffery is tolerated.

> *Major Restrictions:* The Television Advertising Standards (Code of Practice 2) of the Television Authority states: "Advertising matter shall contain no claims intended to disparge competitors and competing products . . . (Section 6.c., as amended in 1975). Consequently, the TA has accepted comparative advertisements only where there exists a significant and tangible difference that can be fully substantiated and is of definite benefit to consumers. No comparisons can be used for medical products.

Self-Regulation: The Association of Accredited Advertising Agents of Hong Kong has Standards of Practice that state: "Advertisements shall not contain disparaging references to products and services of other advertisers. However, substantiated competitive claims inviting comparison with a group of products or with other products in the same field shall not necessarily be regarded as disparaging (Article J)."

Practice: Competitive advertisements represented some 5 percent of advertising expenditures in 1976, and this proportion may soon double. The packaged detergents industry is the main user of comparisons, which remain restricted to the television medium. Major advertisers tend to use them sparingly.

Prospects: The Television Authority is tending to discourage the use of comparisons in view of their increasing popularity.

ITALY†

Basic Legislation: Under Clause 2 of Article 2598 of the Civil Code (1942), any reference to someone else's products is generally considered to amount to denigration of the products or activities of a competitor, and thus represents a

† The assistance of Maurizio Fusi, legal specialist on the regulation of advertising in Italy, is gratefully acknowledged.

forbidden act of unfair competition (also covered by Clause 3). Similarly, appropriation of the merits of a competitor's product or business is considered unfair. Trademark legislation is also applicable when confusion between the brands is possible and/or when the merits of the competitor's products are appropriated.

Major Exceptions:
Puffery.
Self-defense.
Completely objective, comparative statements of a technical or scientific nature, and on a subject of general concern to the public, which are necessary to be made but not solely for advertising purposes.
Answering consumer requests for explanations.
Using the results of independent and objective tests; and advertising that one's product has prevailed in competitive tests.

Self-Regulation: The 1977 Code of Advertising Self-Regulation of the Instituto Italiano del l'Autodisciplina Pubblicitaria forbids *indirect* (i.e., not naming names) comparisons "unless they are intended to illustrate under a technical and economic aspect the characteristics and real advantages of the activity or product that is advertised (Art 15, but also 13 and 14)." In such cases, substantiation of the claims must be possible. Some 20 percent of this body's decisions are presently about such indirect comparisons.

Practice: None as far as direct comparisons are concerned.

Prospects: No change although there are pressures from jurists and advertising practitioners in favor of allowing comparison advertising (the Milan court is more tolerant). Passage of the EEC directive on misleading and unfair advertising would require the legalization of comparisons through a more favorable interpretation of Article 2598 of the Civil Code.

JAPAN†

Special Legislation: None.

Interpretation: Under the Unfair-Competition Prevention Law (1934, amended) and the Law for Preventing Unjustifiable Premiums and Misleading Representations (1962, amended in 1972), comparison advertising would be actionable if it were untruthful or misleading about the product's vaunted superiority.

The government has taken a negative position against industry-wide agreements that ban comparison advertising.

A reference to a competitor in a truthful comparative advertisement that injures his reputation, could be considered tortuous under certain cir-
† See Country Analysis of Japan below.

cumstances and dealt with under the general tort provision of Article 709 of the Civil Code.

Puffery appears to be illicit in Japan.

Implementation: Fair Trade Commission and the courts.

Self-Regulation: The Guide for the Improvement of Advertising, prepared by the Japan Chamber of Commerce and Industry, provides guidelines for the use of superiority and other comparative claims.

Some thirty industries have voluntary "Rules for Fair Competition Concerning Representation" (which must be approved by the Fair Trade Commission), which lay down similar standards for superiority and comparative claims, but only two of them prohibit comparison advertising.

At least eight advertising-related associations have similar standards prohibiting the slandering and vilification of competitors through comparisons and/or requiring the substantiation of comparative claims.

Practice: Until now, advertisers have voluntarily refrained from using comparative advertisements for fear that denigration would lead to declining confidence in advertising as a whole; but also as a reflection of Japanese preference for decorum in public competitive behavior.

Prospects: Interest in comparison advertising is developing among advertisers, agencies, the media, and consumer associations in favor of using comparisons—provided appropriate guidelines and/or regulations are developed and applied.

KOREA (REPUBLIC OF)

Special Legislation: Price Stabilization and Fair Trade Law No. 2798 (31 December 1975).

Interpretation: Article 7 prohibits business activities that treat competitors in an unfair or discriminatory manner (Clause 1) as well as false or exaggerated advertising (Clause 5). There is no direct reference to comparative ads, however.

Implementation: Interpretation of what is unfair is left to the Ministry of Commerce and Industry under the Economic Planning Board.

Self-Regulation: The Advertising Code of the Korea Advertising Association (which is patterned after the ICC Code) states: "Advertising should be so designed as to conform to social mores and to good taste . . . and should not be disparaging or slandering of others (Art. 2 and 3)." The Newspaper Advertising Code has similar provisions (Art. 3), while the Broadcasting Ethics Regulations ban slanderous and defamatory advertisements (whether factual or not) as well as superlatives that may be libelous (Art. 78).

Practice: Nil because of cultural values (based on Confucianism) which reject public statements that are critical of others. These have led advertisers to abstain voluntarily from using comparisons. However, in March 1977, three Korean refrigerator companies fought very aggressively over the technical merits of their products. No names were named, but it was fairly clear what the reference brands were. The Ministry of Commerce and Industry called in representatives of the three brands and impressed upon them that their claims were exaggerated and unfair.

Prospects: No significant changes are anticipated in the law, self-regulation, or practice.

NETHERLANDS

Basic Legislation: Articles 1401 and 1402 (tort law) of the Civil Code are interpreted to prohibit unfair competitive practices that unnecessarily harm others; comparisons *may* constitute one of these practices.

>   *Interpretation:* Dutch courts are divided on the subject of truthful comparisons, with no clear declaration of general principle. Misleading or unnecessarily offensive statements are normally ruled to be illegal; and comparisons, to be acceptable, must deal with all relevant product characteristics. Even stating that one's product is as good as another may be considered improper behavior.
>
>   Article 13.A.2 of the Benelux Uniform Law on Trademarks (Benelux Merkenrecht, 1969) allows the owner to oppose any use of his registered trademark that without a valid reason (just motive) would cause him damage.

>   *Major Exceptions:*
>   Comparisons requested by customers.
>   Answers to criticism or provocation.
>   Comparisons of systems and methods.

Self-Regulation: Self-regulation is very important in the Netherlands. There is an official Advertising Council (Reklameraad) for the state-controlled radio and television network, and an Advertising Code Commission (Reklame Code Commissie), which handles the self-regulation of advertising in most other media. This Commission (which includes representatives of two consumer associations) has recently announced that it is permissible to compare "comparable" products, provided: (1) the comparison rests on complete, objective, and controllable data, (2) unnecessarily denigrating statements are avoided, and (3) the statements are not misleading. It accepts references to product tests carried out by consumer organizations if such references are truthful and up to date. The Advertising Board also accepts comparative advertisements but not references to product tests made by consumer associations.

Practice: Less than 1 percent of advertising expenditures in 1976 through print (e.g., cigarettes) and television (soap). Major users include the soap (Unilever with Lux, and Procter & Gamble with Dreft), tobacco (Niemeyer with Roxy Dual Filter Cigarettes), car (Ford), coffee-whitener, and encyclopedia industries (see the Lux comparative ad in Part III).

Prospects: The courts and industry remain divided on the subject, but the trend appears toward greater tolerance—particularly if the proposed EEC directive authorizes comparison advertising. However, the Benelux Uniform Law on Trademarks may well hamper that development unless courts restrict its application to cases of unfair and misleading advertising.

PHILIPPINES†

Basic Legislation: Section 29(C) of Act No. 166 (1951) on Trademarks and Unfair Competition states: "Any person who shall make any false statement in the course of trade or who shall commit any other act contrary to good faith of a nature calculated to discredit the goods, business or services of another . . . shall be deemed guilty of unfair competition."

Interpretation: The use of truthful comparisons has generally not been considered to amount to unfair competition, and the protection of trademarks does not preclude using the name of a competitor.

Implementation: The Fair Trade Board, which has delegated most rule-making to the advertising industry.

Self-Regulation: It is government policy to encourage self-regulation in advertising. The Philippine Board of Advertising used to allow comparative advertising under Rule 4.1.B. of its Code of Ethics, which states that ("Substantiated competitive claims stating material facts inviting comparisons with a group of products or with other products are acceptable"). However, in late 1976, the PBA imposed a moratorium and then a ban on further use of this practice until more positive evidence is available.

Practice: Before this temporary suspension, a growing number of advertisers had launched comparative campaigns, which represented some 5 percent of total advertising expenditures in 1975–1976—particularly in print and posters for soft drinks (Mirinda), feminine napkins (Kimberly Clark), appliances (Sears), baby powder (Mennen), consumer electronics (Sony), and auto-rustproofing. See the Mirinda comparative ad in part III.

Prospects: Dim.

† See the Country Analysis of the Philippines below.

SOUTH AFRICA

Special Legislation: none.

> *Interpretation:* As in the United Kingdom, truthful comparisons are allowed under common law; and so is the use of scientific comparative-test results. Besides, puffery is tolerated.

> *Major Restrictions:* Use of a competitor's registered trademark can constitute an infringement if it is likely to cause injury or prejudice to the competitor (Section 44.1.b. of the Trade Marks Act No. 62 of 1963).

Self-Regulation: The Advertising Standards Authority of South Africa has a Code of Advertising Practice based on the British and ICC codes. As a matter of principle, comparisons are not permitted because they are considered as disparaging: "In particular, advertisements shall not single out a specific product or service for unfavorable comparison (Art. 6.2); and advertisements should not make unjustifiable use of the name or initials of any firm, or take advantage of the goodwill attached to the trade name or symbol of another firm or its product (Art. 7.1 and 7.2)." However, "substantiated competitive claims inviting comparison with a group of products or with other (unnamed) products in the same field, shall not necessarily be regarded as disparaging (Art. 6.3)." Still, retailers cannot compare their prices with those prevailing elsewhere (Art. 5.3.5). General puffery is tolerated ("The best cigarette in the world!") but superlatives making specific claims ("Most miles per gallon!") must be substantiated (Art. 4.1).

Practice: There is really no comparison advertising in South Africa. However, about 1% of 1976 advertising expenditures (print, radio, cinema and direct mail) was used on *competitive* claims (not on direct comparisons). Major users include soap (Unilever), toothpaste (Colgate-Palmolive, Dr. West's), cereals (Kellogg, Post, Food Corporation), batteries (Eveready, Duracell, Atron), car rentals (Budget, Avis, Grosvenor).

Prospects: No changes are anticipated in regulation and self-regulation; but the use of competitive claims may double to 2% in 1977–1978.

SPAIN

Basic Legislation: The statute of Advertising (Law No. 61/64 of 11 June 1964) prohibits advertising activities "which tend to discredit competitors or their products; and generally, all advertising activities which are contrary to correct usages and commercial practices" (Title II, Article 10). Article 132(e) of the Law of Industrial Property (1902) considers as a forbidden act of unfair competition the "publishing of advertisements . . . which tend to depreciate the quality of a competitor's products."

Interpretation: Since these articles do not distinguish between false and true statements, they effectively ban comparison advertising.

Major Exceptions: General comparisons with unnamed competitors, and the use of superlatives.

Implementation: Ministry of Culture (General Directorate for Advertising and Public Relations).

Self-Regulation:

The Advertising Jury of the National Advertising Board reports to the above Directorate.

Some industries (pharmaceuticals, brandy, detergents) have codes forbidding the use of comparisons.

Major advertisers voluntarily refrain from using comparisons.

Practice: Nil.

Prospects: No relaxation is being contemplated.

SWEDEN

Basic Legislation: Marketing Practices Act (1 January 1971, amended 1 July 1976): Articles 2 (on fair practices) and 3 ("A tradesman who . . . omits to deliver information of particular significance to consumers, may be enjoined by the Market Court to give such information . . .").

Interpretation: Truthful statements about a competitor's products can be made, provided they are significantly complete and informative (major differences, including shortcomings, between the compared products have to be mentioned, but the results of comparative tests may be published). Advertisers must be able to prove the correctness of the information provided (this amounts to a reversal of the burden of proof).

Major Restrictions: Vague and unsubstantiated comparisons (e.g., "Our product is better than theirs") are not allowed.

Implementation: The Market Court and the Consumer Ombudsman (who also heads the National Board for Consumer Policies) handles complaints, and decisions are published in special reports. Voluntary agreement is the predominant approach, but the Ombudsman can ask the Market Court to issue a cease-and-desist injunction, order businessmen to provide more information, or refer the case to a public court (mainly in cases of misleading advertising).

Self-Regulation: The ICC Code prevails and is taken into account by the Market Court and the Consumer Ombudsman. There is also a privately organized consulting bureau to which advertisers, agencies, and media can turn for legal advice, and which reviews (on a fee basis) proposed advertisements and ideas that may represent borderline cases.

Practice: Small use (mostly in print) by the car, household appliances, and food industries (some twenty cases a year, apart from automobiles). See the Ford Consul example in Part III.

Prospects: No regulatory change is being contemplated after the major 1971–1976 reforms (until then, even truthful comparisons were generally considered to constitute unfair competition).

Endast Bosch köksmaskin 1001 R klarar degar "mycket bra" visar ny finsk, statlig test.

Nu är det inte längre svårt att välja köksmaskin. En ny finsk, statlig test visar att Bosch 1001 R är den enda köksmaskin som kan ges betyget "mycket bra" när det gäller vetedegar. Den finska undersökningen har omfattat alla de köksmaskiner som är mest sålda i Sverige. Här kan du läsa några av resultaten från den finska motsvarigheten till vårt eget Konsumentverk. Lägg speciellt märke till att Bosch

1001 R också har den överlägset största kapaciteten när det gäller att bereda stora degar (upp till 1,75 l vätska). Även på andra arbeten har Bosch fått fina betyg. Och det är viktigt − en köksmaskin används ju till mycket mer än bakning. Safta, sylta, stoppa korv, mixa och vispa − allt går fort och lätt med Bosch.

	Kenwood Chef	Kenwood Major	Electrolux	Bosch 1001 P	Bosch 1001 R	
Skålens råmaterial	plast	rostfri stål	rostfri stål	plast	rostfri stål	
max. bruksvolym	4 liter	6 liter	7 liter	5 liter	6 liter	
Vispning						Bosch vispar "mycket snabbt" men utan att göra mycket väsen av sig...
Ljud vid vispning dB(A)	82	81	71	74	75	
Grädde och ägg-vitevispning	mycket snabb	mycket snabb	lång-sam	mycket snabb	mycket snabb	
Skummängdens resultat	mycket bra	mycket bra	bra	bra	bra	...och resultaten blir "bra", d.v.s. jämnt och fint skum.
Blandning av fett och socker	snabb	snabb	ganska snabb	mycket snabb	snabb/ långsam*)	
Beredning av seg jäsdeg Vätskemängd i liter min. − max.	0,2 −0,75	0,2 −1,0	0,2 −1,25	0,2 −1,0	0,5 −1,75	Med Bosch 1001 R kan du sätta de största degarna. Det spar tid och arbete. Och resultatet:
Utförande av arbetet	bra	bra	ganska bra	bra	mycket bra	högsta betyg − "mycket bra".
Mixer Blandnings- skålens råmaterial, max. bruksvolym	glas 1,0 liter	glas 1,0 liter	plast 1,0 liter	plast 1,2 liter	plast 1,2 liter	Även när det gäller blandnings-skålens rymd ligger Bosch i topp.
Bett (Knivkors)	löstagbart	löstagbart	fastsatt i bägaren	löstagbart	löstagbart m. nyckel	
Ljud dB(A)	86	86	ej mätt	82	82	
Förfiningsresultat 1) råa grönsaker 2) lök	jämn, ganska jämn	jämn, ganska jämn	mycket jämn, jämn	jämn, ganska jämn	jämn, ganska jämn	Här visar Bosch igen att en köksmaskin kan vara högeffek-tiv utan att vara högljudd!
Köttkvarn Ljud dB(A)	82	82	ej mätt	74	74	
Malning	mycket snabb	mycket snabb	mycket snabb	mycket snabb	mycket snabb	
Övriga iakttagelser	Bruksanvisning och kokbok. Tillsättning av ingredienser under arbetet litet besvärligt.	Kenwood Chefs bruksanvisning och kokbok. Tillsättning av ingredienser under arbetet. litet besvärligt.	Stadig maskin. Bruksanvisning. Vid beredning av deg måste man hjälpa till ganska mycket. Blandar ej en jämn deg.	Stadig maskin. Bruksanvisning och recept. Bra lock.	*) Med rör-armen i stora skålen. Stadig maskin. Bruksanvisning och recept. Mycket bra lock.	

Ovanstående tabell är hämtad ur en opartisk undersökning, utförd av den statliga finska Forskningscentralen för hushålls- och konsumentfrågor.
I tabellen har vissa fabrikat, med mycket liten representation på den svenska marknaden, uteslutits.
Någon aktuell svensk test finns f. n. inte.

BOSCH

Robert Bosch Aktiebolag, 08/22 70 60

A Swedish comparative ad by a German-owned firm.

SWITZERLAND

Basic Legislation: Unfair Competition Act (30 September 1943).

Interpretation: Comparison advertising does not constitute unfair competition as long as it is objective, is not misleading, and is not unnecessarily injurious (Article 1.1).

DIA MOVIE - 31 vom 4.8.77

(Gestaltungsentwurf vom 5.Juli 1977)

1. Bild

> vergleichen Sie !
>
> comparez !
>
> paragonate !

2. Bild

> *1* Liter
> litre
> litro
> _____
> Erdnussoel
> huile d'arachide
> olio d'arachide

3. Bild

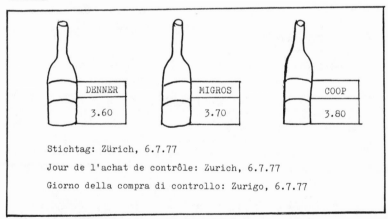

Stichtag: Zürich, 6.7.77

Jour de l'achat de contrôle: Zurich, 6.7.77

Giorno della compra di controllo: Zurigo, 6.7.77

3.1. Die drei Flaschen + stichtag zeigen
3.2. Stichtag weg, Coop-Preis einspringen lassen
3.3. Migros-Preis einspringen lassen
3.4. Denner-Preis einspringen lassen   AV

H. Brun

Example of a Swiss Comparative advertisement.

Major Restrictions:
> In the case of "abuses" ("unnecessarily harmful denigration"), Swiss courts have been rather strict against comparative references that are not really necessary to point out the qualities of the advertiser's goods.
>
> Comparative use of a competitor's trademark on the advertiser's goods or packages constitutes a trademark infringement under the Trademark Law of 26 September 1890.
>
> Only the authorized use of someone else's comparative tests is allowed. The name of the testing organization must be mentioned in the case of commissioned research. The test result must be substantiable and cannot be selectively used.

Self-Regulation: The Schweizerischer Reklameverband (Swiss Advertising Association) Code has allowed the fair use of comparisons since 1973 (Directive No. 11) if they are not untruthful, misleading, or unnecessarily harmful. Some 10 percent of the complaints it handled in 1976 dealt with various kinds of comparison.

Retailers (Pro Marco), chocolate manufacturers (Choco Swiss), and the car trade urge their members to refrain from using comparisons.

The TV network and members of the newspaper association do not accept price comparisons (there is no advertising on radio).

Practice: Relatively minor, and exclusively in print. It is mostly used for consumer non-durables (foods and non-foods), by such major retailers as Migros and Denner, and also by travel agencies.

Advertisers are very reluctant to use comparisons, which are considered costly and divisive in a small country where its industrialists prefer to remain united against their opponents.

Prospects: No regulatory changes are being contemplated.

UNITED KINGDOM†

Special Legislation: None.

> *Interpretation:* British common law permits comparisons that are truthful, it tolerates puffery, and it allows the use of scientific comparative test results. Statutory law essentially deals only with deceptive practices.

> *Major Restrictions:* Using someone's registered trademark in comparative advertisements may be liable to charge of "passing off" one's goods for those of another (Trade Marks Act of 1938). Using his name, however, appears to be legal.

Self-Regulation: Since 1968, the Code of Advertising Practice of the Advertising Standards Authority authorizes the fair use of comparative advertisements, as does the Independent Broadcasting Authority's Statutory Code of Advertis-

† See the Country Analysis of the United Kingdom below.

ing Standards and Practice (radio and television). Stricter standards apply to tobacco and health products, however. ASA has already ruled against some comparative ads for cars.

Practice: Relatively limited and mainly for automobiles (Volkswagen, Fiat, Opel, Mazda, Datsun, Ford), tires (Uniroyal), newspapers, golf balls, (Uniroyal) and car rentals (Swan National). Price comparisons are also common in retail advertising. The print medium predominates (see the Mazda and Opel Kadett examples in Part III).

Prospects: No changes are being contemplated, although the proposed EEC directive *may* require the enactment of specific legislation regarding misleading and unfair advertising but this is being fought by British representatives and trade associations.

UNITED STATES†

Special Legislation: None.

Interpretation: Common law, state and federal statutes, and trademark laws, as well as the Federal Trade Commission Act, generally allow comparisons that are truthful and not misleading (for further details, see the United States section in the chapter on the legality of comparison advertising).

Implementation: Courts and Federal Trade Commission.

Self-Regulation: After accepting the use of comparisons, the media and the advertising self-regulatory body (NAD/NARB) have progressively tightened their guidelines along similar lines; their screening and adjudication processes are becoming more severe, too. (For further details, see the United States sections in various chapters).

Practice:
Media ads (comparing one magazine or medium to others) amounted to 20 percent in 1974.
All networks accept comparative ads; about 2 percent of network commercials, and 8 to 10 percent of *prime-time* network television ads were comparative in 1976.
The top twenty-five general-circulation and women's magazines accept them.
44 percent of advertising agencies in the New York, New Jersey, Philadelphia, and Connecticut areas were handling comparison advertising in 1976—particularly the larger ones.

Prospects: The use of comparisons has probably already reached its limits because of its intrinsic limitations (made evident by experience and research) and of increasing complaints and litigation. More restrictive guidelines are likely too.

---

† Most chapters in Part I include a United States section. See also the various cases and examples in Part III.

WEST GERMANY†

Basic Legislation: Unfair Competition Law (UWG, 1909).

> *Interpretation:* Truthful comparison advertising has traditionally been considered to constitute one of the "acts contrary to honest practices" that can be enjoined under Section 1 of that law. Over a period of time, however, court decisions have extended the number of permissible exceptions. Misleading comparisons are illegal under Section 3, while false or unsubstantiated ones are forbidden by Section 14.

> *Major Exceptions:*
> Comparisons of systems and presentations of new technical improvements when objective and not recognizably directed against specific competitive products.
> Self-defense in answer to a competitor.
> Comparisons at the request of a customer, if verifiable.
> "Necessary" comparisons, as when one's advantages could not otherwise be presented or technological progress demonstrated.
> Unique qualities can be stressed and the use of superlatives are acceptable if specific competitors cannot be identified and if the claim can not be objectively proven.

Self-Regulation: The Zentralausschuss der Werbewirtschaft (ZAW) does not formally oppose comparisons, but is not in favor of them either.

Practice: Minimal—exceptionally by automobile manufacturers (Ford) and supermarket chains (Penny vs. Aldi).

Prospects: Consumer associations and unions favor more comparison advertising, and various jurists have urged legislators to explicitly authorize this practice. However, the federal government appears to be satisfied with the present flexible court-based system—and so are most businessmen. No major changes are thus anticipated.

COUNTRY NOTES

Argentina

A combination of unfair-competition and registered-trademark considerations, as well as restrictions imposed by the Advertisers' Association, effectively prohibit the use of comparisons (Janssen, p. 487).

† See the Country Analysis of West Germany below.

Caribbean Countries

Trinidad and Tobago, Jamaica, and Barbados have statutes similar to the British Trade Marks Act. Comparisons may thus lead to infringement of registered marks. Haiti has a general unfair-competition clause, which may be applicable (Janssen, p. 489).

Chile

General tort provisions and certain criminal statutes are applicable to comparisons (Janssen, p. 489).

Colombia

Truthful comparisons could be considered to be unfair competition under the Commerce Code, which prohibits denigration (Janssen, p. 488).

Costa Rica

The publication of advertisements that tend to belittle the quality of the products or merchandise of a competitor is defined as an act of illicit competition by the Trademarks Law (Janssen, p. 489).

Ecuador

General tort provisions may be applicable to comparisons (Janssen, p. 489).

Finland

Truthful comparisons are allowed if completely truthful and not misleading in any respect (Janssen, p. 475).

Guatemala

No restrictions appear to exist, but there is no practice either.

Iceland

The 1933 Unfair Competition Law and the 1968 Trade Marks Act preclude truthful comparisons, but Scandinavian jurisprudence influences court decisions (Janssen, p. 476).

India

References to a competitor's trademark of the types "as good as" or "a substitute for" are generally permissible under the Trade and Merchandise Marks Act of 1958 (Janssen, p. 483).

Iran

Truthful comparisons are forbidden—under a Decree Governing Advertising Matters (1969)—for discrediting others. They may also amount to unfair competition (Janssen, pp. 490–91).

Ireland

The legislation is very much like that in the United Kingdom.

Israel

The Trademark Ordinance (1972) precludes the unauthorized use of someone else's registered trademark (Janssen, p. 482).

Lebanon

Direct comparisons would probably constitute "unlawful competition" under a 1946 law (Janssen, p. 481).

Luxembourg

Comparisons are forbidden by Article 2.g. of the Grand-Ducal Regulation of 23 December 1974. As in Belgium and the Netherlands, they may also come under the 1969 Uniform Benelux Law on Trademarks.

Malaysia

The Code of Advertising practice forbids explicit comparisons with others.

Mexico

There are no legal provisions against truthful comparisons. However, the Ministry of Health, which grants or denies required administrative "publication permits" for health-related products (pharmaceuticals, food, detergents, toiletries, alcoholic beverages), discourages the use of direct comparisons. American Motors compared its Pacer car to other named makes, but withdrew it after being censored by the Mexican Association of Automotive Dealers. Similar cases involving Volkswagen and Shulton (deodorants) were also handled through professional pressures.

Morocco

The specific mention of competing brands is prohibited.

New Zealand

As in the United Kingdom, there is no major legal restriction against the practice. However, it is probably blocked by voluntary restraint on the part of the Association of Accredited Advertising Agencies' Standards of Practice, the National Press Association, and the government-owned television and radio networks. All are opposed to "knocking copy" that disparages competitors.

Norway

The situation is comparable to that of Sweden and Denmark. Under the 1972 Marketing Control Law, truthful comparisons are allowed if complete and therefore fair (Janssen, p. 475).

Peru

Comparing one's products or services with those of a competitor is one of the specifically forbidden acts of unfair competition listed in the Industrial Property Law (Janssen, p. 489).

Portugal

The 1940 Industrial Property Act precludes making references to a competitor's registered trademark as well as any act "contrary to honest standards and usages"—including references to others (Janssen, p. 477).

Rhodesia

Comparisons appear to be allowed under the Trade Marks Act of 1974 (Janssen, p. 483).

Taiwan

Truthful comparisons appear to be legal (Janssen, p. 490).

Thailand

Trade Mark laws prohibit any public use of another's trade name.

Turkey

The relatively low development of industry, the market, and of advertising itself has precluded the use of comparison advertising.

Uruguay

No specific law covers the subject, but reproducing a registered trademark for profit, without permission of its owner, is forbidden by the Civil Code, the Trademark Law, and the Uruguayan Association of Advertising Agencies.

Venezuela

No specific law covers the subject, but the Code of Advertising Ethics of the National Association of Advertisers opposes the practice (Janssen, pp. 456, 488).

Yugoslavia

Comparisons constitute unfair competition (Janssen, p. 477).

COUNTRY ANALYSES

BELGIUM[1]

Comparative advertisements—even when truthful—are illicit in Belgium, apart from minor legal tolerances. This situation may soon change, however.

[1] The assistance of Messrs. Albert Brouwet (President of the Belgian IAA Chapter), André Lacroix (Director of the Chambre des Agences Conseils en Publicité), Bernard Francq (Belgian

Hence, it is important to understand why comparison advertising is banned, and what forces impinge on the possible removal of this ban.

Legislation [2]

Early Court Decisions: Already in the late nineteenth century, Belgium commercial courts[3] were condemning as an unfair competitive practice advertisements that did not limit themselves to extolling the qualities of one's own products but rather stressed the inferiority of named or identifiable others. This was considered as a *denigration* of another firm, its reputation, products, and/or behavior.

For that matter, *any* reference to another firm was thought to be illicit even if no denigration was involved (e.g., to say that one's products were "as good as" those of a competitor). This was considered as *parasitic behavior,* impinging on a firm's exclusive right to its name and "not to be spoken of"—the only exception being the identification of other brands for which one's product is suitable (e.g., "ABC refills fit Parker Pens").

All along, however, there have been several exceptions and tolerances to these rulings. *Puffery* is one, and so is the use of comparisons to *defend* oneself. A more important exception is comparing *systems and methods,* as when a discount store vaunts its prices, which are lower when compared to traditional outlets. Clearly, the law must allow a firm to stress its novel advantages and "present them intelligibly," even when this requires referring to alternative technologies. However, those "necessary references"[4] that are needed to help consumers understand the advantage of some new system or product must be objective, and a particular competitor or even a specific group of firms (e.g., "downtown department stores") cannot be mentioned.

The condemnation of denigration and of "unnecessary references"—even when truthful—rested, however, on an appreciation by business judges of what were "fair" and "unfair" practices in the light of general rules, commercial customs, and past court decisions (jurisprudence) rather than on any particular legal text.[5]

Recent Regulation: The *royal decree of 23 December 1934* (Art. 1 and 2.b) was the first major legislation dealing explicitly with unfair competitive prac-

legal specialist on the subject), Didier de Wouters d'Oplinter (Director of the Union Internationale des Associations d'Annonceurs), Roger Ramaekers (President of the Conseil de la Consommation), and Louis Viaene (First Counsellor, Ministry of Economic Affairs) is gratefully acknowledged.

[2] Major sources: Bernard Francq, "La publicité commerciale," *Bulletin de l'Institut International de Concurrence Commerciale* (Bruxelles, Belgium: April 1977), pp. 25–78; and A. de Caluwé, A. Delcorde, and X. Leurquin, *La Pratique du Commerce* (Bruxelles, Belgium: Larcier, 1973), Vol. I, pp. 419–46.

[3] Continental European countries usually have separate commercial courts where businessmen serve on a team of specialist judges. Appeals, however, are handled by regular courts.

[4] All comparisons make references, but all references are not necessarily comparative (e.g., "This extract allows you to prepare your own Benedictine-type liqueur").

[5] Article 1382 of the Civil Code, which prohibits harming others, is also applicable.

tices. No longer did businessmen have to wait for some competitor to actually harm them before they could sue. Now, individuals as well as professional trade associations were authorized to ask commercial courts to restrain through a cease-and-desist order whoever engaged in "acts contrary to fair (honest) commercial usages" and *likely* to hurt their reputation, their business, or their capacity to compete.

This decree did not specifically mention comparisons, but they fell under the general category of false, deceptive, and/or malicious statements.[6] As in the past, firms provably hurt by such practices could also sue for damages under the general provisions of civil law.

The *law of 14 July 1971* on commercial practices (which replaced the 1934 decree and assorted regulations) now forbids any advertising using comparisons that are either misleading (e.g., to claim falsely that one is the largest manufacturer of the product), or denigrating (e.g., critical of others even if truthful), or make it unnecessarily possible to identify one or more businessmen—not only competitors (Article 20.2).

This law also includes sections about price comparisons, but the focus is really on misleading advertising (e.g., reference to vague "list" prices is forbidden). In any case, it prohibits comparison with the prices practiced by "named" others (no changes are being contemplated as far as this last rule is concerned).

Apart from being explicit about the ban of comparisons, the 1971 law largely covers the same grounds, exceptions, and tolerances as before. A novelty, however, is that accredited consumer associations as well as the government (for all practical purposes, the Ministry of Economic Affairs) can also ask for cease-and-desist orders against advertisers. Besides, in cases of bad faith, penal action is now possible and can result in fines.

The Benelux Uniform Law on Trademarks (1969) has an Article 13.A.2 that forbids "other uses" of trademarks—besides the more common "passing off" of one's products for those of another.[7] This prohibition would seem to apply to any reference to a registered trade name in comparative advertisements, although there is no jurisprudence to date about it.

Proposed Authorization of Comparison Advertising: The law, as well as most court decisions, has traditionally emphasized the protection of business firms. Doing so, it reflects the highly individualistic character of Belgian commercial law and its traditional favoring of trade over consumer interests when the two conflicted. This situation in turn mirrors the strong political influence of small-and-medium businessmen anxious to avoid "savage" competition, which not

[6] For a discussion of the evolution of this legislation, see: J.J. Boddewyn, *Belgian Public Policy Toward Retailing Since 1789; The Socio-Politics of Distribution* (East Lansing, Mich.: Division of Research, Graduate School of Business Administration, Michigan State University, 1971), pp. 19, 47.

[7] Article 13.A.2 refers to: "Any other use which, in the conduct of business and without a just motive [e.g., in the case of alternative replacement parts] . . . [is] susceptible of harming the trademark owner."

only threatens their renown and economic success but also their social status as "independent" businessmen already buffeted by large corporate firms.[8]

This tradition is now being challenged by the trend toward recognizing the consumer as a major economic actor entitled to have his/her own interests equally defended and promoted by the law—including the right to information. This principle is now generally acknowledged (even by the 1971 law), and it is actively promoted by consumer associations (which can also ask for cease-and-desist orders) and by representative bodies (e.g., the government-sponsored Consumers Council, whose opinion must be solicited on all relevant bills).

Comparison advertising receives some support from this increasing concern with consumer information, from the proposed EEC directive allowing its use, and from various favorable pronouncements by the European Parliament and the Council of Europe (see legal chapter).

Consequently, a 1974 bill by Representative Degroeve[9] proposed to eliminate the 1971 clause forbidding unnecessary references to other firms—thereby authorizing comparative advertisements that are truthful. He justified these amendments by stating that:

> Of course all falsely based and denigrating comparisons should remain forbidden. On the other hand, comparisons referring to the real qualities or to the actual defects of particular products provide consumers with evaluative data which allow them to choose well. Allowing comparison advertising would thus benefit consumers. Should this allowance be abused, competitors would undoubtedly state the truth of the matter, and thus provide advertising useful to honest producers and tradesmen as well as to consumers.

The bill also proposed that the burden of proving the truth of the advertisement should rest with the advertiser, and that penalties should include corrective advertisements (at the discretion of the judge). Degroeve justified reversing the burden of the proof on the grounds that it is normally difficult or costly for the consumer to prove—when he/she asks for a cease-and-desist order—that a product or service does not possess the qualities extolled in an advertisement. Also, court-imposed corrective advertisements would allow consumers to become aware of the untruthful or misleading character of the original ad; and consumer associations would be allowed to sue for damages on behalf of their members in the case of illicit practices (including advertising ones).

This parliamentary bill has been sidetracked in favor of a more extensive revision of the 1971 law. Two drafts (1976 and 1977) of a government bill clearly reveal an intention to extend consumer protection and prerogatives; they include a definite softening of the ban on comparison advertising (there have also been several government pronouncements to that effect).

However, it seems certain that the revised law will be more detailed, restrictive, and punitive in terms of what is allowed and forbidden. Thus, com-

[8] Francq, *op. cit.*, p. 28; Boddewyn, *op. cit., passim.* It seems that most infractions involving comparisons have been committed by smaller firms.

[9] Chambre des Représentants, Session Extraordinaire 1974, *Proposition de loi modifiant la loi du 14 juillet 1971 sur les pratiques du commerce* (29 mai 1974). This bill is now void because of subsequent new elections for Parliament.

parison advertising is likely to be authorized in principle, but to be circumscribed by many requirements, restrictions, and stiff penalties. The use of comparative advertisements may thus be rather difficult and dangerous. This can be ascertained from the following principles and amendments proposed by the government (it is worth noting the negative wording of many statements and clauses):

A. *Principles*

1. It is not enough to forbid misleading advertisements: the proscription should also apply to advertisements whose truthfulness (*véracité, véridicité*) cannot be proven by the advertiser.

2. It seems no longer appropriate to forbid all forms of comparison advertising.

3. In cases of contestations, the burden of the proof (when substantiable) should be on the advertiser who has not stopped an ad contested by the government.

4. Violations (even if done in good faith) should be penalized by fines and (at the discretion of the judge) by corrective advertisements—and even by confiscation of the resulting illicit profits (in cases of repeated infractions).

5. The Ministry of Economic Affairs should be authorized to issue warnings and injunctions to stop illicit commercial practices (including advertisements) as an alternative or a prelude to cease-and-desist and penal actions.

B. *Proposed Amendments (selections)*

- "Is forbidden . . . all advertising which includes misleading [or] denigrating comparisons vis-à-vis one or more vendors; or which includes elements apt to create confusion with another vendor, his products or activity" (Article 20.2 and 20.3).

- "The government can issue warnings, and request that a particular practice be stopped" (Art. 59 bis).

- "Substantiation of all claims can be required by the Government" (Art. 20 bis).

- Article 21 bis provides that: "Will be punished by a fine . . . those who contravene Article 20." (In other words, even infractions committed in good faith could be penalized and not just amenable to cease-and-desist orders; and pursuing a practice after a government warning could lead to a charge of bad faith. Too, penalties could be shared by all involved parties—such as advertising agencies and the printer—not just by the advertiser, as in the case of cease-and-desist orders).

- "In the case of firms with annual sales of at least 50 million BF [about $13 million], the fine will be figured as a percentage of sales" (Art. 64).

- "The judge can order that a corrective advertisement be published; and that the illicitly made profits be confiscated" (Art. 65).

Business and Consumer Positions

The draft of the government bill is being discussed by various formal advisory bodies (Consumers Council, Central Economic Council, and Middle-Classes Council—the latter representing small and medium firms). It will then be debated in Parliament, and may go through several drafts (if only because of new elections and cabinet changes). Altogether, the enactment of these amendments may take anywhere from two to nine years (it took that long for the 1971 law).

Consumers Council: This body groups government-appointed representatives of recognized consumer associations and cooperatives and of consumer-goods industry, distribution, agriculture, and small-and-medium business, together with several experts. As such it provides a good cross-section of the Belgian economy (including consumers), although advertising agencies and the media are not formally represented.

The Consumers Council has already reported on the Degroeve bill and on the government draft.[10] Its two reports deal with many matters—not just comparison advertising—and they are extremely interesting because they reveal very clearly the present views of consumer associations, large producers and distributors (as advertisers), and small-and-medium business[11] vis-à-vis advertising in general.

The following sections focus on comparison advertising as well as on regulations dealing with advertising (reversal of the burden of proof, corrective advertisements, and increased penalization of infractions) to the extent that they bear on comparison advertising.

Comparison Advertising: Consumer representatives like the idea of allowing comparisons, because they would reinforce the informative character of advertising, which they criticize for often being uninformative, misleading, and subjective. However, they caution against incomplete, partial, and relatively erroneous comparisons:

> Advertising arguments should rest only on the intrinsic merits of a product; but remaining silent about its disadvantages seems to conflict with the requirement for truthfulness. Subjective, unverifiable, or irrelevant arguments should be avoided.[12]

[10] Conseil de la Consommation, *Avis sur la proposition de loi Degroeve;* and *Avis sur les principes pouvant être retenus pour la réforme de la loi du 14 julliet 1971 sur les pratiques du commerce,* Documents CC 28 and 29 (Bruxelles, 9 avril 1976).

[11] The Middle-Classes Council has also given its opinion about this government bill, but it does not make any explicit reference to comparison advertising.

[12] Small-and-medium business representatives also opposed intentional omissions that could be misleading. The consumer representatives even suggested that the use of "human images" be forbidden unless necessary for the objective presentation of the product's use and advantages.

It is well to realize that Belgian consumer associations (there were fourteen accredited ones in 1976) are generally suspicious of, if not antagonistic to, advertising. As such, they welcome comparison advertising as a source of additional information and of greater "market transparency"—especially since they sponsor comparative product tests. Yet, their enthusiasm for this new technique is limited, not only because they are aware of some of its limitations, but primarily because of their lingering prejudices against advertisers.

Large as well as small and medium producers and distributors are generally opposed to comparison advertising because it might jeopardize the rules of fair competition: "Competition can be fair (loyal) only if advertisers respect each other." In particular, they raise the following objections:

- It is not fair to use someone else's property—his firm, brands, and general notoriety—to foster one's own interests.

- Comparative advertisements cannot really be fair because advertising is always elliptic: its messages are not like a technical report, and cannot be complete.

- Comparisons cannot be fully objective because advertising ultimately tries to persuade and convince. This one-sided commitment to win is bound to make comparisons either subjective or suspicious.[13]

While accepting the need for promoting consumer interests (including their information), this group—particularly the smaller firms—reminded the government that the 1971 law is also about the protection of "honest traders" against unfair competitive practices, and that this traditional perspective should not be abandoned in the law's revision.

Altogether, it seems that larger firms are opposed to comparison advertising but could live with it; while smaller businesses are afraid of a new technique that would mostly be used by bigger firms with large advertising budgets—and against them, they think.

Reversing the Burden of Proof: All interest groups accept the notion of obliging a challenged advertiser to prove the truthfulness of his claims (whether comparative or not). However, they raise various objections reflecting their respective points of view. In many ways, this provision is much more divisive than comparison advertising itself.

Producers and distributors of all sizes want it restricted to the "objective and measurable" elements in an advertisement. Otherwise, it would be practically forbidden to use themes stressing pleasure, mood, or context, and those reflecting value judgments.

Besides, they argue that the burden of proof should not be used in penal cases since this would amount to presuming the advertiser to be guilty until he

---

[13] For similar views, see the business audience's reactions to Francq's presentation (*op. cit.*) in: "La publicité face aux consommateurs," *Bulletin de l'Institut International de Concurrence Commericale* (avril 1977), pp. 79–94.

can prove his innocence—and negative proofs that "one does not cause something" may be impossible in many cases. Hence, they urge that this reversal be limited to cease-and-desist actions, and that it provide for the protection of trade secrets.

Consumer representatives, on the other hand, want this reversal to apply to all statements made in an advertisement. Otherwise, they fear that limiting it to objective statements would increase the use of subjective arguments in order to avoid having to prove them—advertisements would thus become even less informative than now! Producers and distributors counter this prediction, however, by arguing that any advertiser with an objective advantage would want to use it in his communications.

Corrective Advertisements: All representatives accept that judges be empowered to impose appropriate corrective advertisements. Consumer delegates, however, would like it to be a mandatory penalty—something strenuously resisted by producers and distributors who see it as a disproportionately costly penalty as compared to regular fines. They also think it might confuse consumers at times.

Other Penalties: Making all infractions of Article 20 fall under penal law [14] appeals to *consumer representatives*—especially since accredited associations could sue for damages on behalf of their members. *Producers and distributors* of all sizes, however, want to limit the latter to damages that the consumer associations have personally suffered. Besides, penalizing all infractions (rather than allowing only cease-and-desist actions) would no longer protect an advertiser who acted in good faith.

Fundamentally, the combination of (1) strict truthfulness requirements, (2) reversal of the burden of proof, and (3) penalization of all infractions would amount to obliging challenged advertisers to prove that they are *not* guilty! Also, singling out advertising for penal treatment could lead to the strange situation whereby a firm could be fined for advertising an illicit practice, which by itself is not punishable by fine, but only stoppable by a court order!

All representatives accept formalizing the right of government to issue warnings to apparent offenders, but they object to the use of executive injunctions to stop illicit commercial practices—particularly if a refusal to obey this injunction would lead to some penal action.

Advertisers and Agencies: The Belgian advertising community is presently lukewarm on the subject of comparison advertising. Some advertising agencies favor the removal of the ban because "it would be nice" to have this technique available—especially if comparative advertisements start filtering in from abroad (e.g., through foreign publications and through cable television relaying foreign programs [15]).

---

[14] "Penalization" means that infractions are punished by fines (and possibly other ways) rather than simply having the illicit practices terminated on the basis of a cease-and-desist order.

[15] Consumer representatives on the Consumers Council favor the banning of commercials on foreign programs transmitted through cable television.

On the other hand, major advertisers seem nearly unanimously opposed to legalizing comparison advertising (only one firm—and always the same one—is mentioned as favoring it). Their opposition rests on the traditional European fear of "savage" competition. Also, declining profitability has resulted in major cuts in advertising budgets, and firms are afraid of having to engage in counterattacks once they start being named by their competitors.

Advertisers are also aware of the controversies, complaints, and suits that are likely to result from comparison advertising—based on their understanding of the American experience. They also fear the proposed reversal of the burden of proof, which is likely to accompany any legalization of comparison advertising, and which would require additional time and money expenditures for testing, legal checking, and legal suits. Yet, the recent shift to more immediately "promotional" themes (e.g., special offers) and away from "investment-type" advertising (that creates a long-term favorable image for a company or a product line) may well make comparative advertisements more attractive in the current fight for consumer patronage.

The **media** have no apparent position on comparison advertising.[16] In any case, Belgian radio and television networks are government-owned, and do not accept any commercial advertising.

Self-Regulation

Should the fair use of comparison advertising be authorized, it would benefit from the well-developed Belgian system for advertising self-regulation.[17] Since 1967, there have been an Advertising Code and an Advertising Ethics Jury (Jury d'Ethique Publicitaire) set up as a joint function of advertiser (UBA), agency (CACP), and media associations (several) grouped within the Advertising Council (Conseil de la Publicité). This code makes no reference to comparisons but states that any advertisement must obey the law, be truthful (the Jury can ask for proof), and be in good taste. The Council, however, subscribes to the ICC Advertising Code, which tolerates comparisons.

The Jury handles only complaints that an advertisement is harmful to consumers and/or advertising's general reputation; while disputes among advertisers or with their agencies are handled by the CACP. Many actions are generated on the basis of pre-publication submissions by advertisers or agencies. Close to half of the complaints originate from consumers (not from their associations).

The Jury can only make recommendations and notify the relevant parties and member associations, but the media usually reject advertisements ruled to be unfair. Examples related to comparison advertising include one advertisement dramatizing the lack of comfort in public transportation. It was modified—on Jury recommendation—to be less sharply critical. An unjustified su-

---

[16] The courts decided in a 1952–1953 case that the *Reader's Digest* could not publicize its audience figures in comparison to that of other print media.

[17] A.B. Stridsberg, *Effective Advertising Self-Regulation, op. cit.*, pp. 51–53. See also the publications and reports of the Conseil de la Publicité and of the Jury d'Ethique Publicitaire.

perlative claim was also modified by a beer manufacturer, and an advertisement using unvalidated comparisons about other heating fuels was dropped.

In a recent statement about the proposed revision of the 1971 law on commercial practices (which regulates advertising), the Advertising Council took a rather negative attitude toward comparison advertising.[18] Consumer associations, however, are opposed to the self-regulatory system if it is to be used exclusively or even primarily to handle consumer complaints about advertising. They prefer instead to publicize criticisms in their publications, and to press for legal recourse and redress. Government officials approve of self-regulation but are unlikely to advise a consumer to approach the Advertising Ethics Jury. They are also considering establishing minimum rules for such self-regulatory boards.

Conclusion

Altogether, the Belgian situation reveals that comparison advertising faces deeply seated interests and negative attitudes, but that it has a logic of its own that makes it a natural candidate for legislative reform in countries that ban it. The EEC draft directive on misleading and unfair advertising would, of course, make it necessary to legalize comparison advertising. A similar move on the part of France—a "pilot" country for much Belgian legislation—would also facilitate such a change.

CANADA[19]

Practice

Comparison advertising is definitely on the upswing in Canada. At least some 5 percent of national advertising expenditures are used for that purpose in all media—principally for automotive products (Ford, Volvo, American Motors, and Japanese makes), personal-care and household-products, and soft drink (Pepsi, 7-Up, Coca-Cola) products.[20] Some observers think that this percentage could reach 10 percent by 1978, but others believe that it has already reached its peak. In any case, use is more limited in French Canada.

This upsurge was preceded by much soul-searching on the part of Canadian advertisers, agencies, and media, and the same arguments (pro and con) were used as in the United States, although with a more British accent on the

[18]Conseil de la Publicité, "Projets de législation en matière de publicité; Position du Conseil de la Publicité" (Brussels, 1977), pp. 8–9.

[19] The assistance of Messrs. Rolf James (Project Manager, Association of Canadian Advertisers), Robert Marvin (Executive Director, Advertising Standards Council), K.W. McCracken (Legal Counsel, Association of Canadian Advertisers), R.E. Oliver (President, Canadian Advertising Board), K.G. Decker (Chief of Misleading Advertising Division, Consumer and Corporate Affairs Department), and Ms. Jo-Ann Christian (National Research Chairman, Consumers' Association of Canada), is gratefully acknowledged.

[20] A 1976 study of 3,580 advertisements in the print and television media determined that about 2 percent of them were direct comparisons, with another 17 percent indirect ones (e.g., "Than any other [unnamed] brand"). G.H.G. McDougall, A Study of Comparative Advertising in Canada (Ottawa: Consumer Research Council Canada, 1976). These ads were in English.

necessity of "fair play" in advertising. The symbiosis between the two countries' business systems ultimately led to Canadian adoption of this practice, which had been legal all along—apart from some questions about the use of someone else's registered trademark (see below).

Legislation [21]

No federal[22] law or regulation prohibits truthful comparative advertisement. However, Subsection 36(1) of the Combines Investigation Act (about competition) prohibits: (1) materially false or misleading representations to the public, and (2) statements that are not based on "an adequate and proper test thereof."

In applying this Act, the Department of Consumer and Corporate Affairs follows 1976 comparison-advertising guidelines in deciding about initiating an inquity that may lead to possible prosecution (violations are punishable by fine and imprisonment).

Essentially, this Department favors comparison advertising for contributing to better consumer information and decisions as well as to greater care in preparing advertisements.

The Canadian Trade Marks Act forbids the use of someone else's *registered trademark* on products or packages "in a manner likely to have the effect of depreciating the value of the goodwill attached thereto" (Section 22.1);[23] while its Subsection 7(a) provides that: "No person shall make a false or misleading statement tending to discredit the business, wares or services of a competitor" in the context of using a trademark or the trade name of a business.

The Department of Consumer and Corporate Affairs has recommended that Section 22 be eliminated to allow the use of rival trademarks in order to encourage competition, and the Patent and Trade Mark Institute of Canada is willing to have Section 22 amended to accept "accurate and non-misleading statements by competitors as to the comparative advantages of their products in relation to trademarked products of others."

However, this proposed revision is dormant because of the strong opposition expressed by a special 1974 committee of the Canadian Bar Association, which recommended that all forms of comparison advertising be banned. In any case, the very fact that an amendment has been recommended reveals that some doubt remains about the legality of using registered trademarks in comparison advertising under this Act.

[21] The major source used here is: Werner Janssen, Jr., "Some Foreign Law Aspects of Comparative Advertising," *The Trademark Reporter,* Vol. 64 (1974), pp. 484–87. The assistance of Messrs. K. Wayne McCracken and Reuben M. Bromstein is also gratefully acknowledged regarding this legal section.

[22] There is also relevant provincial and municipal legislation that complicates the determination of the legality of comparisons—for example, the various Provinces' Business Practices Acts. Also, the Food and Drugs Directorate limits the use of comparisons in nutritional claims, and bans it in the case of drugs. Furthermore, all ads dealing with foods and drugs must be approved by the Health Protection Branch of the Department of National Health and Welfare.

[23] There is an important 1968 Clairol case about the use of a registered trademark on a defendant's wares or their packages. For details, see Janssen, *op. cit.,* pp. 484–85.

CANADIAN GOVERNMENT GUIDELINES *

1. *Generalized Superiority Claims:* Comparative data should not be used to imply general superiority for a product unless such a claim would be accurate over a comprehensive range of normal conditions of use for the product. If the superiority of the product is limited to a certain range of conditions, then any superiority claim should be qualified to reflect that limited range. *For example:* if a brand of gasoline were to be advertised as producing better mileage than several competitive brands and the claim would be accurate under highway driving conditions but inaccurate under city conditions, this limitation must be clearly expressed.

2. *Performance Tests*

   a. Any tests on which superiority claims are to be based should be conducted according to normally accepted scientific principles, and the tests should be reliable to at least a .05 level of confidence. *For example:* if one brand of rope is represented as being stronger than a competitor's, then adequate tests should exist to demonstrate that the brand of rope would be significantly stronger than the competitor's, at least in 95 out of every 100 comparisons.

   b. In any claim of performance superiority, there should be a difference in performance that is meaningful to consumers, and not merely measurable by instruments. If an air conditioner, *for example,* is advertised as being quieter than a competitor's brand and in fact the noise level registered only a few decibels lower (a difference of three decibels is about the smallest difference a normal human ear can discern), no claim should be made to that effect.

3. *Demonstrations*

   a. Comparisons demonstrating the relative effectiveness of competing products should be shown under equivalent conditions. *For example:* a demonstration of the different effect of two types of paints on a wall should be displayed under equal lighting conditions. Thus, the advertiser's product should not be shown in relatively soft light while the competitive product is displayed in a harsh light.

   b. Demonstrations of the relative effectiveness of products should not attempt to compare a product in a use for which it was not intended or under a method of application for which it was not intended. *For example:* various oven cleaners are designed to be applied in different ways since some are intended for immediate scrubbing following application, whereas others are designed to be scrubbed only after a waiting period of several hours. Obviously, if an advertiser of the first type of oven cleaner were to compare his product with a cleaner of the second type, both products would have to be used as intended and directed by the manufacturer.

Source: Canadian Government, Consumer and Corporate Department, *Misleading Advertising Bulletin* (4 November 1976), pp. 2–3.

Self-Regulation [24]

The Manual of General Guidelines for Advertising of the Canadian Adver- tising Advisory Board (CAAB) has several sections on comparative advertis- ing, dangling comparisons, superlatives, visual representations, and test and survey results, that give limited approval to comparisons.

Furthermore, Section I on "Test and Survey Results" lists a number of

[24] For further details, see: A.B. Stridsberg, *Effective Advertising Self-Regulation* (New York: International Advertising Association, 1974), pp. 57–62. The CAAB has adopted in principle the ICC Code of Advertising Practice.

points about validity and deception—including instructions to avoid comparisons of an advertiser's best line with a competitor's lower-priced or poorer quality lines, as well as overall performance claims that select only favorable factors and ignore those in which the competitive product or products are superior. Whenever possible, tests should be conducted under conditions that can be duplicated, and research data should be available on request to any recognized enforcement body. The CAAB has already sustained complaints about advertisements because selected factual comparative data were used to imply overall superiority.

CANADIAN ADVERTISING ADVISORY BOARD
SELECTED GUIDELINES

II. *Comparative Advertising*

Consumer information often becomes more meaningful through factual comparisons. It is, therefore, the current opinion of the Councils that such communication techniques have a legitimate basis in today's advertising milieu. However, it should be noted that large sections of the media community in Canada reject comparative advertising, since this form of advertising is particularly susceptible to abuse, and can lead to unfair or false disparagement of competition. From the viewpoint of the advertising industry itself, comparative campaigns based on confusing counter-claims seriously undermine the credibility of the whole advertising process.

The following guidelines indicate how to avoid the unethical use of comparative advertising.

1. When competitors' names are mentioned or shown, they should be used only in the context of a factual comparison.
2. Products identified in comparisons must actually be competitive with one another.
3. Comparisons must be between related, or similar features, properties, qualities, ingredients, e.g., compare MacIntosh apples with MacIntosh apples. (The sections on Test and Survey Results and Visual Representations are particularly relevant here.
4. The elements involved in the comparisons should be measurable *and* significant in terms of value or satisfaction to the consumer.
5. Selected, factual comparative data should not be used to imply *overall* superiority. If the claim is total, the comparison should be comprehensive, and include those in which the competitor excels.

III. *Dangling Comparisons*

Dangling Comparisons are simply the use of incomplete comparisons—''10 per cent faster.'' Than what? Because the comparison is not completed, the message provides little real information.

This does not necessarily mean that dangling comparisons are *always* deceptive, but caution should be exercised through the application of these two guidelines:

1. When a dangling comparison implies a general comparison with all competitive products, the company should have valid research data available to back up whatever claim is made, e.g., "Fastest by far" with reference to a car implies all other available comparable models in the market have been tested. Such substantiation need not appear as support in advertising. However, the company must be prepared always, if called upon, to substantiate to the media or the Advertising Standards Council, not only dangling comparisons, but any "more than" completed comparisons as well.

2. If the dangling comparison refers only to an improvement in the product itself, this should be made clear, e.g., "New 'X' gives you 20 percent more than ever." Of course, eliminating the dangling comparison is even better—"New 'X' gives 20 percent more 'Y' than ever before, where Y equals flavour, long life or whatever.

IV. *Superlatives*

The use of superlative claims in advertising should follow the same norms of substantiation as those of dangling comparisons. The more specific the superlative, the easier its substantiation: For example, "largest selling," "the most popular," "the smallest," "the largest" can be verified more readily than "the best," "the greatest," "the highest quality," "the most effective," etc. If the superlative cannot be substantiated, it should not be used (see Exceptions, below). For example, in a period of flexible pricing the promise "lowest prices in town" is almost meaningless, and may well be misleading.

A useful guideline for superlatives: Be as specific as possible so that adequate substantiation can be readily provided.

Exceptions:

1. *Hyperbole*
   Although exaggerated claims or promises are generally deceptive, there are types of exaggerations *which are clearly understood by the receiver to be an intended exaggeration.* This is what hyperbole means. Those superlatives which are hyperbolic are an exception to the above guidelines. For example, "the greatest show on earth" or "the fastest 'something' in the West," "Everybody loves Wet Smacks" are acceptable simply because they are received as obvious exaggerations (hyperboles). But the technique should be used with care and not be abused.

   Humor is often a good vehicle for the hyperbolic communication of superlatives.

2. *Subjective Comment*
   Some superlative claims represent opinions or personal evaluations of product or service qualities—flavour, fragrance, styling appeal—that usually cannot be proven or disproved. They are permissible so long as they do not convey a misleading impression.

   Unless self-discipline is exercised in the use of superlatives, of course, they tend to become meaningless words.

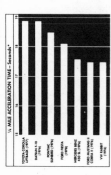
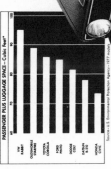

> V. *Visual Representations*
>
> It is certainly legitimate to show a product or service and their effects in the most appealing and dramatic fashion; it is also important to represent them faithfully.

Other associations, such as those in the field of proprietary drugs and toiletries, also authorize the fair use of comparison advertising; the (public) Canadian Broadcasting Corporation has also come to accept them.[25] On the other hand, some major dailies apply acceptance criteria that effectively ban comparative advertisements.

Consumerist Reactions

The Consumers' Association of Canada (CAC) conducted a survey among its members in 1977, that turned out to be very negative regarding comparison advertising—possibly as a reflection of more general attitudes against advertising among action-oriented CAC members.[26] The CAC, however, remains essentially favorable to the use of comparisons though doubtful about the substantiation of claims made in all advertisements.

Prospects

Numerous criticisms are still being directed at the practice of comparison advertising on the well-known grounds that it leads to disparagement and a reduced credibility for advertising in general, and that it allows lesser-known brands to "hitchhike" on the good reputation of others. Opposition comes mainly from some advertisers and lawyers; while consumer associations remain somewhat skeptical.[27] Still, the United States example and the national government's support (partly in emulation of the U.S. Federal Trade Commission) have led to a growing practice that may already have peaked.

DENMARK[28]

Practice

The use of comparison advertising has recently increased in Denmark. A November 1976 analysis by Roepstorff (*op. cit.*) of 1,900 advertisements re-

---

[25] Canadian Broadcasting Corporation, *Commercial Acceptance Policy Guidelines* (1976); and "Guidelines for Clearance of Competitive Comparisons" (1 July 1976). However, the standards for children advertising rule out toy advertisements that make direct comparisons with previous-year models or with competitive makes, even when the statements or claims are valid.

[26] For the detailed findings, see the chapter on "Comparison Advertising: Beneficial or Not?," which also reports the negative findings of McDougall (pp. 66–68).

[27] "Open Way for Comparative Ads, Canada Meet Told," *Advertising Age* (12 May 1975), p. 6.

[28] This section is based on a manuscript especially written for this volume by Bjorn U. Roepstorff (Cand. Jur., HD; Assistant Manager Forenede Assundandorer A/S). See also his article: "Sammenlignende Reklame," *Orientering* (September 1977), pp. 5–10. The assistance of Benedicte Federspiel (Cand. Jur.) of the Forbrugerradet (Consumers Council) is also gratefully acknowledged.

vealed that some 17 percent were comparative in one form or another. Most of these 320 ads only made indirect references to "other" or "leading" brands, or amounted to superlative statements, but 32 (or 1.7 percent) were direct comparisons.

They were used mostly by the automobile and insurance trades and by radio-TV retail stores—besides the more traditional comparisons by media trying to sell their publications to advertisers and their agencies. They were in print for the most part, since there is no commercial television or radio in Denmark.

Legislation

This development owes much to the relaxation of self-regulation and to the recent enactment of the Marketing Practices Act (No. 297 of 14 June 1974—effective 1 May 1975).

Originally, the 1912 Fair Competition Act was applied in the light of the Advertising Code of the International Chamber of Commerce. As was mentioned in a previous chapter, earlier versions of this code were rather negative toward comparison advertising—a situation made worse by the incorrect translation of "should be avoided" into the Danish "must be avoided." After the 1966 and 1973 revisions, the ICC Code became more tolerant toward this practice.

The new 1974 Marketing Practices Act does not refer specifically to comparison advertising, but its Article 1 requires that commercial activities be conducted in accordance with "proper [fair] marketing practices." Article 2.1. forbids "any false, misleading, or unreasonably incomplete indication or statement likely to affect the demand for or supply of goods, real or personal property, and work or services." Article 2.2 prohibits practices that, because of their form or reference to irrelevant matter, are "improper" in relation to traders and consumers.

Thus, Article 2.1 applies to truthful comparisons that are nevertheless misleading; while Articles 1 and 2.2 deal with any comparison—whether truthful or not—that could be considered unfair ("improper") to other businessmen or to consumers. These provisions also protect non-competitors (e.g., creditors and suppliers), and apply to business and consumers associations as well as to product-testing organizations (Article 2.4).[29]

The unauthorized use of someone else's registered or commonly used trademark in principle constitutes an infringement of the 1959 Trade Marks Act and of Article 5 of the 1974 Marketing Practices Act. However, the strong consumer-orientation of the latter legislation appears to tolerate it when such use is clearly intended to assist consumers. On the other hand, simply using someone else's name to further one's commercial position ("coattail-riding") may be

---

[29] However, consumer associations cannot normally complain or sue on behalf of their members. The 1974 Act also protects "public" consumers (e.g., a governmental purchasing unit), but does not seem to apply to government advertising. Thus, the Consumer Ombudsman recently exonerated the Ministry of Finance which had compared its bonds to alternative forms of private investment.

considered "parasitic" and therefore "improper" according to Article 2.2 of the 1974 Act.

The Consumer Ombudsman supervises the implementation of the Marketing Practices Act, using "his best endeavors by negotiation" to insure compliance with the law. Otherwise, he brings the matter before the commercial courts, which use the ICC Code as a guideline. The Ombudsman, however, has until now mainly dealt with consumer complaints. Businessmen resort, for the most part, to the courts when they cannot settle their complaints privately.

Few comparison-advertising cases have so far come to the attention of the Ombudsman. Most have dealt with improper price comparisons in relation to "suggested" or "normal" retail prices. He has ruled that such references are acceptable only when "guided" prices are in fact widely used. Other cases bore on products that were not truly comparable, not readily available in other stores, or not compared along a sufficient number of attributes. A language school that claimed to be "The only specialist in intensive language training" was found guilty of misleading consumers and of acting unfairly toward competitors, since its claim could not be substantiated. These decisions to date parallel those made previously under the Danish self-regulatory system.

Self-Regulation

The Danish Advertising Board (Dansk Reklamenaevn) was disbanded after the 1974 Act became operative in 1975 because advertisers felt that businessmen and consumers could now refer their complaints to the Consumer Ombudsman. Before its demise, this Board stated in 1971 that comparative advertisements are acceptable if completely truthful, relevant, and fair.

Of some five hundred complaints handled by the Board from 1971 to 1975, 16 percent dealt with comparative ads. Its decisions stressed—among others—that comparisons should be substantiatable; that differences among compared products be significant; that a reasonable selection of attributes be included; that products be truly comparable (particularly in the case of price comparisons) or that significant differences be mentioned; and that denigration (including the humorous ridiculing of a competitor) and undue generalizations be avoided.

Prospects

The practice of comparison advertising is picking up speed in Denmark now that some firms are aggressively using it. Most businessmen still stay away from it, considering comparisons as unfair and/or dangerous for the overall image of advertising and business. On the other hand, consumer associations are basically positive if comparisons live up to the above mentioned standards. The proposed EEC draft directive on misleading and unfair advertising (see above) would provide additional support to the Danish position toward comparison advertising.[30]

[30] This draft directive also provides for various sanctions (e.g., corrective advertising), which are now missing in the Danish legislation.

Its future will depend on how advertisers behave themselves. Some observers fear that too many comparisons will violate both the Marketing Practices Act and the ICC Advertising Code. In such a case, the Ombudsman may well issue strict guidelines, and commercial courts will be kept busy. However, no ban of comparisons appears likely.

JAPAN[31]

Practically no comparisons are used in Japanese advertising. This situation reflects a preference for gentle suggestions over strong contrasts and exaggerated claims in advertising. Besides, open attack and denigration of rivals is scrupulously avoided on account of the cultural tradition of "respecting each other's face."[32]

However, there are a few examples of indirect hints at the competition. In the launching of the new film Sakuracolor-24, popular comedian Kinichi Hagimoto was shown holding in one hand a conventional 20-frame roll of film, and in the other the new 24-frame film. He said: "Four extra frames, but the price is the same. Which is more profitable? Give it a good thought." In this example, the expression is so reserved that at first glance the comparison intended is not very obvious. Similarly, a Nissan Sunny ad observed that: "The neighbor's car looks small"—probably referring to Toyota's Corolla, but without elaborating and stressing the comparison.

This tradition of not slandering or vilifying competitors explains the near absence of comparison advertising, which does not suffer from any regulatory or self-regulatory ban.

Legislation

In Japan, no law or regulation prohibits truthful comparison advertising. The 1962 (amended 1972) Act Against Unjustifiable Premiums and Misleading Representation, which is a subsidiary law of the Anti-monopoly Act (Act Concerning the Prohibition of Private Monopoly and the Maintenance of Fair Trade), deals only with untruthful and misleading representations (including comparisons) on account of exaggerated claims.

Thus, Article 4 of this Act forbids:

1. Representations apt to entice customers unjustifiably, and to prevent fair competition because they may cause them in general to assume erroneously that the merchandise or service is markedly superior to the actual merchandise or service, or to those of competitors, in terms of quality, standards, and other matters.
2. Representations apt to entice the customers unjustifiably, and to prevent fair competition because they may cause them in general to assume er-

[31] The assistance of Mr. Tadataka Ibusuki, Executive Secretary of the Advertising Problems Office of Dentsu Advertising Ltd. (Tokoyo), and of the IAA Japanese Chapter is gratefully acknowledged.
[32] Satoshi Mukai, "Japan–U.S. Contrast in Advertising Expressions," *Dentsu's Japan Marketing Advertising* (January 1977), pp. 54–56.

roneously that the merchandise or service is markedly more advantageous to the [buyer] than the actual merchandise or service, or to those of competitors in terms of price and other terms of sale.

Regarding truthful comparisons, the Staff Office of the Fair Trade Commission has taken the position that "it is desirable because it offers information useful to the consumers. However, since comparison advertising challenges competition in a most acute form, it is prone to create intense cut-throat competition. Whether to engage in this kind of advertising is for the industries themselves to decide."

Self-Regulation [33]

Various trade and industry associations have developed codes of conduct that bear on the use of comparisons.

Japan Chamber of Commerce and Industry: Typical of advertising codes providing voluntary controls regarding comparison advertising is the "Guide for the Improvement of Advertising" prepared by the Japan Chamber of Commerce and Industry. In its section dealing with "Standards of Expression in Advertisements," it allows comparisons as long as the rules regarding "superiority" and "comparative representation" are observed:

1. *Superiority*
   a. Superiority shall be expressed on the basis of data that are objectively appropriate, and after strict substantiation of the facts. Besides, when dealing with facts, the organization having made the survey as well as the period of the survey shall be clearly identified. Examples of words used in indicating superiority include: "First in the world; First in Japan; Only this company; Ranking first; First; Number 1; Top-Ranking; Without a peer; Most suited to; Highest; Largest; Smallest; All; 100 percent; and All-powerful."
   b. Even though superiority of *part* of the merchandise or part of the quality, performance, or efficacy may be a fact, expressions that may be mistaken to mean superiority as a *whole* shall be avoided.
   c. Even though superiority of production volume, sales volume, export volume, rate of popularity, etc., may be a fact, use of words indicating superiority shall be avoided when the difference with the competition is small.
   d. Expressions that could be misconstrued to apply to different conditions shall not be used.

2. *Comparative Expressions*
   a. When comparing in terms of quality, performance, efficacy, prices, etc., one's merchandise with that of other firms, these comparisons shall be based on objective facts, and not contravene basic principles.

---

[33] For further details, see: A.B. Stridsberg, *Effective Advertising Self-Regulation* (New York: International Advertising Association, 1974), pp. 93–95. There is a Japan Advertising Review Organization (1974) similar to the U.S. National Advertising Review Board.

    b. The expression of comparative prices (for the same quantities) shall
be made on the basis of facts which can be proved by the advertiser;
and fictitious prices shall not be used in comparisons.

    c. Words, charts, and photographs referring to the merchandise of an-
other firm and deemed by a third party to be clearly slandering and
vilifying of it shall not be used. Also, when making comparisons
with the merchandise of another company, ambiguous expressions
shall not be used—for example: "Thing in general use; Conventional;
Everything else; The usual thing; Things in use so far; Something
else; Anywhere else; and Unprecedented."

As can be seen, this code of conduct is rather strict and detailed, and it
largely precludes the use of puffery.

Industry: Article 10 of the Act Against Unjustifiable Premiums and Misleading
Representation provides for the approval by the Fair Trade Commission of industry-wide codes of conduct. There are many of them which derive some
quasi-legal character from this legislation.

Thus, some thirty industries have voluntary "Fair-competition Rules
Regarding Representations," and they parallel those of the Japan Chamber of
Commerce and Industry. They often deal with superiority and comparative
claims in such fields as real estate, margarine, milk, canned goods, meats,
chocolate products, biscuits, chewing gum, ice cream, cosmetics, dentifrice,
automobiles, and dog food. Only two of them (automobiles and cosmetics) prohibit comparison advertising, but the Fair Trade Commission has taken a negative position against industry-wide agreements that ban it.

Advertising Industry: All advertising associations have ethical principles and
rules for voluntary self-control. While not all of them deal specifically with
comparison advertising, they all prohibit expressions slandering and vilifying
other companies through comparative expressions, or they require substantiating one's facts.[34] Leading advertising-related organizations having such rules
include:

- Advertising Federation of Japan
- Japan Advertising Review Organization
- Japan Advertisers Association
- Japan Newspaper Publishers and Editors Association
- National Association of Commercial Broadcasters in Japan
- Magazine Advertising Association of Japan
- Japan Advertising Agencies Association

There are no prohibitions of comparison advertising, but advertisers have
used it very little and continue the practice of voluntary restraint.

[34] For example, Rule 5 of the Advertising Code of the Japan Advertising Agencies Association
(1971) provides that "Advertisements must not abuse, slander or attack others." Rule 13 of the
Newspaper Advertising Code of the Nihon Shinbun Kyokai (1958) provides that a newspaper may
reject or reserve the right to publish an advertisement when "in order to emphasize the superiority
of the product, person or institution it is advertising, it slanders or denigrates others."

The Japan Advertising Review Organization does not subscribe to the ICC Code of Advertising Practice, but like other advertising bodies uses it for reference purpose—though not to the point of endorsing comparison advertising.

Prospects

Lately, Japanese advertisers, agencies, the media, and consumers have expressed interest in comparison advertising. As in other countries, it is favored by some for making it easier for consumers to become more aware of differences in the distinctive features of the advertised goods and services. Consumer associations (which are rather powerful in Japan) are not, however, pressing the government and/or industry to have its use increased. In advertising circles, on the other hand, many remain apprehensive over its demerits and fear that the denigration of other firms could lead to forfeiting trust and confidence in advertising as a whole.

Since opinion thus remains divided on this subject in a country noted for its preference for consensus, it could take quite a while to resolve this impasse. In such a case, fairly detailed industry guidelines would probably be developed to constrain the use of comparison advertising.

PHILIPPINES[35]

This country provides the interesting example of having recently banned all uses of comparison advertising under rather unusual circumstances.

Legislation

There is no regulatory obstacle to the use of comparisons. Section 29(C) of Act No. 166 on Trademarks and Unfair Competition (1951) states: "Any person who shall make any false statement in the course of trade or who shall commit any other act contrary to good faith of a nature calculated to discredit the goods, business or services of another . . . shall be deemed guilty of unfair competition." However, the use of truthful comparisons has generally not been considered to be unfair, and the protection of trademarks does not preclude using the name of a competitor.

Self-Regulation

The implementation of this Act is left to the Fair Trade Board. However, it is the Filipino government's policy to encourage self-regulation in advertising. This role has been deputized to the Philippine Board of Advertising (PBA) by the Philippine Council for Print Media (a private media-industry body) and the Broadcast Media Council (a semi-government agency), both of which were

[35] The assistance of the IAA Philippine Chapter is gratefully acknowledged—particularly that of Ms. Maria Lourdes Mijares of Advertising and Marketing Associates, who is Study Committee Coordinator of the Philippine Board of Advertising for comparison advertising. Messrs. O.P. Lagman, Jr. (Executive Director of the PBA) and Antonio R. de Joya (IAA–Philippines President) were also most helpful. Information provided by Pepsi-Cola Bottling Co. of the Philippines was used in the discussion of the Mirinda case.

created by a Presidential decree in 1974. The PBA acts in consultation with the Fair Trade Board, other government agencies, media associations, and consumer groups.

The resulting PBA Code of Ethics until late 1976 allowed comparative advertisements under Rule 4.1.B: "Substantiated competitive claims stating material facts inviting comparisons with a group of products or with other products are acceptable."

Practice

This rule was interpreted by some advertisers as allowing true comparisons naming names, so that a number of comparative campaigns were launched until they represented some 5 percent of advertising expenditures in 1975–1976—particularly in print and through posters for soft drinks (Pepsi's Mirinda), feminine napkins (Kimberly Clark's New Freedom), consumer electronics (Sony's Trinitron), baby powder (Mennen's), household appliances (Del Rosario's and Sears), and auto-rustproofing.

This growing practice generated some definite controversy and opposition which came to a boil when Mirinda (a Pepsi brand) challenged Royal TruOrange (a local San Miguel brand) in a manner reminiscent of the "Pepsi Challenge" in the United States.[36] It advertised in 1976 that "45 percent of Royal TruOrange drinkers prefer Mirinda." This claim was challenged by San Miguel, and the Philippine Board of Advertising requested that it be substantiated. The Pepsi-Cola Bottling Company of the Philippines refused to submit the raw data of the taste-test survey on the grounds that they belonged to Consumer Pulse, Inc. (CPI), which conducted it and sold the results only to Pepsi.

CPI then argued that it was bound by the International Chamber of Commerce's Code of Marketing Research Practice, which restricts revealing the identity of informants to outsiders. Nevertheless, CPI was willing to grant the PBA's request to examine the data, but on the conditions that they be inspected on CPI premises and that CPI would determine what information to show to the PBA representatives.

Moratorium and Ban

The PBA was not agreeable to any condition being set, and it banned the Mirinda "challenge" ad from the media when the requested data were not submitted before the PBA-set deadline. It then drafted new rules regarding comparison advertising that were very similar to U.S. guidelines. While allowing comparisons, they stressed that all facts deemed relevant by the PBA should be provided "without delay upon demand," and that confidentiality should not be invoked as a reason for denying access to them.

[36] Various Fall 1976 issues of *Business Day, The Times Journal,* the *Philippines Daily Express* and *Sunday Express* were used to prepare this synopsis. The ads only appeared in print, following the PBA suspension of comparative advertisements, which prevented extensions to television and radio.

The proposed rules were submitted for evaluation to PBA member organizations and to the Fair Trade Board, which supported them. However, at the October 1976 PBA-sponsored Philippine Advertising Congress, they were rejected for being "too vague." Instead, a sixty-day moratorium was imposed on *all* comparison advertising, and the Philippine Association of National Advertisers (PANA) was empowered to set up a Special Study Committee to review the issue.

The matter of drafting new guidelines was thus left to the *advertisers* themselves on the ground that they are the principal ones involved in the issue of comparison advertising. The PANA panel heard various firms and groups, including consumer[37] and market-research organizations. In December, 1976, the PANA committee (made up entirely of advertisers) advocated continuing the ban on direct comparisons on the grounds that:[38]

1. The contention that direct comparative advertising ultimately provides the consumer with better information has not been established and is highly questionable.
2. Direct comparative advertising tends to erode the credibility of its practitioners and the industry as a whole.
3. Direct comparison advertising leads to wastefulness of financial and human resources to the detriment of consumers.
4. The settlement of conflicts arising from direct comparison advertising requires "the establishment of universally accepted criteria for the comparison of product features, independent sophisticated testing facilities, and an efficient and acceptable adjudication body of experts," none of which exists today.
5. Direct comparison advertising would seem to be offensive to the observed cultural values and behavior patterns of the Filipino.

It is in the spirit of full appreciation of the delicate issues surrounding direct comparison advertising that the Philippine Association of National Advertisers strongly recommends to the Philippine Board of Advertising to:

1. Disallow or suspend *all* direct comparison advertising in all media until more conclusive evidence of its positive effect on consumers is established.
2. Seek to establish the validity of the hypothesis that direct comparison advertising can effectively improve the perception of an average Filipino consumer of the attributes of products and services.
3. From experience in countries that allow direct comparison advertising, strive to secure data which might indicate the effects of direct comparison advertising on the *attitudes* of the consumer in particular and the business establishment in general.

[37] The Consumers Union of the Philippines took a strong stand against comparison advertising, but it seems that other segments of the consumer movement approved of comparison advertising, without feeling strongly about it—as is true of most consumer associations around the world.

[38] The following is based on: "Direct Comparison Advertising: A Position Drafted by the Special Study Committee of the Philippine Association of National Advertisers." This report contains various inaccuracies such as stating that comparisons are banned in West Germany, Norway, Brazil, and Japan.

In the meantime, we call on the advertising industry to concentrate its efforts instead on the development of more solid and infinitely more positive growth areas of Philippine advertising. As professional practitioners of advertising, we firmly believe that we have to provide consumers with the necessary information to make the best possible purchasing decision according to their needs. We believe this can best be achieved by stating the true merits of one's own product or service, or even by comparisons which do not directly name another product or service competing in good faith.

This recommendation was accepted by the PBA, which enforces it now that the Fair Trade Board has endorsed it. Ads which do not name the competition but make it readily identifiable were also banned eventually. Mirinda (Pepsi) then switched to indirect comparisons, and capitalized on the controversy to maintain a high profile.

Prospects

One may certainly deplore that the foreseeable fate of comparison advertising in the Philippines has been precipitated and largely decided on the basis of an imitation of the U.S. ''Pepsi Challenge''—certainly not the best illustration of the use of comparison advertising, and one whose screening and substantiation have led to acrimonious confrontations both in the United States and the Philippines. Also deplorable are the facts that: (1) self-regulation in the matter of comparison advertising was largely delegated to a group of advertisers who did not practice it, (2) the Fair Trade Board chose not to spearhead or supervise the investigation, and (3) no serious ongoing study of the problem seems to be underway, despite pious vows to the contrary in the PANA Committee's report (see above).

Yet, the issue is bound to come up again now that the Philippine Board of Advertising and the Fair Trade Board are working more closely together (two FTB representatives sit on the PBA ad-screening committees).[39]

[39] A basic agreement (21 June 1977) between the Department of Trade and the Philippine Board of Advertising provides that:

(1) All cases and/or complaints of alleged violations of accepted fair trade practices or laws involving the use of mass media advertising brought before the Department of Trade or any of its instrumentalities be referred to the Philippine Board of Advertising for proper hearing and adjudication.

(2) The PBA be authorized to screen all advertising as may fall within the jurisdiction of the Department of Trade. In this connection, at least two senior officials of the Department of Trade shall be appointed by the Secretary of Trade, who shall participate in the activities of the screening committees of the Philippine Board of Advertising.

(3) The Philippine Board of Advertising shall submit its screening procedures to the Department of Trade for endorsement; and

(4) The sanctions provided for by law will be imposed by the Department of Trade upon recommendation of the Philippine Board of Advertising on parties found guilty of violating existing laws and/or governmental rules and regulations relative to fair trade practices in the use of mass media for advertising.

This broad delegation of powers is ironic in the light of a comment appearing in the PANA Committee report: ''Adjudication of conflicts arising from direct comparison advertising requires: (1) the establishment of universally accepted criteria for the comparison of product features for all products, (2) independent sophisticated testing facilities, and (3) an efficient and acceptable adjudication body of experts. Unfortunately, none of the above exists at the moment.'' How then can PAB do its job about any type of advertising?

Thus, the PBA has recently come up with stricter rules for advertising in both print and broadcast media. Among others, it states that:

> When a dangling comparison implies a general comparison with all competitive products, the companies should have valid research data available to back up whatever claim is made. For example, "fastest by far," with reference to a car, implies all other comparable available models in the market have been tested. The company must always be prepared to substantiate the claim when asked by the PBA. This rule also applies to the phrase "more than" when comparing products or claiming usage of products (Article 6).[40]

Clearly, the future of comparison advertising in the Philippines is dark at this point in time, and immediate favorable developments appear unlikely.

UNITED KINGDOM[41]

Practice

Comparison advertising has been used in the United Kingdom since at least 1968. No estimate of expenditures are available, but comparative advertisements are unlikely to exceed 1 or 2 percent of the total. The car industry is the major user of such ads (Volkswagen, Fiat, Opel, Mazda, Datsun, Ford, Saab, and BMW), but they are also utilized by newspapers, golf ball (Uniroyal) and tire manufacturers; and price comparisons are very common in retail advertising. All media use it—particularly print.

Clearly, the use of comparison advertising has been rather limited in the United Kingdom even though it is permissible under both British law and voluntary regulation (see below). This self-restraint appears to reflect both a cultural reluctance to attack the competition through "knocking copy" and the realization that it is difficult to compare without being misleading or unfair.

Law[42]

British common law allows comparisons that are truthful—whether to affirm that one's product is equal or superior to another or that the latter is inferior in some way. Trade "puffery" is tolerated, and the courts are reluctant to provide judicial determination of which competing product is in fact better. Furthermore, the authorized use of test results from independent laboratories is lawful.

False and malicious statements are actionable under common law, how-

---

[40] "Stricter Rules for Advertising Approved," *The Times Journal* (29 October 1977), p. 24.

[41] The assistance of Messrs. A.E. Pitcher (Chairman of the U.K. Chapter of the IAA), James O'Connor (Director of the Institute of Practitioners in Advertising), Peter Smith (Deputy Director, Advertising Standards Authority), R.G.C. Hunt-Taylor (Secretary of the Advertising Association), Peter Woodhouse (Head of Advertising Control, Independent Broadcasting Authority), and Hugh Holker (IAA World President) is gratefully acknowledged.

[42] Major sources used include: Werner Janssen, Jr., "Some Foreign Law Aspects of Comparative Advertising," *The Trademark Reporter*, Vol. 64 (1974), pp. 478–82; and Bernard Francq, "La publicité comparative," *Bulletin de l'Institut International de Concurrence Commerciale* (Bruxelles, Belgium: April 1977), pp. 25–78.

In the past, our claim that the Plus 6 flies further used to take quite a bit of believing.

So we were determined to prove it beyond a shadow of a doubt.

We did it by developing a test machine with two tees and a double headed club which enable two balls to be fired off at the same time and therefore under identical conditions.

The green at our testing range is 190 yards from the hitting machine – the distance equivalent to a good drive by an amateur.

Then we fired off the Dunlop 65, the Penfold Ace GL 100, the Slazenger + Black and the Titleist simultaneously with the Plus 6, giving each brand the benefit of 100 hits.

91 Plus 6 balls, in some cases more, reached the green, whereas the best competitor only made it with 81 balls and the worst with 11.

We have even evolved a portable version of our testing machine which we set up at tournaments so that we can carry out our two-tee tests in front of everyone.

However, since you can only hit one ball at the same time, we suggest you make sure it's a Uniroyal Plus 6.

UNIROYAL

The tee for two

ever, on grounds of "slander" of goods or of title (specific damages need to be proven), and deceptive statements can be challenged under the criminal provisions of the Trade Descriptions Act of 1968. Using someone else's registered trademark (not just his name) in comparative advertisements *may* also entitle the owner of the mark to restrain publication by seeking an injunction and/or an award of damages on grounds of the user's having "passed off" his goods for those of another.[43] The general purpose of this area of the law is to guard

[43] Under the Trade Marks Act of 1938, Section 4(1) forbids: ". . . importing a reference to some person having the right as proprietor or as registered user to use the trademark or to goods

consumers against being misled by false statements and to protect a firm's goodwill and trademarks.

Self-Regulation [44]

These same purposes are the object of the well-developed British system for self-regulation in advertising. The Advertising Standards Authority (ASA)[45] supervises the self-control system, ensuring that the British Code of Advertising Practice (BCAP) is kept under continuous review, and is properly, fairly, and effectively applied by the CAP Committee.

This Committee includes representatives from some twenty associations of advertisers, agencies, and all types of media. It has a number of special-purpose subcommittees or panels that meet as needed to consider specific subject matter. Comparative advertisements are often referred to the Committee's Copy Panel for consideration of their acceptability.

Television and radio, however, are controlled by the Independent Broadcasting Authority (IBA) in accordance with statute that requires them to have their own Code of Advertising Standards and Practice.

The ASA and CAP Committee share a common permanent Secretary and Secretariat, which performs four major functions as far as print advertisements are concerned: (1) general guidance through bulletins, and confidential pre-publication advice on copy and the suitability of products, (2) investigation of complaints from public and competitors, (3) monitoring of newspapers and magazines on a random basis, and (4) developing support for advertising self-regulation among the industry, government, and the general public.

As far as broadcasts are concerned, the Independent Broadcasting Authority (IBA) must insure that no misleading ads are aired. Consequently, television and radio advertisements are checked against the requirements of the IBA Code before transmission. Broadcasting companies, through their associations (Independent Television Companies Association and Association of Independent Radio Contractors), play an important part in this acceptance procedure, and give advice to advertisers and agencies on individual script submissions.

Since 1974, Section II.5 of the British Code of Advertising Practice clearly authorizes the fair use of comparative advertisements "in the interest of vigorous competition and public information," but Sections II.4, 6, 7, and 8 are also relevant: [46]

4. *Truthful Presentation*

4.1 All descriptions, claims and comparisons which relate to matters of objectively ascertainable fact should be capable of substantia-

with which such a person as aforesaid is connected in the course of trade." The mark, however, must have been registered in Part A of the Register.

[44] For details about the British system, see: A.B. Stridsberg, *Effective Advertising Self-Regulation* (New York: International Advertising Association, 1974), pp. 119–30 ("United Kingdom").

[45] ASA is financed by the Advertising Standards Board of Finance, which represents all major U.K. advertising organizations.

[46] Advertising Standards Authority, CAP Committee, *The British Code of Advertising Practice* (incorporating amendments to January 1976), (London, 1976), p. 5.

tion; and advertisers and advertising agencies are required to hold such substantiation ready for production without delay to the CAP Committee or the Advertising Standards Authority.

5. *Comparisons*

5.1 Advertisements containing comparisons with other advertisers, or other products, are permissible in the interest of vigorous competition and public information, provided they comply with the terms of this section and the next following section of the Code.

5.2 All comparative advertisements should respect the principles of fair competition and should be so designed that there is no likelihood of the consumer being misled as a result of the comparison, either about the product advertised or that with which it is compared.

5.3 The subject matter of a comparison should not be chosen in such a way as to confer an artificial advantage upon the advertiser.

5.4 Points of comparison should be based on facts which can be substantiated and should not be unfairly selected. In particular:

1. the basis of comparison should be the same for all the products being compared and should be clearly stated in the advertisement so that it can be seen that like is being compared with like.

2. where items are listed and compared with those of competitors' products, the list should be complete or else the advertisement should make clear that that the items are only a selection.

6. *Denigration*

6.1 Advertisements should not unfairly attack or discredit other products, advertisers or advertisements directly or by implication.

7. *Exploitation of name or goodwill*

7.1 Advertisements should not make unjustifiable use of the name or initials of any firm, company or institution.

7.2 Advertisements should not take unfair advantage of the goodwill attached to the trade name or symbol of another firm or its product or the goodwill acquired by its advertising campaign.

8. *Imitation*

8.1 Advertisements should not be so similar in general layout, copy, slogans, visual presentation, music or sound effects to other advertisements as to be likely to mislead or confuse.

These rules (as well as the law) apply to most products and services, but cigarette and hand-rolling tobacco advertisements ''should not claim directly or indirectly any health advantage of one brand over other brands, except on evidence which has been accepted by the health authorities.'' [47] Further provisions

[47]*British Code of Advertising Practice, op. cit.,* p. 60 (Rule 2.1).

state: (1) "Claims such as that a particular product gives *more* satisfaction . . . should not be made unless they can be substantiated by objective evidence" and (2) "Claims to brand leadership among any section of the community or in any area or country should not be made unless capable of substantiation." [48]

It is the practice of the ASA to publish monthly lists of complaints together with their resolution. Comparative advertisements have been included in such lists since their inception in 1973, but their proportion is miniscule as a reflection of the paucity of such ads in the United Kingdom. They typically deal with problems of substantiation of claims, the value of goods, and denigration. Since May 1977, ASA has upheld three complaints involving comparative advertisements for cars that were considered to be unfair.

Similar rules on comparisons and denigration appear verbatim in the Independent Broadcasting Authority's Code of Advertising Standards and Practice (Paragraphs 20 and 21), which applies to radio and television broadcasts. Television and radio companies—like any other advertising media—can of course impose stricter standards and may reject any advertisements they wish.

Thus, the Independent Television Companies Association has issued the following provisions: [49]

> Although ITCA has, of course, always accepted comparative advertisements, it has not previously accepted advertisements which named rival products or services. This is mainly because of the possibility that a comparison with a named rival product may imply that the advertised product, which may have an acknowledged advantage in one respect, is equal to or better than the rival product in every respect. This is almost never the case, and such comparisons may, therefore, mislead or confuse rather than help the consumer. There is also the possibility that the competitor's trademark may be infringed by the use of his name or by showing his product.
>
> The naming of other brands may, however, be justified in certain circumstances, and it has been decided that in future the specific identification of another product or service by name may be acceptable in a comparative advertisement subject to the following conditions:
>
> i) The comparison must be based on irrefutable factual evidence acceptable to ITCA and, if appropriate, ITCA's technical consultants.
> ii) The comparison must be stated accurately and factually and no unjustified conclusions may be drawn from it, or implied, regarding other aspects of the products.
> iii) The comparison must be significant in consumer terms.
> iv) Legal advice must be taken by the advertiser that the advertisement does not infringe the legal rights of any competitor, and ITCA must be informed of such legal clearance.
> v) The advertisement must comply with paragraphs 20 and 21 of the IBA Code in the spirit as well as in the letter.
> vi) Transmissions of the advertisement may have to be suspended pend-

---

[48] *Ibid.*, p. 60 (Guidelines for Cigarette Advertising, No. 3.1.3; 3.2.2; and 3.4.1). There are also special rules applying to medicinal and related products.
[49] ITCA, *Copy Clearance Bulletin No. 3.*

ing further investigations if a reasonable objection is received by ITCA.

The use of comparative advertising can easily distort facts and, by implication, convey information that can be misleading to the consumer and unfair to competitors. This is especially so when the comparison is selective and when the competitive product is named or otherwise specifically identified. Each case will be considered by ITCA on its merits, and agencies and advertisers are advised to discuss any proposals with ITCA at the earliest possible stage.

This note of guidance does not apply to advertisements for medicines, treatments and health claims, which may not name or otherwise specifically identify competitive products or services.

Trends

No major change seems likely in British usage and regulation, and the 1977 IAA opinion survey reported on pp. 68–69 above revealed favorable reactions toward comparison advertising among the British public.

The Advertising Association (representing all the major British associations in this field) has taken a rather strong stand against various items and terminologies included in the proposed EEC directive on misleading and unfair advertising (see above). In particular, it objects to the requirement of statutory restrictions on advertising when the British would prefer to continue their practice of relying mainly on voluntary regulation. It appears that their objections will be met in the final directive.

WEST GERMANY[50]

Regulation

There is no specific German law dealing with comparison advertising. Instead, its regulation falls under the general framework of the 1909 Law Against Unfair Competition ("UWG") whose Section 1 states: "Anyone who, in the course of competitive business activity, commits acts contrary to honest practices, may be enjoined from continuing such acts, and held for damages."

Original Rulings: The interpretation of this section (including the vague expression "honest practices" also translated as "good habits" or "business ethics")

---

[50] Major sources: Janssen, *op. cit.*, pp. 161–64; Francq, *op. cit.*, pp. 50–62; Warren S. Grimes, "Control of Advertising in the United States and Germany," *Harvard Law Review*, Vol. 84, No. 8 (June 1971), pp. 1769–800; Marlies Löhr, "Vergleichende Werbung im Spiegel der Rechtsprechung," *Markenartikel* (November 1974), pp. 498–504; Georg Wronka, "Vergleichende Werbung: Reizvokabel ohne Reiz," *BAG-Nachrichten* (7/1976), pp. 18–20; ZAW, *Diskussionspapier zur Werberechtspolitik* (Bonn, 1976); and Gerhard Schricker, "Die wettbewerbsrechtliche Beurteilung der vergleichenden Werbung in Deutschland" in *Problemi Attuali di Dirritto Industriale* (Milan, Italy: Giuffré Editore, 1977), pp. 1037–53. The assistance of Professor Helmut Soldner, of Uwe Goettsche (International Advertising Director of Gruner & Jahr, Hamburg), of Volker Nickel of the German Advertising Industry Central Committee (ZAW), and of H. Dieter Löhr (Markenverband) is gratefully acknowledged.

has been left to the jurists and the judges. Hence, the legality of comparison advertising can only be inferred by a longitudinal analysis of court decisions.

Originally, German courts used this Section 1 to rule against comparisons on the grounds that an advertiser acted unfairly when he sat as judge of the merits of competing products. This prohibition was reinforced in 1931 when the Federal Supreme Court (Bundesgerichtshof) ruled in a landmark decision that it is contrary to good business ethics to advertise one's own performance by comparing it with that of a competitor. This decision was extended even to cases where the comparison was based on facts and presented objectively.

While Section 1 of the Unfair Competition Law originally provided the basis for the general prohibition of truthful comparisons, misleading comparisons remain illegal under Section 3; while false (unsubstantiated) ads are prohibited by Section 14 (which in fact imposes a reversal of the burden of proof on the advertiser).

The opposition to comparisons, however, is now giving way to a more balanced interpretation in the light not only of what is in the interest of business competitors but also of other market participants (suppliers, customers) and of the community at large. This has been achieved through court decisions rather than legislative changes, however.[51]

Defining Comparison Advertising: The German courts differentiate between "subjective" and "objective" comparison advertising:

> It is *subjective* if a reference to a manufacturer's or advertiser's personal status, race, religion, or political opinion sheds a negative light on his products or services. Rulings against such subjective comparisons have remained consistent over time.

[51] In 1962, the Parliamentary Group for Consumer Interests of the Social Democratic Party proposed to the Bundestag the introduction of a law specifically permitting comparison advertising. In reply, the Federal Vice Chancellor prepared a study concluding that a reformulation of the existing Unfair Competition Law to permit comparison advertising would be inappropriate for the following reasons:

    a. The Unfair Competition Law was specifically designed to be very broad and unspecific in nature in order to provide a high degree of flexibility in judging "unfairness" according to changing business and societal needs.

    b. A separate law on comparison advertising would start a wave of demands for other specific laws about advertising and marketing practices, which are presently lumped together under "unfair practices."

    c. The legalization of comparison would have to be defined under a "complete-comparison" basis where all features of the products are compared, including negative ones. This would create unsurmountable legal problems in defining a complete comparison since the number of relevant product features vary among consumers. Also, it would be inconsistent with the nature of advertising which requires simple elliptic messages. Furthermore, the necessity of long and (expensive) advertising would put smaller, financially less powerful companies at a disadvantage. Thus, a legal definition of "complete comparison" would substantially limit the use of comparative ads.

    d. A comparative survey undertaken in 1960 by the University of Munich indicated that the present German legal stand on comparison advertising displayed a high degree of similarity with other Common Market countries.

Hence, in 1964, the Federal Cabinet decided that the existing Unfair Competition Act would not be changed. See: *Bericht des Bundesministers der Justiz über die Möglichkeit einer wahrheitsgemässen vergleichenden Werbung* (Bonn, 24 February 1964).

Objective comparison advertising refers to advertising which either directly identifies or implicitly suggests the competitive brand.

Regarding the latter, it is well to emphasize that the courts' definition of comparison advertising goes beyond the explicit naming of competitors. It also includes any indirect reference to competitive products when a majority of the readers can logically deduce who the implied competitors are. For example, a daily newspaper in a small community with three competitors advertised that it had "higher readership among young adults." This was ruled to constitute comparison advertising because the competitors could readily be identified. In general, the smaller the number of competitors in a certain area, the more the courts tend to classify such ads as comparative.

Evolution of Court Rulings: While retaining the basic prohibition of comparison advertising, the courts eventually developed four categories of conditions under which it would exceptionally be permitted:

1. Comparison of production, product, service and/or distribution *systems,* without any explicit reference to a specifically designated competitor.
2. *Clarification of new technical developments and differences* which cannot be explained in any other way. In other words, if you have built a better mousetrap, you can say so.
3. Comparisons *in response to inquiries by consumers* concerning competitive products, provided: (a) there is an actual inquiry (e.g., members of a consumer association request competitive price information from a sales office), and (b) factual and verifiable information is provided. This kind of comparison is obviously not addressed to the general public.
4. Comparison *for defensive purpose* against false or deceptive advertising. Thus, the manufacturer of a new additive for concrete advertised that it furthered the life of concrete. The Association of Concrete Manufacturers reacted with a comparison of product tests that pointed out the lack of supportive test data for the new product. The court accepted the association's comparative approach as reasonable since it drew attention to the potentially harmful effects of an untested new product.

In 1961, the Federal Supreme Court ruled that the legality of comparison advertising is not necessarily confined to these four clear-cut categories, but should be assumed whenever there is a "sufficiently substantiated reason" *(hinreichend begruendeter Anlass)* for it.

In the late 1960s and early 1970s, the interpretation of this "sufficiently substantiated reason" was broadened to provide better representation of consumer interests. This shift of emphasis from producer to consumer is reflected in a 1976 Federal Supreme Court decision stating that in judging whether there is a "sufficiently substantiated reason," one cannot simply refer to the fact that the case falls within the four categories of exceptions identified by earlier court decisions. Instead, admissibility must also be evaluated in terms of the advertisement's contribution to consumer information.

This means that a "sufficiently substantiated reason" can also be assumed in cases where: (1) the advertiser is unable to demonstrate his offer in any other way but through comparison and (2) there is an interest on the part of the public (particularly consumers) for factual information, which can also foster competition.

Accordingly, legal experts now present the following extended categories for comparison advertising:

1. *Comparison for defensive purpose* against major damage resulting from false or deceptive advertising (see above).
2. *Comparison in response to inquiries* by consumers concerning competitive products (see above).
3. *Comparison for correction of false consumer conceptions or misperceptions about a product or service.* Thus, a feed manufacturer lost substantial market share to a new product on account of perceived inferior feeding quality. To regain his market position, he used a comparative advertisement to indicate that for the same price, his competitor's product actually offered less feeder. The court ruled this comparison to be legal since it helped clarify a misconception.
4. *Comparison for information.* Originally intended to explain and relate new developments to existing products (see above), this concept has become progressively extended to any information that furthers competition by providing better market information to the consumer. Thus, the advertisement of a jewelry store stating that certain specifically designated brands could be bought "40 percent below suggested price" in his store, was adjudged to be legal—the "sufficient reason" being that it contributed to market transparency. In delineating the borderline between acceptance and rejection, the consumer and public interests are used as major criteria. Thus, court decisions have been unfavorable in the case of comparative advertisements that single out a specific competitor without engaging in an objective and broad comparison.

Altogether, the list of cases admissible under the concept of "sufficiently substantiated reason" is now theoretically unlimited. Indeed, many legal experts think that today comparisons are generally permitted, and only illegal under certain conditions. Besides, the Zentralausschuss der Werbewirtschaft (ZAW)—the self-regulatory body of the German advertising industry—has repeatedly declared that comparison advertising is legal in West Germany. Moreover, numerous demands—particularly on the part of the unions and consumer associations (e.g., AGV)—for an improvement of consumer information through (among other things) comparative advertisements have been countered by the argument that comparison advertising is already legal, and that therefore these demands would be pointless.

However, the latest decisions of the Federal Supreme Court have reemphasized the general prohibition of comparison advertising,[52] which remains legal only when all three of the following conditions are met:

1. There is a "sufficiently substantiated reason."
2. The statements made are true or, at least, the comparative ad in its entirety appears to be truthful.
3. The statements, by their very kind and nature, remain within the limits of information necessary for a factual comparison.

Conversely, there is insufficient reason when the comparison is not necessary—as in cases of denigrating competitors by making such statements as: "Don't buy from dealers with the lowest prices" or "Don't fall into the trap of believing high discount offers."

Consistent with the consumer-interest viewpoint, and with demands for greater access to product information, the German courts under the principle of freedom of speech have granted product-testing institutions (e.g., Stiftung Warentest) the right to publicize their findings. Accordingly, companies can compare their products with those of competitors, and refer to their higher quality or lower price, as demonstrated by an independent testing institution.

Practice and Prospects

Notwithstanding these legal developments, the practice of comparison advertising remains miniscule in West Germany. There are occasional comparative ads about cigarettes, cars, food discount chains (Aldi vs. Penny), and media, but most are relatively mild.

To explain this situation by the lack of confidence German advertisers have in comparison is somewhat questionable in view of the fact that German companies use this method quite frequently in international marketing (e.g., Bosch, Volkswagen, and BMW in Scandinavia, the United Kingdom, and the United States).[53]

The true reason appears to lie much more in the widespread uncertainty about the legality of comparison advertising. This is evidenced by the fact that a 1976 Ford–Taunus outdoor poster was acclaimed as "revolutionary" and much discussed in the advertising press, although it only stated: "Dear driver— particularly Ascona, Audi, Passat, Fiat, and R-12 drivers: The New Ford Tauns is here!" Besides, the Ford Advertising Department objected strenuously to this comparative campaign developed by Ford's sales promotion agency.

Another factor is that the right to complain and petition the courts for injunctive relief is available to businessmen, to trade associations, and to *bona fide* consumer organizations (since 1965) even if none of their members have

---

[52] Schricker, *op. cit.*, p. 1045.
[53] The reaction of Volkswagen to a Ford–Taunus comparative ad was: "Each firm has its own style—certainly this would not be ours!" Yet, Volkswagen/Audi uses much stronger comparisons extensively in the United States and the United Kingdom.

Oben der Penny-Stein des
Anstoßes („Keiner ist billiger
und besser"), unten die
aufsehenerregende Aldi-Antwort:
Werbung mit offenen Preis-
und Qualitätsvergleichen.
Zum Beispiel: Leinsamen-
schnitten, 500 g, Aldi-Preis
—,89 DM, Penny-Preis 1,68 DM.

Aber auch Markenartikel,
bei denen Qualitätsunterschiede
nicht ins Feld zu führen sind,
werden verglichen, zum Beispiel
1 Liter Amselfelder: Aldi-Preis
3,48 DM, Penny-Preis 4,13 DM.
Die beiden Kontrahenten
einigten sich aber umgehend
darauf, die Streitobjekte aus
dem Verkehr zu ziehen.

This ALDI (discount food chain) handout was designed to counteract PENNY's general claim that "Nobody is cheaper and better." A private settlement between the two companies ended this brief foray into "competitive" and "comparative" advertising.

been directly affected by such arts. This situation reveals that the German system depends primarily on privately initiated action rather than on public enforcement of the Unfair Competition Act.[54] This helps explain why the use of comparison advertising has so far been extremely limited in Germany, and frequently invites litigation—since so many private parties can initiate or threaten legal pressures—with the unsuccessful defendant having to bear all legal costs.

More generally, Germans still express aversion against what they call harsh "criticizing" comparisons of the U.S. type. For that matter, the ZAW does not encourage it for fear of too much advertising aggressivity creating an unfavorable image for the industry—at a time when marketing has been much criticized by the powerful unions and by certain consumer groups.

Still, the latter favor more comparisons,[55] and the two leading German political parties' programs for greater consumer information include the legaliza-

[54] There are other legislations centering on such products as food, wine, and drugs that are enforced through criminal and civil remedies available to the public authorities.

[55] Thus, the Consumer Federation has urged the enactment of legal conditions for the sensible use of comparison advertising; and the Consumers Council has come out in favor of comparative *price* advertising.

tion of comparisons beyond the extent officially authorized so far.[56] Similar pressures come from the proposed EEC directive on misleading and unfair advertising (see legal chapter).

Altogether, one can expect *some* increase in German comparative advertisements due to improving legal clarification, more examples, and greater support from consumer and political constituencies.

[56] These parties are the Social Democrats (SPD) and the Christian Democrats (CDU). For a discussion of these political views, see: Dankwart Rost, "Was die Werbung von Bonn zu erwarten hat," *Markenartikel* (10/1976), p. 415.

Part Three

STRATEGIES & CAMPAIGNS

Comparison Advertising: Strategies & Campaigns

THE THIRD AND LAST part of this report on comparison advertising includes various analyses of actual campaigns. First, comparative approaches are classified according to a framework devised by Neil O'Sullivan in his analysis of recent automobile ads in the United Kingdom.

Second, two in-depth analyses of the by-now famous U.S. "Pepsi–Coke" and "Datril–Tylenol–aspirin" comparative campaigns are presented on the basis of materials collected and interpreted by Stephen Copulsky.

Third, shorter analyses sample comparative ads around the world. They include: (1) a variety of *products:* consumer non-durables and durables, industrial goods, and services; (2) as many *countries* as possible (unfortunately good copies were not always available); and (3) a spectrum of ads illustrating the strengths and weaknesses of comparison advertising as well as *good and not-so-good executions* of this novel and spreading technique (additional examples can be found in previous parts of this report). These analyses are based on what advertisers and/or their agencies reported in the questionnaires mailed to a large number of firms, about half of which did not answer or declined to provide the relevant information. Vita Toros helped obtain many of these ads; and Rita Bari gathered and checked the information provided by advertisers and agencies from many countries.

Finally, a sample of headlines and ads illustrates the fierce comparison-advertising battles in the office-equipment business, where Xerox and IBM hve provided superb targets for hitchhikers.

SIX DIFFERENT
COMPARISON-ADVERTISING APPROACHES[1]

"Look at Me!

This approach can help an unfamiliar company or brand register with the consumer such key items as name and approximate size and price class. In the automobile business, for example, car buyers hardly think in terms of feet and inches, but place a car within a "group" such as "Cortina size." Thus a British ad for the Opel Manta, which is relatively unknown in the United Kingdom, does not denigrate the brand leader, but uses his name to immediately identify the relevant class of car:

> Before you buy a Ford Capri,
> Shouldn't you drive a Sporty Opel Manta?

This is a useful stage for a newcomer. With reasonable followup, the customer will get used to the new brand name. But the advertiser should then move away from comparisons, and allow his agency free creative rein to invest his brand with its own distinctive personality without providing further free endorsements for the brand leader.

"Shorthand: Quickly Establishing Value for Money"

The objective of this type of comparison advertising (somewhat similar to the "Look at me!" approach) is primarily to establish a "value for money" platform *quickly,* by reference to more expensive competition.

Thus, a 1973 Ford Consul ad was headlined:

> It's worth noting that many of the features on a Ford Consul 2500 are by ▮
> means unique [other cars illustrated in the ad, have them too].
> It's only unique at its price.
> The Ford Consul 2500.
> From £1330.

Research had told Ford that the public was not fully aware of the high level of technical sophistication of its car. Hence, this ad compares the Ford Consul's specifications with much more expensive cars that are known for their technical excellence (Jaguar XJ6's width and length, Fiat 130's V6 cylinder engine and top speed, Rover 2000 SC's individual front seat, and Mercedes 220's suspension), and then seals the "value for money" message by signing off boldly with the Consul's price.

The limitations of this approach center on its being a short-term expedient which does very little to build a *distinct personality* for the product. Further-

[1] This section is based on the thought-provoking presentation by Neil O'Sullivan (at the time Marketing Director of Ford of Britain) on the topic: "Is Comparison Advertising an Effective Marketing Device?" held by the U.K. Chapter of the International Advertising Association in London on 13 October 1977. In view of his industry affiliation, Mr. O'Sullivan dealt exclusively with automobiles, but his observations are more broadly applicable.

more, there is the risk that the reader will fail to take seriously an ad that compares prestigious makes with a rather more humble entrant.

"Features List"

This frequently used technique provides a tabular comparison of a number of significant features (e.g., luggage space, miles per gallon, number of service dealers). Like the "Look at me!" ad, the purpose is to register name, size, and price; and then to establish what "value for money" the newcomer represents. Thus, a Datsun ad's headline ("In the Executive 2-litre class, Audi, BMW, Mercedes, Volvo, etc., make the [Datsun] LAUREL SIX remarkably good value!") is followed by a 32-point comparative analysis, including its lower price.

Such advertisements appear to satisfy consumer demand for meaningful information about comparable and competitive products in a seemingly objective manner. A weakness of that approach is that this recitation of features fails to spell out the benefits that the consumer derives from them. To do so would require even more space and possibly lose the reader's attention. Consumers may also be suspicious about what's left out in the comparison. (This problem, however, can be mitigated by listing one's shortcomings—an approach used by Buick's Opel 5, which acknowledged that it finished Number 2 in a five-car comparison.[2]) Incomplete comparisons can also lead to complaints that they are misleading, and thus increase litigation and regulation.

"Single-Feature Comparison"

Concentrating on one feature allows the advertiser a much greater degree of creative freedom, and it gets more attention. Volkswagen has used this approach in the United Kingdom, focussing on, among other things, its less frequent need for servicing ("Fiat, Datsun, Vauxhall, and Leyland all get you here [the service station] quicker") and on the safety of the Polo's passenger compartment, which is built like that of the Mercedes 450SE and Volvo 244GL.

This type of comparison advertising can of course be terribly misleading in its manifold implications that everything else is equal. This danger, however, exists in non-comparative advertisements, too.

"Association"

Here the advertiser strives openly to improve his product's image by comparing it with the acknowledged leaders of the prestige luxury class of car. The problem here is that stating that your car is "Like a Rolls Royce" tends to be read as "But definitely *not quite* a Rolls Royce!" It confirms that the comparator really *is* the ultimate; and it begs the question whether the buyer should settle for anything else.

Of course, this approach can be used to position an automobile not against

---

[2] Volkswagen capitalized on this confession by headlining in a subsequent U.S. ad: "General Motors names Rabbit best of five economy cars tested . . . Volkswagen does it again."

a superior car but vis-à-vis the true competitor. Thus, various U.S. Ford ads have compared themselves to Cadillac, Peugeot, or BMW but not to draw away from that market. The goal, instead, was to upstage General Motors' unmentioned Chevrolet ("My parking ticket said Cadillac. But my car is a Ford Granada!") The target of some comparative ads is therefore not always what it seems—but will the consumer get that message?

"Hitching A Ride"

A British VW Polo ad features its similarity to the brand-leader Ford Fiesta, but then adds: "Actually, they're about as alike as the Beetle and the Prefect"—implying that there is much more to a Volkswagen.

This approach may be valid if the brand leader is spending very heavily in the same medium. Otherwise, "the hitchhiker provides the ride" by giving additional exposure to the competitive product—as happened in the Datril–Tylenol–aspirin contest (see case below). This is particularly true if the ad creates confusion about the sponsor's identity.

TWO IN-DEPTH STUDIES

DATRIL vs. TYLENOL, AND THE ANALGESIC MARKET[1]

In the spring of 1975, Bristol-Meyers began its national introduction of Datril. Like Tylenol, it is an acetaminophen non-aspirin, over-the-counter drug for use in the relief of headache pain without creating the stomach upset that might be caused by aspirin. Johnson & Johnson (J&J), whose McNeil Laboratories make Tylenol, virtually owned this non-aspirin analgesic market at the time of Datril's introduction, marketing it with promotion and advertising aimed only at physicians. A budget of under $2 million (with only $83,000 in measured media) had given Tylenol an over 10 percent share of the rapidly growing $440 million total analgesic market, making it the Number 4 brand among all analgesics.

Comparative Claims

Datril's introductory campaign on television and in print consisted of comparison *price* advertising against Tylenol. Its ads pictured a 100-tablet bottle of Datril selling at $1.85, compared with $2.85 for the same-size Tylenol. "Since they are both the same," claimed the ad, "there is no reason to keep paying more for Tylenol." The ad ran despite a prior telephone call from the president of J&J to the head of Bristol-Myers, warning that an immediate and substantial price cut in Tylenol would invalidate the ad. After it appeared, J&J immediately protested to the National Advertising Division(NAD), the Council of Better Business Bureaus' unit that investigates advertising complaints.

Bristol-Myers withdrew the first ad (which was rejected by the television networks after complaints by J&J) and replaced it with a slightly toned-down version: "Datril can cost less. A lot less. You save when you shop for the best prices. Why spend more?" This commercial was also rejected by the networks after J&J filed complaints based on market surveys of Datril and Tylenol retail prices. Bristol-Myers tried deleting "a lot less" from the ad and then created an entirely new version:"Compare prices. Depending on where you shop, Datril can cost less." A price-cutting battle between the two companies ensued.[2]

[1] This case was prepared by Stephen Copulsky, Marketing Assistant, Dollar Savings Bank of New York, and author of: "Comparative Advertising of Consumer Products" (unpublished MBA thesis; Graduate School of Business Administration, New York University, May 1977). It is based mostly on articles from *Advertising Age* (1975–1977) and on additional information provided by McNeil Laboratories (Johnson & Johnson) and by Bristol-Myers. The assistance of Nancy Giges (Associate Editor of *Advertising Age*) is also gratefully acknowledged.

[2] Besides cutting Tylenol's price, Johnson & Johnson also moved this product from the sales force that handles its ethical drugs to the one that handles its Band-Aid and Micrin products; and it began planning its first consumer ads. "A Pained Bayer Cries 'Foul'," *Business Week* (25 July 1977), p. 142.

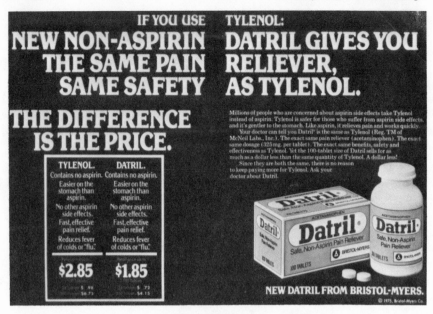

J&J continued to protest the ads, claiming that their rapid price reductions matched Datril's declining price and made the ads false.

ABC and NBC television networks requested that the two companies conduct a joint price survey, but J&J and Bristol-Myers could not agree on where, when, and how many times to conduct such a survey. Thus, prices for a 100-tablet bottle of Tylenol in the New York metropolitan area reportedly varied from as low as 69 cents to as high as $3.95. CBS from the outset of the controversy, had disallowed virtually all of the Datril ads.

The rapidly changing campaign made it difficult for the National Advertising Division to respond to complaints by J&J. Early reports indicated that NAD was preparing to rule that the Datril commercials left an overall misleading impression on viewers. However, the rapid revisions in the ads apparently delayed such a ruling. Prior to making a final judgment on the campaign, NAD was advised by Bristol-Myers that for the latter's own reasons, the advertising was being discontinued. Therefore, the NAD withheld judgment.

Bristol-Myers finally offered a harmless version of the ad, showing a woman stating, "I buy whichever one costs less. Compare prices and save money." There were no objections to this ad. Datril also ran ads during the summer of 1975 and early in 1976 offering a one-dollar refund with proof-of-purchase; Tylenol then counteroffered one-dollar rebates in co-operative ads in the fall of 1975.

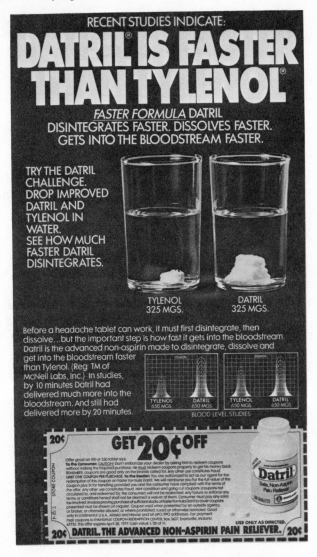

In the spring of 1976, a new Datril-Tylenol dispute erupted. Datril began advertising that it "delivers more pain relief faster than Tylenol." Its ads claimed: "In studies, on the average ten minutes there was much more Datril in the bloodstream than Tylenol. At twenty minutes, almost twice as much." Tylenol claimed that the "faster formula" ads were false and misleading because the differences were based solely on how tightly packed the tablets were (which determined how fast they dissolved), and because tests were based on an earlier formulation of Tylenol, which in its newer version dissolves just as rapidly as Datril. Complaints were filed with the networks, NAD, the Proprietary Association, and all medical journals.

Bristol-Meyers once more revised the ad to read: "Datril has been improved to dissolve faster, so it delivers much more pain reliever when you really want it. At just ten minutes, Datril averaged 70 percent more in the bloodstream. And Datril had significantly more even at twenty minutes. Much more pain reliever. Faster than Tylenol."

Still, J&J maintained its "false and deceptive" charge, and added that the Datril ads did not distinguish between the 325 mg. and (new) 500 mg. Tylenol formulas. Bristol-Myers responded that the J&J charges were themselves false, and that its test results for Datril were valid. J&J said that it was more concerned with this comparison than with the previous price comparison since a superiority claim was involved, which the consumer could not verify as he/she could the price claim. Bristol-Myers eventually withdrew the ad.

Meanwhile, Tylenol had great success introducing a 500 mg. tablet (before Datril did so), and centering its first consumer advertising on this extra-strength tablet. It began a full-fledged consumer campaign in the early summer of 1976 with ads that claimed: "You can't buy a more potent pain reliever without a prescription." Several months later, a 500 mg. Datril was introduced on the market.

Results

In the first four months of its comparison price campaign, Datril captured 15 percent of the non-aspirin analgesic market that itself began to grow at a 40 percent rate (up from the 25 percent rate of previous years). It thereby earned a 2 percent share of the total analgesic market so that Raymond Baker, a creative supervisor at Ted Bates (Datril's ad agency), called the Datril effort a prime example of comparison advertising that works.

However, Tylenol's market share also continued to grow during the Datril campaign. A year after the Datril advertising had begun and prior to any major Tylenol consumer advertising, Tylenol had captured an additional 4 percent of the total analgesic market for a 14.7 percent share—enough to become the Number 2 analgesic behind Anacin. Meanwhile, Datril's share remained at about 2 percent.

After Tylenol started advertising its new 500 mg. extra-strength tablet, it became—by the end of 1976—the Number 1 analgesic. It obtained a 15.9 percent market share in January–February 1977, while Datril's share slipped to 1.8 percent after reaching about 2.5 percent earlier. Tylenol's gains were lessened to some degree by a reduced profit margin, although they were earned with a smaller ad budget ($4 million) than Datril ($6.2 million), Bayer ($10 million), Bufferin ($13 million), and Excedrin (10 million).

A clear winner in the Datril-Tylenol comparison advertising battle, however, was the consumer, since prices for non-aspirin analgesics were reduced substantially and new formulas (500 mg.) were introduced by both companies.

Interpretation

Why did Bristol-Myers introduce Datril with a comparison-advertising price battle? There is no simple answer to this question. Baker explained that an advertiser with a competitive advantage is probably wasting ad dollars if he is not telling the consumer what his benefit is in specific direct comparison to competitors.[3]

More specifically, it was reported that Bristol-Myers in two earlier tests apparently had proved to its own satisfaction that there was not room for a Tylenol-like "me too" product at a comparable price. In the test markets, with advertising based solely on the benefits of a non-aspirin pain reliever, sales were sluggish. On the other hand, in a five-month test of Datril in Peoria, Illinois, and Albany, New York, Datril had huge sales when advertised as costing a dollar less than Tylenol.[4]

Another problem for Bristol-Myers was that the company did not want Datril to cannibalize the sales of Bufferin or Excedrin, its two major aspirin analgesics. Thus, the company may have been reluctant to introduce Datril with a campaign showing its benefits against aspirin.

The relatively meager results for Datril have been variously interpreted. For Professor Barbara Coe of New York University, Datril's challenge illustrates "how very difficult it is for a new brand to unseat a leader."[5] In another vein, the Director of the Business Planning Group at the University of Denver Research Institute, believes the J&J's price reductions for Tylenol were very predictable, and that "Bristol-Myers might well have succeeded better with an indirect approach hitting at local markets and regional weaknesses, that is, stealing away small pieces of the juicy bone."[6]

Copulsky of W.R. Grace think that a better alternative would have been to position Datril as the only alternative to Tylenol, saying: "There's only the leader and us. No one else counts." Avis used this "Number 2" strategy very effectively in the rental car market, and Datril might thereby have been able to keep its introductory price at or near Tylenol's and enjoy a high profit margin.[7]

In retrospect, comparison price advertising was not successful for Datril. Although the campaign allowed Datril to rapidly gain a foothold in the market, the strategy did not appear to offer an opportunity for sustained growth. Fur-

[3] "Tylenol Exec Speaks Out on Datril Price Ad," *Advertising Age* (29 March 1976). p. 1.
[4] "A Painful Headache for Bristol-Myers?" *Business Week* (6 October 1975), p. 78.
[5] Bernard Wysocki, Jr., "Punching Is Furious in Tylenol-Datril Fight for Non-Aspirin Users," *Wall Street Journal* (24 May 1976), p. 1.
[6] W.E. Matthews, "Do Marketers Ever Learn?" *Marketing News* (21 November 1975), p. 4.
[7] William Copulsky, "Tylenol–Datril 'Poker Game' Analyzed from Marketing Strategy Viewpoint," *Marketing News* (12 March 1976), p. 7.

thermore, Datril's advertising gave a free ride to Tylenol, which had previously been sold without consumer advertising. Undoubtedly, consumer awareness for Tylenol soared—as it did later on when Bayer and Anacin also attacked Tylenol (see below).

Tylenol's price-cutting reaction to Datril's price threat must have occurred much more rapidly than Datril expected, and credibility for Datril's advertising may have been hurt substantially by consumers being able to price the two competitors and discover that prices were about the same. Datril's second comparison campaign, stressing faster action, did not appear to have any noticeable impact on consumers—perhaps due to credibility problems created by the first campaign.

Comparisons Spread to Other Analgesics

In the fall of 1976, Bristol-Myers dropped any mention of Tylenol in its Datril advertising but referred instead to the "leading non-aspirin pain reliever." Datril then positioned its 500 mg. tablet not against Tylenol but against generic aspirin. With actor John Wayne as spokesman, Datril 500 was advertised as a headache remedy more gentle for the body than aspirin. Late in 1977, Bristol-Myers used a new comparison-advertising approach for Datril 500, with ads positioning it against prescription pain relivers. They stated "According to two major medical studies, the extra-strength amount of non-aspirin in Datril 500 [two tablets] was significantly more effective in relieving pain. More effective than both Darvon Compound-65 and Darvocet-N 100." The ads also included coupons for fifteen cents off the regular price.

Due to the success of Tylenol, a heated and controversial comparison advertising battle started taking place throughout the analgesic market. Thus, Bristol-Myers transferred its comparison advertising against Tylenol from Datril to Bufferin (a buffered aspirin which Bristol-Myers also makes), claiming that: "Bufferin can reduce painful swelling and inflammation. Tylenol cannot. And with Bufferin, like Tylenol, there's far less chance of stomach upset than with Bayer or Anacin." Another comparative ad for Bufferin claimed that it delivers pain reliever sooner than Bayer or Anacin; and unlike those two, it also protects the stomach.

American Home Products (AHP), maker of Anacin, also entered the comparative arena with ads that have resulted in a court ruling against this company. One Anacin ad claimed that: "Anacin can reduce inflammation that comes with most pain. Tylenol cannot. . . . Your body knows the difference between the pain reliever in Adult Strength Anacin and other pain relievers like Tylenol."

Johnson & Johnson filed complaints with the media, but when AHP brought a legal action against J&J, charging harassment, the latter countersued to prevent Anacin ads from making claims for an anti-inflammatory action not found in Tylenol. According to J&J, aspirin and acetaminophen are equally effective analgesics at label-recommended dosages, while aspirin has an anti-

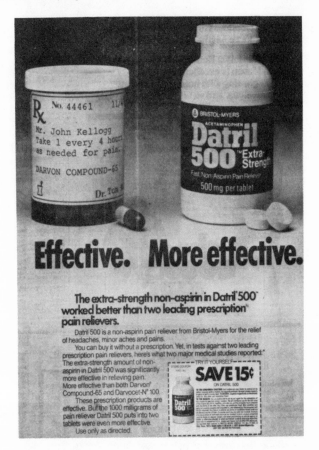

Effective. More effective.

The extra-strength non-aspirin in Datril 500 worked better than two leading prescription pain relievers.

Datril 500 is a non-aspirin pain reliever from Bristol-Myers for the relief of headaches, minor aches and pains.

You can buy it without a prescription. Yet, in tests against two leading prescription pain relievers, here's what two major medical studies reported:

The extra-strength amount of non-aspirin in Datril 500 was significantly more effective in relieving pain. More effective than both Darvon Compound-65 and Darvocet-N 100.

These prescription products are effective. But the 1000 milligrams of pain reliever Datril 500 puts into two tablets were even more effective. Use only as directed.

SAVE 15¢

inflammatory effect only at higher-level dosages, which are prescribed by physicians mainly for those suffering from rheumatoid arthritis.

In August 1977, a federal judge ruled in favor of J&J, and restrained AHP from representing Anacin "as a superior analgesic generally or a superior analgesic for conditions which are associated with inflammation or have inflammation components."[8] Anacin decided to comply with this court ruling (although it may appeal it) and announced a decision to discontinue the comparison ads. Subsequent television ads by AHP only stated that: "Anacin contains the pain reliever recommended by doctors 4 to 1 over the pain reliever in aspirin substitutes." This ruling will probably restrict other analgesic marketers from referring to anti-inflammatory action lacking in Tylenol (the previously mentioned

[8] Nancy Giges, "Judge Rules for Tylenol; Anacin Ordered to Halt Inflammation Ad Claims," *Advertising Age* (22 August 1977), pp. 1, 62. J&J was able to obtain a rapid decision in the case because the company asked for an injunction, rather than for damages, against AHP. Such a quick decision disproves the belief that an advertising campaign will have run its course before a legal ruling is made in a court action. See the legal chapter for further discussion of this application of the Lanham Act. J & J filed another suit against AHP in February 1978, charging violation of this court order.

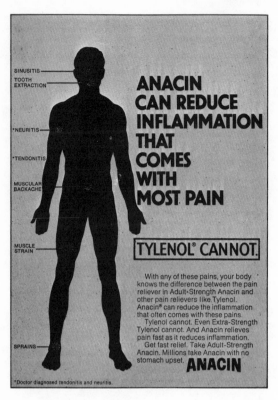

commercials for Bristol-Myer's Bufferin also made such claims, as have ads for Sterling Drug's Bayer).

The comparison advertising battle escalated when Johnson & Johnson began using controversial ads for Tylenol. They positioned it against generic aspirin without directly naming competitors but with such bold headlines as: "Why doctors recommend Tylenol more than all leading aspirin brands combined" and "Why hospitals dispense Tylenol more than all leading aspirin brands combined."

In response to these Tylenol ads, Sterling Drug used comparison ads for Bayer aspirin that made attacks of an unprecedented nature and startled the advertising community with such headlines as: "Tylenol, shame on you!" Bayer accused the Tylenol ads of misleading consumers by referring to doctor recommendations of Tylenol vs. aspirin "brands," when in truth (Bayer said) many doctors tell patients to take aspirin without mentioning a specific brand by name. Actually, "Doctors recommend Aspirin more than twice as often as they do Tylenol!" Bayer claimed. The Bayer ads also mentioned the danger of possible side effects from Tylenol, and disputed the J&J claim that Tylenol was safer than aspirin. Another Bayer comparison ad was headlined: "No, Tylenol is *not* found safer than aspirin," citing a recent Food and Drug Administration (FDA) report to support this claim. In response Johnson & Johnson charged that the Bayer ads were false and misleading, and threatened to file suit against

Makers of
Tylenol,
Shame on you!

Sterling Drug. Related ads for Bayer were shown on television, although they did not specifically mention Tylenol. They stated that, according to the FDA, "aspirin substitutes were not found safer than aspirin."

In September 1977, the National Advertising Division of the Council of Better Business Bureaus questioned the controversial Tylenol ads that had prompted the harsh Bayer response. NAD thought that consumers might erroneously interpret the ad to mean that doctors recommend Tylenol or aspirin substitutes more than aspirin as a generic category. Although J&J had survey information to the contrary, the company announced that the ad had been discontinued.

Despite the attacks against Tylenol (and possibly, in part, due to the additional exposure provided by the comparison ads), its market share continued to rise. In late 1977, Tylenol held a 21 percent share of the $650 million analgesic market, followed by Anacin (14 percent), Bayer (11 percent), Bufferin (9.8 percent), Excedrin (7.5 percent), and Datril (1.8 percent). Yet, Tylenol's advertising expenditures have been well below those of its competitors (see above).

The Food and Drug Administration has recently been investigating the labeling and advertising of non-prescription drugs. In July 1977, a scientific panel submitted a report to the FDA, recommending that the FDA simplify allowable label claims for analgesics by banning references to specific illnesses or symptoms such as neuritis, arthritis, or fever of cold and flu. The panel urged a short and general label statement: "For temporary relief of occasional minor aches, and pains, and headache" and "for reduction of fever." It also said that it found no basis for claims that acetaminophen is safer than aspirin, but urged that both pain relievers carry warning labels about possible harm from overdoses.

Drug manufacturers will undoubtedly fight against many of the panel's recommendations. However, FDA Commissioner Donald Kennedy predicted that it will eventually adopt tight labeling restrictions "that will be used by the Federal Trade Commission [FTC] as the basis for requiring accuracy and honesty in the advertising of non-prescription drugs." He also stated: "For pain-relief drugs specifically, we fully expect that the all too prevalent addiction to 'adjective-itis' and misleading comparisons will disappear from the TV tube and from magazine and newspaper ads." [9]

In December 1977, the FDA complained to the FTC and to the two companies that Bayer Aspirin and Tylenol in their "advertising battle" were causing confusion that jeopardizes the "public's confidence in self-medication products" by taking information out of context from an FDA news release and/or by pointing out the negative aspects of a competitor's product but not of his own. [10] The FDA also asked Sterling Drug (Bayer) to drop its current ads; the latter agreed to do so in late 1977.

Conclusion

Most of the above ads have been withdrawn for "marketing" reasons and/or following court and NAD action. Still, this battle of the analgesics illustrates many of the criticisms addressed against comparison advertising: possible consumer confusion generated by conflicting claims, vicious "name-calling"

[9] R.L. Gordon, "Tight Label Rules on Analgesics Will Cure Adjective-itis: FDA Chief," *Advertising Age* (11 July 1977), pp. 1, 179.

[10] *New York Times* (14 December 1977), p. D11; and *Advertising Age* (19 December 1977), pp. 2, 8. Technically, the FDA has no legal control over product advertising, but turns over its complaints to the FTC for action. The *Advertising Age* article also points out that Sterling Drug produces Panadol, the leading U.K. brand of acetaminophen. Whereas in the United States Sterling Drug has claimed that Tylenol has not been found to be safer than aspirin, its U.K. Panadol packages mention: "For safer relief of pain!"

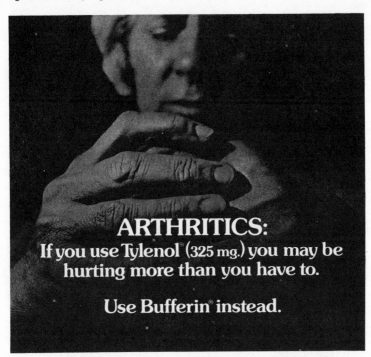

ARTHRITICS:
If you use Tylenol® (325 mg.) you may be
hurting more than you have to.

Use Bufferin® instead.

**Bufferin can reduce painful swelling and
inflammation. Tylenol cannot.**

And with Bufferin, like Tylenol, there's
far less chance of stomach upset than
with Bayer® or Anacin.®
So use Bufferin for hours of relief
from minor arthritis pain.

Because arthritis can be serious, if pain persists more than ten days
or redness is present, consult your doctor immediately. If under medical
care, do not take without consulting a physician.

Read and follow
label directions.

©1976 Bristol-Myers Co.

battles among competitors, charges of false and misleading advertising (sustained in court in one case), and unintended results (Tylenol's gains against those that named it and gave it greater visibility). It also revealed the vulnerability of price comparisons, which can be readily matched and whose truth can be challenged when prices are not uniform within an area. Finally, further government regulation may well ensue.

One can also question the execution of these comparative compaigns since Datril may have been poorly positioned against Tylenol, and the latter's name may have been too prominently displayed in its competitors' ads. Too, there were other marketing changes (product, price) that—as usual—prevent reaching a final conclusion about the net effectiveness of any advertising campaign. Fortunately, there was some consumer gain in terms of reduced prices and product improvement that resulted from these controversial comparative ads.

B. *PEPSI* against *Coke* [11]

This comparison-advertising campaign is believed to be the first one for the soft-drink industry and for a major advertiser whose superiority claims are based strictly on taste-test research.

Challenge and Counter-Challenges

The original Pepsi comparison ads, which ran on television, radio, and in print, asked consumers to take the "Pepsi Challenge." Commercials showed a blind taste test being administered to people who claimed to be regular Coke consumers. Since a majority of them had chosen Pepsi as tasting better than Coke, Pepsi made the claim that: "Nationwide, more Coca-Cola drinkers prefer Pepsi than Coke."

This campaign was developed in early 1975 to overcome what was called the "Southwest problem." In the Dallas–Fort Worth market, Pepsi held only an 8 percent market share, compared to 28 percent for Coke. Nationally Coke was the Number 1 brand with a 26.2 percent market share, and Pepsi was second with a 17.4 percent share.

Pepsi considered the Dallas taste-test campaign to be highly successful since during the early stages of the campaign, their share of the Texas market doubled. However, the results were clouded by drastic discounting—first by Coca-Cola soon after the Pepsi spots were aired, then by Pepsi, and finally by other competitors, until six one-quart bottles of soft drinks in Dallas were retailing for about 79 cents. Although Coca-Cola reacted in Texas primarily with a higher ad budget and heavy promotional expenditures, it also ran comparison ads for Coke, with people saying they preferred it over Pepsi. According to Coca-Cola, their Dallas market share is now above pre-challenge levels.

In the spring of 1976, a year after its Dallas experience, Pepsi made plans for expanding the campaign to other cities. It did not restrict its challenge to cities where it was second to Coke, as had been expected, but even where it was Number 1 (as in Michigan). Anticipating this move, Coke launched a blind taste-test television effort nationally for its sugar-free Fresca, with ads claiming: "If you're a Pepsi drinker, Fresca has a surprise for you . . . one out of three Pepsi drinkers chose Fresca." Coke also began a comparison-advertising campaign for Tab (its virtually calorie-free cola diet-drink) against Pepsi Light (a reduced-calorie but not sugar-free cola with a lemon taste): Tab was advertised as "lighter than Light."

In June 1976, Coke began a retaliatory campaign in Dallas with highly un-

[11] This case was prepared by Stephen Copulsky, Marketing Assistant, Dollar Savings Bank of New York, and author of: "Comparative Advertising of Consumer Products" (unpublished MBA Thesis; Graduate School of Business Administration, New York University, May 1977). It is based mostly on articles from *Advertising Age,* and on additional information provided by the Pepsi-Cola and Coca-Cola companies. The assistance of Nancy Giges (Associate Editor of Advertising Age) is also gratefully acknowledged.

Radio TV Reports

41 East 42nd Street New York N.Y. 10017
(212) 697-5100

PRODUCT:	PEPSI COLA		7F0051
PROGRAM:	DICK VAN DYKE SHOW	8/18/76	30 SEC.
	WPIX-TV	(NEW YORK)	7:24PM

1. MAN: What we're doing is a taste test.

2. ANNCR: In recent side by side blind taste test, nationwide,

3. more Coca Cola drinkers prefer Pepsi than Coke.

4. Here's Wendy Young of Bronxville taking the same kind of test.

5. MAN: Which one do you prefer?
WENDY YOUNG: I liked 'L'.

6. MAN: What did you pick? YOUNG: Pepsi. (LAUGHS) That's incredible. That is really incredible.

7. I chose Pepsi. I'll probably be drinking Pepsi from now on.

8. ANNCR: Coca Cola drinkers, let your taste decide. Take the Pepsi challenge.

An Early version of the "Pepsi Challenge."

usual TV commercials hinting that the Pepsi blind taste test was not valid. In the Pepsi ads, the letters "M" and "Q" had been used to designate glasses of Pepsi and Coke respectively. The Coke ads told of a bias for the letter M over Q, with an on-camera spokesman stating that: "Here's a fascinating report. Two glasses, one marked M and the other marked Q. Both glasses contain the same thing. Coca-Cola. We asked people to pick the one that tasted better. Most of them picked M even though the drinks were the same. You know what that proves? It proves that people will pick M more often than Q. It's odd, but people like the letter M more than Q. So M has an advantage. Now in recent TV commercials, Pepsi-Cola put itself up against another cola, and Pepsi Cola called itself M." The commercial ended there. Market observers speculated that Pepsi must have been making inroads in some areas to elicit such a dramatic response from Coke, the Number 1 soft drink.

Pepsi-Cola Senior Vice-President Alan Pottasch said that he thought the Coke M/Q commercials were "silly" and "deceptive" since Pepsi had similar results in other cities with other letters. In Dallas, Pepsi dropped the commercials, and substituted spots from San Antonio and Corpus Christi, where Pepsi was labeled "L" and Coke was labeled "S." Pepsi again won the taste test. A Coca-Cola's spokesman responded to the ads, saying that his company tests showed a definite bias for the letter "L" over "S."

In the important New York metropolitan market (over 6 percent of total U.S. soft-drink sales), Coca-Cola took the offensive with a comparison-advertising campaign claiming that "New York prefers Coca-Cola to Pepsi 2 to 1," based on a "study of consumer preferences." Industry sources said that Coke chose New York to "teach Pepsi a lesson. If you want to keep others in line by showing your muscle, you do it where everyone can see and where it hurts."

According to Pepsi, however, the Coke strategy was based on sales, and had nothing to do with taste. Pepsi therefore quickly began running "Pepsi Challenge" ads in New York and Los Angeles, insisting that "Nationwide, more Coca-Cola drinkers prefer Pepsi than Coke." A widely distributed Pepsi "fact sheet" claimed that: "When consumers do have a freedom of choice (as in food stores), Pepsi has outsold Coke for more than a year." Coke, however, disputed the claim.

At this point, the National Advertising Division (NAD) of the Council of Better Business Bureaus—the ad industry's body for self-regulation—became concerned over the claims and counterclaims of the two companies and their effect on advertising credibility, and it ordered an evaluation of their broadcast and print copy.

The comparison battle became more heated with ads by Coke attempting to ridicule the Pepsi campaign, and to point out that "one sip is not enough." The new Coke campaign included a "taste test" ad in which a tennis ball was preferred over both Coke and Pepsi because the taster liked fuzz, an ad that tried to use a monkey as a taster, and another in which the would-be taster walked off the set before the test was completed.

An advertising creative man suggested that Coke was trying to embarrass Pepsi enough to get the "Pepsi Challenge" spots off the air. Another theory was that Coke aimed at getting consumers so confused about taste tests that both the Coke and Pepsi tests would "turn them off." In such a standoff, the theory went, Coke comes out ahead by virtue of its traditional preeminence in the marketplace.

In November 1976, at the National Soft Drink Association's annual convention, Coca-Cola announced a halt to its comparison advertising counter-effort. Industry representatives reacted with immediate and prolonged applause. Donald Keough, Coca-Cola Company's Executive Vice-President, announced a "genuine and firm intention to return to constructive advertising." He said that while some comparison advertising can be valuable for consumers, Coke opposed the destructive tendency of highly subjective comparisons, in that such advertising is counter-productive and can only work to the detriment of the industry. Mr. Keough warned that he hoped it would not be necessary to reconsider the decision. Pepsi's plans, however, remained unchanged by this announcement, and the "Pepsi Challenge" is still being used selectively in various markets.

In April 1976, NAD reached final judgment on the validity of claims made in the Pepsi and Coke comparison ads. It recommended a modification for Pepsi ads that had claimed: "Nationwide, more Coca-Cola drinkers prefer Pepsi than Coke" and "Nationwide, more people who drink Coca-Cola prefer Pepsi." NAD found that the independent market-research organization that had

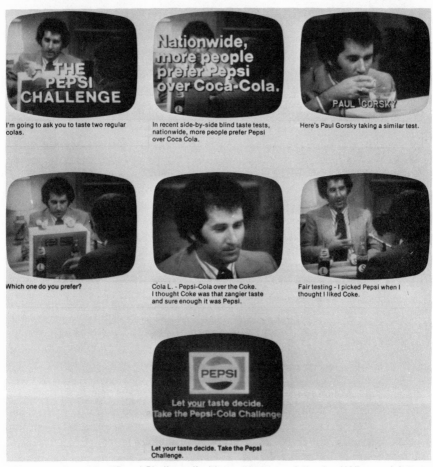

I'm going to ask you to taste two regular colas.

In recent side-by-side blind taste tests, nationwide, more people prefer Pepsi over Coca Cola.

Here's Paul Gorsky taking a similar test.

Which one do you prefer?

Cola L. - Pepsi-Cola over the Coke. I thought Coke was that zangier taste and sure enough it was Pepsi.

Fair testing - I picked Pepsi when I thought I liked Coke.

Let your taste decide. Take the Pepsi Challenge.

A later version of the "Pepsi Challenge" with modifications, following NAD complaints.

conducted the taste tests had vaguely defined the term "Coca-Cola drinker" so that it could include consumers who drank Coke but favored different soft drinks. At the time of the NAD judgment, Pepsi was using modified ads that had eliminated the questioned expression and which were found acceptable by NAD, the three television networks, and the National Association of Broadcasters. The newer ads stated: "We conducted taste tests among people all across the country. Nationwide, more people prefer Pepsi over Coca-Cola."

NAD also objected to Coca-Cola ads that stated that Coke taste tests using two differently lettered glasses of identical Coke "proved that people like the letter 'M' more than they like the letter 'Q'." The NAD said that "although the claim of letter preference could theoretically be correct, in this case the respondents were specifically asked to compare soft drinks (although they were the same) and not the letters used to label the glasses. In addition, the study provided was not designed to be nationally projectable.'' Coca-Cola advised the NAD, prior to its having reached a final judgment, that the ads had been discontinued for marketing reasons, with no further plans for future use.

Results and Interpretation

The Pepsi/Coke comparison-advertising battle began because Pepsi apparently felt that it had little to lose with a radical change in advertising strategy—especially in the Dallas market where it had an unusually low market share. The standard Pepsi and Coke advertising had become so non-competitive as to create an opportunity for a hard-hitting campaign. Once Pepsi experienced success in some markets, there was no reason not to expand into others. Pepsi must still believe that the comparison campaign is successful, since it is continuing to use the ''Pepsi Challenge'' in selected local markets; meanwhile, the ''Have a Pepsi Day'' campaign continues nationally.

The perplexing question, however, is: Why did Coke enter the comparison advertising arena? Traditionally, the brand leader ignores comparison challenges from below, since a response seems to acknowledge the validity of the challenge and harms the aura of being Number 1. According to industry observers, the more Coke ducked the ''Pepsi Challenge,'' the worse the situation seemed to become. One Coke bottler—noting that there had been no research conducted that could tell whether the ''Pepsi Challenge'' would be effective in dislodging Coke as the Number 1 soft drink—said: ''We couldn't afford the risk of having to play catchup.'' Despite the floundering appearance of the Coke counter-effort, Coca-Cola sources said that every commercial was carefully calculated and tested to meet a specific objective.

Ironically, Coke sales continued to grow where comparison advertising ran, so that the immediate losers in the Pepsi/Coke comparison-advertising battle were other soft-drink companies which could not match the heavy expenditures for advertising, promotion, and price-cutting. Sensing that the ''Pepsi Challenge'' was not a serious threat to its own sales, Coke was able to withdraw from the comparison-advertising battle that it had reluctantly entered.

Nevertheless, in May 1977, Coke again began using ads that poked fun at the Pepsi taste test, although the new ads made no direct mention of Pepsi. A Coca-Cola spokesman denied that the new ads were a return to the ''subjective comparative advertising'' criticized by its Executive Vice President several months earlier, and an advertising executive from the New York Coca-Cola Bottling Company said that the new ads were part of the overall ''Coke adds life'' national campaign.

Although Pepsi has had some success with its comparison advertising campaign in the United States, a representative of the Coca-Cola Company stated that—as of September 1977—the ''Pepsi Challenge'' had been unsuccessful in foreign markets due either to its lack of consumer appeal or to the inadmissibility of such comparison advertising from a legal standpoint. Thus, Coca-Cola reported that Pepsi has tried it without success in Sydney, Australia; Norway; Rio de Janeiro, Brazil (although it has been reintroduced there); Athens, Greece (where government authorities have ordered it to be removed from the air); and Chile (where it was prevented from being exposed to the public by the government). Pepsi-Cola, however, retorted that the "Challenge" has been generally successful where allowed by regulations (e.g., Canada, Brazil, and Australia).[12] The Philippine advertising industry's ban on comparison advertising is a direct outcome of this use of taste tests by Pepsi's Mirinda (see the Philippine country analysis in Part II, and the Mirinda case below).

Conclusion

According to many observers, the Pepsi and Coke comparative campaigns generated a lot of silliness, somewhat discredited consumer–opinion tests, and hurt advertising's image. The resulting negative government and industry reactions in various countries are also to be deplored. These outcomes hardly compensate for the market shares temporarily gained by these companies and for the sporadic price cuts linked to these campaigns.

[12] Letters from Messrs. J.F. Brandhorst, Jr., Corporate Advertising Manager, Coca-Cola Company; and J.F. Corbani, Vice President Marketing Services, Pepsico International.

SEVENTEEN COMPARATIVE CAMPAIGNS

ALLEGHENY (USA)

COMPANY: ALLEGHENY AIRLINE (USA)   *Date:* 1977

PRODUCT: Air transportation: Allegheny vs. American, TWA, Pan Am, and others.

MEDIA: Magazines, television, and newspapers.

_____

REASON(S) FOR USING A COMPARATIVE FORMAT: To establish Allegheny as an acceptable competitive alternative to better known airlines, on the basis of Civil Aeronautics Board data:

- "Did you know Allegheny is 22 American cities bigger [77] than American [55]?"
- "Did you know Allegheny is 20,000 U.S. flights [292,647] bigger than TWA [271,258]?"
- "Did you know Allegheny is 2 million passengers [10,905,000] bigger than Pan Am [8,257,000]?"

_____

ADVANCE CHECKING BY A GOVERNMENT AGENCY: No
                    SELF-REGULATORY BOARD: No
                    MEDIA: Yes (the networks asked to see all supporting data)

CHANGES MADE: None

_____

READERSHIP OR TV RATINGS: Awareness of Allegheny has doubled.

MARKET RESULTS: "We believe [that sales were increased by these comparative ads]: traffic was up in 1977."

_____

COMPLAINTS, HEARINGS, LEGAL ACTION: American Airlines complained to the NAD self-regulatory board, which ruled in favor of Allegheny.

OTHER REACTIONS: TWA started its "on time" comparative campaign.

_____

This information was provided by Jim Tower of J. Walter Thompson, Washington, D.C.

Did you know Allegheny is 2 million passengers bigger than Pan Am?

Passenger Totals	
ALLEGHENY	**10,905,000**
Pan Am	8,257,000

Source: CAB, latest available 12-month data. Does not include 1,431,000 passengers flown by the 12 Allegheny Commuters.

When you're a big airline you count passengers by the millions.

When you're a good airline you never forget that every passenger is a person.

At Allegheny we mean to be as good as we are big. (And you're starting to know how big we are.)

Come fly Allegheny. Relax in the comforts of our single-class jet cabins.

We've got the cities you want. The business-day schedules you want. The discount fares you need, so you and your family can travel without breaking the bank.

And one thing more. We've got people who care about other people, which everybody wants.

Next time you fly, let us show you how good we really are. Just see your travel agent or call Allegheny. Welcome aboard!

ALLEGHENY®

It takes a big airline.

COMPANY: CARTE BLANCHE (USA)   *DATE:* 1977

PRODUCT: Credit card: Carte Blanche vs. American Express and bank cards.

MEDIA: Television spots in New York and Chicago areas, and magazines.

REASON(S) FOR USING A COMPARATIVE FORMAT: Overall intent was to provide the consumer with a truthful and credible message—namely, that no one credit card is acceptable everywhere.

ADVANCE CHECKING BY A GOVERNMENT AGENCY: No
                              SELF-REGULATORY BOARD: No
                              MEDIA: Yes (networks' continuity departments)

CHANGES MADE: None

READERSHIP OR TV RATINGS: None used for the ads.

MARKET RESULTS: New applications for Carte Blanche were running 17 percent ahead of forecast some four months after the beginning of this campaign.

COMPLAINTS, HEARINGS, LEGAL ACTION, OTHER REACTIONS: None

This information was provided by Mr. D.S. Kitchen, Vice President—Marketing, Carte Blanche, Los Angeles, California.

"WITHOUT IT, SOMETHING IS MISSING."

"I have a Carte Blanche card but I need an American Express card and a bank card, too."
Raymond J. Mulligan, President, Liggett Group Inc.

"Because there isn't any one credit card in the world that's accepted everywhere...not even Carte Blanche."
John C. Emery, Jr., President, Emery Air Freight Corp.

"That's why I carry American Express and a bank card. And that's why I carry Carte Blanche."
Robert F. Weltzien, President, Timex Corp.

"I agree. Everyone should have at least three of the best credit cards in the world. Including me. And I'm the President of Carte Blanche."
Ken Dunsire, President, Carte Blanche Corp.

To apply for a Carte Blanche card,
fill out an application today or call this toll free number:
800-325-6400

CARTE BLANCHE. One of the credit cards you should have.

CHEVROLET (BRAZIL)

COMPANY: CHEVROLET DEALERS OF BELO HORIZONTE (BRAZIL)
DATE: December 1976–January 1977

PRODUCT: Cars: Chevrolet vs. Ford, Fiat, and others.

MEDIA: Newspapers, outdoor advertising, radio, and television.

REASON(S) FOR USING A COMPARATIVE FORMAT: The comparative format was chosen to capitalize on the publicity generated by the Sao Paulo Auto show—in fact, creating mini auto-shows at selected Chevrolet dealers in order to increase consideration of Chevrolet products.

ADVANCE CHECKING BY A GOVERNMENT AGENCY: Yes
SELF-REGULATORY BOARD: No
MEDIA: Yes

CHANGES MADE: None

READERSHIP OR TV RATINGS: None, but initial dealer reaction was very positive.

MARKET RESULTS: Sales did increase, but "it becomes increasingly difficult to isolate this campaign's role in the entire program [which had other components]."

COMPLAINTS, HEARINGS, LEGAL ACTION, OTHER REACTIONS: None

This information was provided by Jens Olsen, General Manager of McCann Erickson Publicidade Ltda., Sao Paulo, Brazil.

Headline: "They are confident about what they sell, and are not afraid to compare. Come to the Comparative Auto-Show of our Chevrolet dealers in Belo Horizonte."

COMPANY: THE CONTINENTAL INSURANCE COMPANIES (USA)
DATE: 1977

PRODUCT: Continental's Insurance Store vs. Allstate and State Farm Insurance Co.

MEDIA: Magazines.

REASON(S) FOR USING A COMPARATIVE FORMAT: The comparative ads were intended to differentiate Continental's agents ("The Insurance Store") from their better known national rivals. A direct comparison seemed the best way to accomplish this purpose.

ADVANCE CHECKING BY A GOVERNMENT AGENCY: No
SELF-REGULATORY BOARD: Yes, with NARB in terms of basic creative and copy approach.
MEDIA: No
CHANGES MADE: NARB suggestions were incorporated in the final ad series.

READERSHIP OR TV RATINGS: Some 16 percent of all adults and 24 percent of all college-educated adults became aware of "The Insurance Store" within a 2.5-year period. This is considered good for an insurance campaign and generally better than with non-comparative ads.

MARKET RESULTS: Increased sales were not a specific goal, but greater awareness and differentiation were. Continental agents reacted very positively to the campaign, and that probably helped the sales pictures.

COMPLAINTS, HEARINGS, LEGAL ACTION: "None since we do not disparage them or their products . . . we simply point out advantages our agents offer that theirs do not."

This information was provided by Jack Disbrow, Manager of Advertising Services, The Continental Insurance Companies, New York.

Which one can do more for you?

Here are three of the best places where you can buy insurance for your car, your home, and yourself.

The agents at all three can do a good job for you.

But the agent at one—The Insurance Store—can actually do more. Because he offers you more.

For example, the agent at Allstate sells only Allstate Insurance.

And the agent at State Farm sells only State Farm Insurance.

But the agent at The Insurance Store offers you a wide selection of leading insurance companies—including us, Continental Insurance.

And each one of his companies has its own special capabilities and expertise.

So whatever insurance you need, he's in the best position to give you the specific companies, policies, and prices that best match your needs. And budget.

Today, there are over 6,500 Insurance Stores ready to serve you.

To find your nearest one, just check the Yellow Pages for the nearest agent listed under Continental Insurance.

He offers you more.

The Insurance Store
featuring
Continental Insurance
From Subsidiaries of The Continental Corporation

COMPANY: BUCKINGHAM CORP. (USA)   *DATE:* 1977

PRODUCT: Scotch whiskey: Cutty 12 vs. Chivas Regal.

MEDIA: National and local magazines.

REASON(S) FOR USING A COMPARATIVE FORMAT: To create brand awareness for Cutty 12 among upper-income Scotch drinkers in a context of "prestige equivalency" to dominant Chivas Regal, although also pointing out significant taste differences between the two brands. In the deluxe-priced, twelve-year-old Scotch category, Chivas Regal is *the* standard, so that a direct comparison with it helped achieve quicker consumer product positioning for Cutty 12. Various comparative ads were used on that theme.

ADVANCE CHECKING BY A GOVERNMENT AGENCY: No
SELF-REGULATORY BOARD: No
MEDIA: No

READERSHIP OR TV RATINGS: Starch readership ratings scored about 20 percent higher than liquor ad norms.

MARKET RESULTS: Slow turnover rate in liquor business as well as difficulty in obtaining distribution for new products have traditionally made it difficult to measure sales impact. However, there is reason to believe that this advertising has resulted in "a worthwhile level of consumer trial—particularly in bars."

COMPLAINTS, HEARINGS, LEGAL ACTION: An earlier ad was challenged in federal courts by Chivas Regal, but no restraining order was obtained. There were no other complaints or significant reactions by others.

OTHER REACTIONS: [This comparative campaign has received a lot of attention in the literature of comparison advertising because of some of its aggressiveness and "coattail-riding" character.]

This information was provided by John Miller, Vice President Advertising, The Buckingham Corporation, New York.

WHAT'S THE DIFFERENCE BETWEEN
CUTTY 12 AND CHIVAS REGAL?

Both are expensive and 12 years old.
But you don't buy Cutty 12 for its
similarities to Chivas. You buy it for
the differences. Like taste. Many
people find Cutty 12 impressively
smooth and more flavorful. But
without that slightly heavy, smokey
quality of some other 12 year olds.
And, though it's more than
acceptable to serve a prestigious
Scotch in its own bottle, Cutty 12
arrives in a more unusual vessel.
A ship's decanter. And Cutty 12 is
certainly more exclusive. It's the
12 year old currently on the tip of
only the most discerning tongues.

CUTTY 12.
THE 12 YEAR OLD THAT TASTES
EVEN BETTER.

COMPANY: FORD MOTOR CO. AB (SWEDEN)   DATE: 1972–1974

PRODUCT: Cars: Ford Consul vs. Volvo, Saab, and Opel Rekord.

MEDIA: Metropolitan and local newspapers.

REASON(S) FOR USING A COMPARATIVE FORMAT: Primarily to instantly position the new model against the major domestic manufacturers Volvo and Saab. Secondly, to emphasize the independent rear suspension (USP) on the Consul, which none of the others can offer.

ADVANCE CHECKING: The ads were thoroughly checked with an outside agency specializing in Swedish marketing laws.

CHANGES MADE: No significant changes were made, although additional substantiation was provided.

READERSHIP OR TV RATINGS: No testing.

MARKET RESULTS: No information available regarding the effectiveness of this comparative approach.

COMPLAINTS, HEARINGS, LEGAL ACTION: None

OTHER REACTIONS: This campaign received a lot of attention because it was one of the first comparative campaigns in the automobile business.

This information was provided by Lars-Johan Haggard, J. Walter Thompson Co. AB, Stockholm, Sweden.

I Ford Consul får du delad bakaxel-komfort. Den komforten får du arken i Volvo, Saab eller Opel Rekord.

Åkkomfort och väghållning. Skillnaden i åkkomfort och väghållning mellan Ford Consul och Volvo 142/144, Saab 99 och Opel Rekord beror på Ford Consuls delade bakaxel. Den som åker betydligt mjukare och bekvämare i Ford Consul. Du märker det framför allt när du kör på en gropig väg. Gupp och andra ojämnheter utjämnas mera i Ford Consul än i Volvo, Saab och Opel. Särskilt som den delade bakaxeln i Ford Consul är kombinerad med en bredare spårvidd, ett större axelavstånd och en lägre tyngdpunkt (jämfört med Volvo, Saab och Opel).

Provkör och jämför Ford Consuls åkkomfort. Det hjälper inte ens att t ex Saab har sin berömda framhjulsdrift, eftersom den mjukare och bekvämare gången beror mer på hjulupphängningen än på var drivhju-

len sitter. Provkör och jämför Ford Consuls åkkomfort. Vi tror att du själv kommer att märka att du åker mjukare och bekvämare i Ford Consul än i Volvo, Saab och Opel. Och frågan är väl om inte just åkkomforten är den viktigaste och mest betydelsefulla skillnaden för dig som bilköpare när du ska välja bil.

Naturligtvis finns det andra skillnader dom fyra bilarna emellan. Men det finns också mycket som är gemensamt.

Utrymmena. Alla fyra bilarna är stora, komfortabla och välutrustade. Du har gott om utrymme i alla. Dom är gjorda för fem som vill sitta bekvämt. Och dom har alla fyra ett väl tilltaget bagageutrymme. Lätta att lasta i och ur.

Bredast invändigt totalt sett är Ford Consul. Längsta kupéutrymmet har Volvo. Bredast i armbågshöjd är Saab. Och högst i tak har Opel. Men även här ska du pröva själv och känna i vilken av bilarna du har mest rörelsefrihet.

Motorerna. Alla fyra bilarna har bra motorer. Ford Consul och Saab har visserligen den modernaste

motorkonstruktionen, den med överliggande kamaxel. Volvo har stötstänger och Opel högt liggande kamaxel.

Alla fyra bilarna ligger i samma prisklass. Du får med andra ord en Ford Consul till ungefär samma pris som en Volvo, Saab eller Opel, trots att Ford Consul har den delade bakaxel-komforten.

Consul-modellerna. Du kan få din Consul som 2- eller 4-dörrars Sedan, 2-dörrars Kupé, 5-dörrars Kombi eller som 2-dörrars GT. Samtliga modeller har halogenljus och strålkastartorkare. Och du får den med en 2,0 liters på 99 hk DIN (73 kW eller 113 hk SAE). En 2,3 liters på 108 hk DIN (79 kW eller 123 hk SAE). Eller med en 3,0 liters V6:a på 138 hk DIN (101 kW eller 157 hk SAE). Gör som många andra gjort. Ta med dig din Volvo, Saab eller Opel till en Ford-återförsäljare. Och provkör och jämför Ford Consul med din bil. Det är riktigt skönt att vara lite otrogen ibland.

Alla jämförelser avser Volvo 142/144, Saab 99, Opel Rekord och Consul L.

Provkör Ford Consul 1974. Och jämför med Volvo, Saab och Opel Rekord.

TYSKA FORD CONSUL

"In the Ford Consul you get divided rear-axle comfort. That comfort you will not get in the Volvo, Saab, or Opel Rekord. Try out the Ford Consul 1974. And compare with Volvo, Saab, and Opel Rekord."

COMPANY: FORD DIVISION (USA)   *DATE:* 1976

PRODUCT: Cars: Ford Granada Sports Coupe vs. Mercedes 450 SLC Sports Coupe.

MEDIA: Magazines.

REASON(S) FOR USING A COMPARATIVE FORMAT: "We wanted to show that a Ford Granada looked like one of the finest European sports cars, and had remarkable performance for a car with a modest price. Naming the competition made for clearer communication. It praises the competition, while it takes advantage of the similarities between the two cars. It backs up the visual similarities, which we used in early stages of Granada advertising, with specific product facts."

ADVANCE CHECKING BY A GOVERNMENT AGENCY: No
SELF-REGULATORY BOARD: No
MEDIA: No, apart from providing the necessary data to substantiate all claims.

READERSHIP OR TV RATINGS: "Above average recall."

MARKET RESULTS: "Granada is a highly successful car."

COMPLAINTS, HEARINGS, LEGAL ACTION, AND OTHER REACTIONS: None

---

AUTHORS' COMMENT: [This kind of ad is obviously not addressed to the Mercedes market. It can be interpreted as either an attempt to "upgrade by association" and/or an attempt to "upstage" its real but unnamed competitors. Thus, another Ford advertisement states: "The 1977 Ford LTD has the full-size of a Cadillac but is priced like a down-sized Chevrolet."]

This information was provided by Bertram Metter, Senior Vice President, J. Walter Thompson Co., New York.

Remarkable achievement.
$23,976*

Mercedes 450 SLC Sports Coupe

Remarkable achievement.
$4,189*

Ford Granada Sports Coupe

Manufacturer's suggested retail price excluding title, taxes, destination charges.

Pictured at top is perhaps the world's finest sports coupe, and a remarkable achievement in automotive engineering.

From its fully independent suspension system to the design of its interior, the Mercedes 450 SLC is a possession of pride for those who can easily afford its formidable price tag. Those who cannot, please read on.

The second car pictured above is a dramatically styled edition of one of the best-selling cars in America:

New Ford Granada Sports Coupe

You may notice that the Granada Sports Coupe is virtually the same size as the Mercedes 450 SLC. (See specifications) But no car can be categorized "sports coupe" in its dimensions alone.

For road performance at the sporting level this Granada is equipped with a heavy duty suspension, heavy duty shock absorbers, heavy duty rear springs and steel-belted radials. Inside it features reclining bucket seats, leather wrapped steering wheel and floor shift. Wiper/washer

SELECTED SPECIFICATIONS	MERCEDES 450 SLC	GRANADA SPORTS COUPE
WHEELBASE (IN.)	111.0	109.9
LENGTH	196.4	197.7
WIDTH	70.5	71.2
HEIGHT	52.4	53.3
BODY CONST.	UNIT	UNIT
ENG. DISPLACEMENT (CU. IN.)	275.8	200 (OPT. 250, 302, 351)
COMP. RATIO	8.0:1	8.3:1 (200 CID)
BORE X STROKE (IN.)	3.62 X 3.35	3.68 X 3.126
†GEAR RATIO: 1ST	2.31:1	2.46:1
2ND	1.46:1	1.46:1
3RD	1.00:1	1.00:1

†These are automatic transmission gear ratios.

controls are positioned for instant reach on turn signal lever, European-style.

And to further enhance the performance of your car, the Granada Sports Coupe offers a great range of special equipment to order from. Including a powerful 351 CID V-8 engine and SelectShift transmission. Even 4-wheel disc brakes are available (Granada is one of the few American cars to offer them).

A sporting choice

If money is really no object, you should certainly consider the Mercedes 450 SLC. It is a remarkable achievement in automotive engineering. Under any circumstances, consider the new Granada Sports Coupe. Starting at $4,189* it is a remarkable achievement by almost any standard.

See your local Ford Dealer

FORD GRANADA

FORD DIVISION

215

COMPANY: FREDGAARD (Denmark)   *DATE:* 1977

PRODUCT: Radio-TV chain stores: Fredgaard vs. Fona.

MEDIA: Print.

REASON(S) FOR USING A COMPARATIVE FORMAT: From image analyses, we knew that FONA had achieved a high level of consumer awareness, whereas the rest of the trade was mentioned in a more random fashion. Since we wanted to obtain a higher level of awareness, we chose to position ourselves against FONA as the preferred alternative to the largest and best-known competitor.

ADVANCE CHECKING: By using a message where we praise and present FONA in a favorable light, we avoided legal problems and complied with the ICC Advertising Code. Therefore, we did not need to seek advance approval of our ad.

READERSHIP RATINGS AND MARKET RESULTS: Not provided by the respondent.

COMPLAINTS, HEARINGS, LEGAL ACTION: None from FONA.

SPECIAL COMMENT: [This comparative ad gives a relatively balanced picture of both chain stores. As such, it is not likely to mislead consumers nor is it unfair to FONA. However, there are other sizable competitors that were not included in the comparison—and this may be unfair and therefore contravene the Danish Marketing Practices Act.]

This information was provided by B.U. Roepstorff, based on data provided by the Fredgaard company.

"FREDGAARD: The most reasonable alternative to FONA." In the copy Fredgaard acknowledges Fona's size as well as its products, prices, and services. Then, it points out that the two firms are very similar in these matters (apart from size) so that consumers might as well buy from one as from the other.

COMPANY: UNILEVER (NETHERLANDS)   *DATE:* April–June 1976

PRODUCT: Detergent: Lux vs. Dreft.

MEDIA: TV and print.

REASON(S) FOR USING A COMPARATIVE FORMAT:

Dreft (Procter & Gamble) had been running a "Brand X" campaign for a number of years, claiming that one teaspoon of Dreft dishwashing liquid washed more dishes than Brand X because Dreft was so concentrated. In the past, this claim was true, although it did not state that Dreft, relatively speaking, was also more expensive than most dishwashing liquids.

This campaign was hurting sales of Lux, which in price and concentration level was positioned very near to Dreft. Besides, in the last few years, only three brands remained in the Dutch market (about 60 percent of volume is taken up by cheaper private–label brands). Because of this, Unilever had indications that consumers associated Brand X with Lux dishwashing liquid.

At the end of 1975, Lever changed the formula of Lux to exactly the same active-detergent concentration level as Dreft . Subsequently, the management of Lever asked Procter & Gamble to stop Dreft's advertising, as it was no longer true. Brand X could only be one of the other two

---

TRANSLATION OF THE LUX LIQUID COMMERCIAL

Of course you know the dishwashing test of Dreft against Product X, a well-known dishwashing liquid detergent.

Well, Lux dares to take on that test . . .

With the same teaspoon and the same amount of Lux . . .

and look . . . after that pile of dishes,

Lux still foams just as well . . .

And then even cleans such a greasy pan.

Lux lasts just as long and does the same amount of dishwashing.

There is just one important difference: for Lux you pay less! [voiced]

Lux has just as much dishwashing power, but cheaper.

Nou die test durft Lux best aan hoor...

schuimt Lux nog even goed...

Lux evenveel afwas wel voordeliger.

U weet wel die afwastest van Dreft tegen produkt X, een bekend afwasmiddel

en kijk... na die hele stapel borden

Met Lux doet u even lang en wast u net zo veel af...

met een zelfde theelepel en evenveel Lux...

en krijgt dan ook zo'n vette pan nog schoon

brands: Lux or Dubro (also from Unilever), and the comparison with Lux could no longer be made. Procter & Gamble refused.

To force Procter & Gamble to stop their campaign as well as publicly setting things right, Lever together with its advertising agency (JWT), decided to run a comparative campaign rather than go to court.

The TV commercial simply stated that Lux dares to take on the Brand X role in the Dreft test, showing that one teaspoon of Lux cleans exactly as many dishes and pans as one teaspoon of Dreft, with one major difference: Lux costs less.

In this way, it satisfied legal and self-regulatory requirements, since the comparison was made on all relevant consumer points (long-lastingness, cleaning efficiency, and price) without being derisive of Dreft.

ADVANCE CHECKING: The TV commercial was checked in advance in storyboard form with the Dutch TV authorites (Advertising Council and STER). They heard Unilever's arguments and agreed to run the commercial, with no changes requested. An outside lawyer was also consulted to check the legality of the ads, and to prepare for a possible court action.

REACH: The TV commercial was shown twenty-one times (which means a reach of about 68 percent and a frequency of about 4.3). Also, three page-dominating advertisements were run in newspapers, with a national coverage of about 80 percent.

MARKET RESULTS: In terms of sales, Lux's decline of the last few years was stopped; and during the campaign, sales actually increased. Sales have stabilized since. Dreft, through very large price discounts, got a lot of additional volume sales at the expense of the cheaper private brands. The consumer was the main winner, since he was able to buy either of the two leading brands, Lux and Dreft, at a low price.

COMPLAINTS, HEARINGS, LEGAL ACTION: Three times the Lux-Dreft case was brought before the Advertising Council (Reclame Raad), the official body that also handles complaints about TV advertising.

The first complaint came from somebody who was apparently studying the workings of the Reclame Raad and made regular complaints to test its functioning. His complaint was found ungrounded. The second one came from Procter & Gamble. Again, the complaint was rejected, so Lux continued to run is TV commercial. The third complaint also included the Dreft campaign, since obviously either Lux or Dreft was not telling the truth (this was exactly what Lever was waiting for). The Reclame Raad's decision was that Procter & Gamble was forbidden to further run its "Dreft versus Brand X" campaign.

OTHER REACTIONS: This campaign evoked a lot of journalistic interest as articles were written about it in the trade and consumer press and there were discussions on TV news programs. Reactions were generally sympathetic to Lux—partly because the original Dreft campaign was thought by many consumers and consumer organizations to constitute very irritating advertising. Procter & Gamble, when forced off the air, reacted with massive consumer price cuts, so that Lux's claim that it was cheaper was no longer true. These factors led the managements of Lever and Procter & Gamble to stop the fight, and the Lux comparative commercial was withdrawn after some two and one-half months of running.

OTHER COMMENTS: The legal consultant brought up the matter that Procter & Gamble could possibly sue Unilever on the ground that the latter was using someone else's brand to its benefit but without the former's permission (Benelux Merkenrecht—Uniform Law on Trademarks). However, since brand awareness of Lux was as high as or higher than Dreft, Procter & Gamble could not claim that Unilever was using the Dreft brand name to build up awareness of Lux. It is not clear what the judge would have decided in this case, but Procter & Gamble never went to court.

Interestingly enough, when a few months later a fairly unknown cigarette brand ran a full-page newspaper ad comparing their nicotine and tar content with that of a large number of other named brands, the same lawyer, in the service of one of the big tobacco companies, attacked this ad in court on the grounds of the Benelux Merkenrecht, stating that the fairly unknown brand was benefiting from the high brand-awareness of the other cigarette makes, and without their permission. The court, in this case, decided that he was right, and the comparative advertisement was forbidden.

This information was provided by Mr. B.B.H.L.M. Hoogeweegen of J.W. Walter Thompson (Amsterdam).

COMPANY: MAZDA CAR IMPORTS (U.K.)   *DATE:* June–July 1977

PRODUCT: Cars: Mazda vs. Polo, Chevette, Renault 5, and Fiesta.

MEDIA: National press.

_____

REASON(S) FOR USING A COMPARATIVE FORMAT: With only 1 percent of the market, research showed that there was not only an awareness and educational job to be done for the Mazda Hatchback, but also a need to position it against better-known models and to highlight its price competitiveness.

_____

ADVANCE CHECKING BY A GOVERNMENT AGENCY: No
                  SELF-REGULATORY BOARD: No
                  MEDIA: Automatic

_____

READERSHIP OR TV RATINGS: None

MARKET RESULTS: "Sales results were incredibly good—obviously due to the standard marketing mix of product, price, distribution and, hopefully, advertising!"

_____

COMPLAINTS, HEARINGS, LEGAL ACTION, OTHER REACTIONS: The hatchback market is very competitive in the United Kingdom, and many comparative campaigns have been run in 1977.

_____

This information was provided by Mr. M.J. Rudd of Mazda Car Imports (GB) Ltd., England.

The Polo, Chevette, Renault 5 and Fiesta just don't compare with the new Mazda Hatchback.

	FORD FIESTA S	VW POLO L	VAUXHALL CHEVETTE GL	RENAULT 5 GTL	MAZDA HATCHBACK 1300 DL
TOP SPEED (MPH)	86.4	80.7	88.9	82.6	88.9
0-60 MPH (SECONDS)	15.0	18.3	15.1	18.9	14.3
PETROL GRADE	4	2	4	4	2
TURNING CIRCLE (FT)	29.7	29.0	28.5	30.0	27.4
MAXIMUM FRONT LEGROOM	38.5"	40"	38"	38"	40.5"
MINIMUM REAR LEGROOM	24"	22"	18.5"	23.8"	24"
REAR WASH/WIPE					STANDARD
LAMINATED WINDSCREEN					STANDARD
RUBBER BUMPER INSERTS		STANDARD		STANDARD	STANDARD
TINTED GLASS					STANDARD
HEAD RESTRAINTS					STANDARD
CIGAR LIGHTER	STANDARD		STANDARD	STANDARD	STANDARD
PANEL LIGHT DIMMER	STANDARD				STANDARD
CARPETS	STANDARD	STANDARD	STANDARD	STANDARD	STANDARD
CLOTH UPHOLSTERY	STANDARD	STANDARD	STANDARD		STANDARD
CLOCK	STANDARD		STANDARD		STANDARD
TRIP METER	STANDARD		STANDARD	STANDARD	STANDARD
RECLINING SEATS	STANDARD	STANDARD	STANDARD	STANDARD	STANDARD
DAY/NIGHT MIRROR	STANDARD	STANDARD	STANDARD	STANDARD	STANDARD
LOCKING FUEL CAP		STANDARD	STANDARD		STANDARD
HEATED REAR WINDOW	STANDARD	STANDARD	STANDARD	STANDARD	STANDARD
PRICE	£2,513.00	£2,487.00	£2,390.00	£2,397.00	£2,323.00

We don't want to "knock" the Polo, Chevette, Renault 5 and Fiesta.

They're all excellent cars.

But in most of the 22 areas shown in the chart, they aren't quite as excellent as the new Mazda Hatchback.

Performance, for example. None of the others matches Mazda's 0-60 acceleration, and only the Chevette matches its top speed.

Take passenger space. The Mazda's rear legroom is equalled only by the Fiesta, while its front legroom is unbeatable.

Its turning circle is the smallest, making it exceptionally easy to manoeuvre in towns.

(Turning circle, performance and legroom figures in the chart are from "Motor" 7 May 1977.)

It uses two-star petrol, unlike the Renault, Chevette and Fiesta.

It's the only one with a laminated windscreen, a safety feature the US Government considers important enough to be compulsory on all cars.

It's the only one with head restraints, another safety feature the US Government considers important enough to be compulsory on all cars.

It's the only one with tinted glass to cut down driver fatigue, and a rear washer-wiper for visibility.

And it has such features as cloth upholstery (which the Renault hasn't got), rubber bumper inserts (which the Chevette hasn't got), cigar lighter (which the Polo hasn't got), and locking fuel cap (which the Fiesta hasn't got).

And how much extra do you pay for all this?

Silly question.

The Mazda Hatchback 1300 DL's basic price is £67 less than the Chevette GL, £74 less than the Renault 5 GTL, £164 less than the Polo L and £190 less than the Fiesta S. (These prices include VAT, car tax and seat belts, but not delivery or number plates.)

The Mazda Hatchback comes with a choice of 985 cc or 1272 cc engines, with three or five doors. Prices start at $2,033*.

There are 253 Mazda dealers in this country, any of whom will be happy to arrange a test-drive and tell you about our low-cost insurance scheme and our 12 month unlimited warranty.

For the address of your nearest dealer, please post the coupon below. You don't need a stamp – we pay the postage.

Mazda
HATCHBACK

Price includes Car Tax, VAT and inertia seat belts. Delivery and number plates extra. For Fleet, Military and Export sales write to Mazda Car Imports (GB) Ltd., North Farm Industrial Estate, Tunbridge Wells, Kent TN2 3EY.

To: Mazda Car Imports (GB) Limited, FREEPOST, Longfield Rd., Tunbridge Wells, TN2 3EY, Kent. Please send me the name of my nearest Mazda dealer and details of the Mazda Hatchback.

Name:_____ Address:_____

Please tick if under 17 □

223

COMPANY: PEPSI-COLA BOTTLING CO. (PHILLIPPINES)

DATE: September 1976.

PRODUCT: Orange soft drink: Mirinda vs. Royal TruOrange (San Miguel Co.).

MEDIA: Newspapers for twelve days before the comparative campaign was blocked by the Philippine Advertising Board (PBA).

REASON(S) FOR USING A COMPARATIVE FORMAT: The strategy was to build brand-awareness and trial via a dramatic, attention-getting format. Comparison advertising was believed the most appropriate technique to use in view of: (1) Mirinda's superiority (it was the winner of the blind taste test against Royal TruOrange), (2) its gross sales inferiority (Royal TruOrange outsold it 4 to 1), and (3) its much lower brand-awareness and image (Royal TruOrange was like a generic name in the orange soft-drink category). (There was no *"Pepsi* Challenge," because it is the leading cola drink in the Philippines.)

ADVANCE CHECKING BY A GOVERNMENT AGENCY: No

SELF-REGULATORY BOARD: Yes (PBA)

MEDIA; No

CHANGES MADE: Final headline had to include (45 percent) instead of simply stating "about half."

READERSHIP OR TV RATINGS: The two newspapers (four full pages each) had a combined circulation of 350,000. However, the unusual comparative taste-test format, plus the protest from the competition as well as the ban (temporary at first) discussed in the press, drew tremendous publicity for Mirinda, despite the campaign's limited run.

MARKET RESULTS: They are not directly measurable because—with the suspension of the ad—Mirinda's retail price was dropped from 40 to 30 cents. The combined "Mirinda Challenge," price cut, and other promotions improved sales volume by 274 percent versus three months before, and by 373 percent versus the year before. Dealers also became much more willing to carry Mirinda.

COMPLAINTS, HEARINGS, LEGAL ACTION: The Philippine Board of Advertising, acting upon a complaint from San Miguel Co., asked for sub-

stantiation of the test results. Refusal to unconditionally comply with this request led the PBA to suspend the print ad after twelve days, despite its prior approval. This suspension prevented extension of this comparative campaign to television and radio. A sixty-day ban ensued and was ultimately followed by an indefinite one. For a while, Mirinda used an indirect comparative ad ("the leading orange soft drink") but ads making unnamed competitors readily identifiable were also proscribed later on (see the Philippine country synopsis for further details).

OTHER REACTIONS: Press coverage was intense and much polarized.

———

This information was provided by Mr. V.S. Quimbo, former Mirinda Brand Manager in the Philippines.

COMPANY: R.J. REYNOLDS SCANDINAVIA AB (SWEDEN)

DATE: 1977

PRODUCT: Cigarette: More vs. Prince.

MEDIA: Newspapers and magazines.

———

REASON(S) FOR USING A COMPARATIVE FORMAT: To launch a new long brown cigarette on the Swedish market, which was unfamiliar with them, and was likely to think of them as cigars. Since the major target was cigarette-smoking females, and their preferred brand is Prince, a comparison with the latter was indicated. Too, it was important to identify More as a cigarette, and this suggested comparing it to a well-known Swedish cigarette. Research had also revealed that smokers look at ads featuring their own brand, so that by comparing More to the most popular cigarette, greater awareness of the former could be achieved. Other comparative ads were also used, giving less prominence to Prince.

———

ADVANCE CHECKING BY A GOVERNMENT AGENCY: No.
SELF-REGULATORY BOARD: Yes
MEDIA: Yes

CHANGES MADE: None

———

READERSHIP OR TV RATINGS: In Sweden, there is no regularly measured recall research, and no specific study was made of the effectiveness of this comparative campaign.

MARKET RESULTS: Sales goals were achieved within six months and exceeded thereafter.

———

COMPLAINTS, HEARINGS, LEGAL ACTION: None

OTHER REACTIONS: A great deal of interest was generated by this first comparison of one cigarette to another, and by the introduction of a totally new type of cigarette.

———

This information was provided by Mr. Bo Seifert of Perceptum Information AB, and Mr. Povl van Deurs Jensen of R.J. Reynolds Scandinavia AB (Stockholm, Sweden).

MER CIGARETT.

(Räcker längre)

NY
CIGARETT
LÅNG (3,5 cm längre än Prince)
BRUN
MER (Räcker längre)

More

Den första 120 mm långa cigaretten som lanserats i Sverige.

OPEL KADETT (UNITED KINGDOM)

COMPANY: OPEL (UNITED KINGDOM) *DATE:* September 1976–May 1977

PRODUCT: Cars: Opel Kadett vs. Allegro, Volkswagen, Renault, Peugeot, Ford, and Fiat.

MEDIA: Magazines.

REASON(S) FOR USING A COMPARATIVE FORMAT: The strategy was to improve overall awareness of both brand (Opel) and model (Kadett), and to emphasize its highly competitive price position. (Other versions were prepared to position additional Opel models [Ascona, Rekord, Manta] against better known comparable models.)

ADVANCE CHECKING BY A GOVERNMENT AGENCY: No
SELF/REGULATORY BOARD: Yes. Code of Advertising Practice (CAP) Committee cleared ads in principle for general approach.
MEDIA: Yes

CHANGES MADE: One magazine referred the Rekord ad to CAP because of an apparently identical claim with Peugeot, regarding leadership in Europe. Opel's claim was upheld, but the wording was amended for clarification sake.

READERSHIP OR TV RATINGS: "Impossible to evaluate due to the low level of expenditure."

MARKET RESULTS: "Cannot [be determined]; there are too many variables."

COMPLAINTS, HEARINGS, LEGAL ACTION: There was a consumer complaint to the Advertising Standards Authority (ASA) alleging that it was unfair to compare the Opel Kadett to the VW Golf instead of to the cheaper VW Polo [Rabbitt]. The Agency justified this choice to ASA's satisfaction.

OTHER REACTIONS: This campaign was not considered controversial, but was praised for honesty by *Motor Magazine* in a review of car advertisements, because Opel listed cheaper cars too.

This information was provided by Mr. Mike Longhurst of McCann-Erikson Advertising Ltd., London, United Kingdom.

228

229

COMPANY: ROYAL DOULTON (USA)   *DATE:* 1977

PRODUCT: Crystal glasses: Royal Doulton vs. Waterford.

MEDIA: Magazines.

———

REASON(S) FOR USING A COMPARATIVE FORMAT: "Waterford is the best known crystal in the market. While in every way the two lines are comparable, it was deemed necessary to provide the consumer with a valid advantage in purchasing Royal Doulton—namely, that if a breakable product is broken, replacement costs only half the original price. Further, our resources to build a traditional image are limited so that a traffic-stopping advertising/marketing scheme made the available funds more productive." [Royal Doulton also ran a comparative ad against Lenox china ("The china of Stoke-on-Trent, England vs. the china of Pomona, New Jersey"), which the latter countered in the *trade* press ("Remember what happened the last time the British attacked a Trenton headquarters!") and by providing comparative information for retail-store salesclerks.]

———

ADVANCE CHECKING BY A GOVERNMENT AGENCY: No
                   SELF-REGULATORY BOARD: No
                   MEDIA: No

———

READERSHIP OR TV RATINGS: "We cannot specifically measure it . . . but this ad has generated the second highest consumer write-in response of our entire product program."

MARKET RESULTS: "An increase in sales to our accounts was noted and attributable to the campaign—apparently due to salespeople in the stores becoming excited at having a good selling tool for their product, which is up against the better known Waterford name and consumer-acceptance level."

COMPLAINTS, HEARINGS, LEGAL ACTION: None

———

OTHER REACTIONS: "Interestingly, we have received, for replacement, merchandise manufactured by other crystal companies—in addition to our own." [This, of course, may reveal consumer confusion.]

———

This information was provided by Nancy E. Oliver-Clarke, Advertising/Sales Promotion Manager, Doulton & Co., Inc., Carlstadt, New Jersey.

This is when you'll be twice as glad that you own Royal Doulton crystal instead of Waterford.

If you should inadvertently break a beautiful piece of Royal Doulton crystal stemware, the catastrophe is now minimized by half. Because from now on, at any time throughout the life of the pattern, we will replace your broken stemware for only half the suggested retail price then in effect.

But how desirable is our crystal intact?

For one thing, it's full lead crystal. More than 30%. It's hand-blown and hand-cut. So light dances and shimmers in and around our multi-faceted crystal stemware with the sparkle of precious jewels.

In fact, every attribute we have, Waterford has. Except for our "Simply Smashing Breakage Policy." And, since accidents *do* happen, you will be twice as glad that you chose Royal Doulton crystal instead of Waterford.

How our "Simply Smashing Breakage Policy" works.
1. Carefully wrap stem and part of bowl from broken Royal Doulton stemware.
2. Include the pattern name and item, your name and return address, and a check, to Royal Doulton, for half the current suggested retail price, plus $1.00 insurance and postage.
3. Mail to Doulton and Co., Inc., 400 Paterson Plank Road, Carlstadt, N.J. 07072. Your replacement delivered in approximately four weeks.

Royal Doulton
English Crystal

Royal Doulton Water Goblets, left to right: Sherbrooke, $14.50; Rochelle, $17.50; Carlyle, $26.00; Balmoral, $19.50

231

COMPANY: SLAZENGER (AUSTRALIA)   *DATE:* Summer 1977

PRODUCT: Golf ball: B51 Slazenger/Dunlop 65 vs. Spalding Hot Dot/P.G.F. Status.

MEDIA: Weekend newspaper (*Sun Herald*).

REASON(S) FOR USING A COMPARATIVE FORMAT: Comparisons were used to answer a series of advertisements that had already been prepared by the Spalding Company, which made less specific claims but which implied the superiority of the Spalding golf ball—a superiority of performance which was simply not the case. The strategy was simply to place some facts before the golfer to show that the Slazenger B51 golf ball would in fact out-perform the Spalding ball.

ADVANCE CHECKING BY A GOVERNMENT AGENCY: No
                    SELF-REGULATORY BOARD: No
                    MEDIA: No

READERSHIP OR TV RATINGS: None available.

MARKET RESULTS: None available.

COMPLAINTS, HEARINGS, LEGAL ACTION, OTHER REACTIONS: This ad was withdrawn because both Slazenger and Spalding lodged complaints with the Disparaging Committee of the Australian Media Accreditation Authority. Both companies agreed to withdraw their ads due to the difficulty of proving the validity of the comparisons they made.

This information was provided by Mr. Graham Sawyer of Leo Burnett Pty. Ltd., Sydney, Australia.

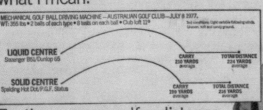

233

COMPANY: TOSHIBA AMERICA, INC. (USA)   *DATE:* 1977–1978

PRODUCT: Photocopiers: Toshiba vs. Xerox.

MEDIA: Consumer, business, and office trade magazines.

REASON FOR USING A COMPARATIVE FORMAT:

Situation Analysis

1. "Toshiba's brand awareness is extremely low, particularly in the office-equipment field."
2. "Current budget limitations do not afford us the opportunity to position ourself through a corporate campaign in keeping with the image of quality and prestige that our parent company, Tokyo Shibaura Electric Co., Ltd., has established in Japan and Europe."
3. "Xerox is the leader in copier placements and awareness. They hold about 70 percent share of the low to medium copier placements."
4. "The Toshiba BD-702A copier is less expensive, more compact, and offers more versatility than the Xerox 3100 (which represents the bulk of Xerox installations)."

Strategy

"We selected a comparative format to position our company as a leader by comparing our BD-702A copier with the established giant's model 3100. This could be done effectively using one-page black and white, whereas a corporate campaign would have looked weak in one color. Secondly, we felt that a straight non-comparative product approach would not sufficiently distinguish Toshiba from the other 16 brands competing for the remaining share of the business."

ADVANCE CHECKING BY A GOVERNMENT AGENCY: No
                              SELF-REGULATORY BOARD: No
                              MEDIA: No

"The ad copy was checked by both DKG, Inc.'s legal department and our own attorneys. All feature claims were substantiated and price comparison qualified to insure we were comparing apples with apples."

READERSHIP OR TV RATINGS: "No Starch report has been done to evaluate readership. However, based on the media department estimates, 3 out of 4 professional/managerial types will be reached by our ad."

MARKET RESULTS: "It is difficult to relate the exact increase in sales to this comparative effort because we are still in the process of establishing national distribution through independent office-equipment retailers. However, we received almost double the number of inquiries from this cam-

O.K. XEROX, TRY AND COPY THIS.

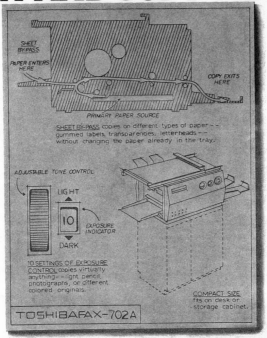

paign as compared to previous efforts in the same media. And our overall sales of the equipment increased.''

———

COMPLAINTS, HEARINGS, LEGAL ACTION, AND OTHER REACTIONS:
None

———

This information was provided by Mr. J.I. Hunt, Advertising Manager, Business Equipment Division, Toshiba America, Inc. (New York).

235

COMPANY: LEYLAND (AUSTRALIA)   *DATE:* Fall 1977

PRODUCT: Cars: Triumph 2500 vs. Peugeot, Toyota, and Volvo.

MEDIA: Newspapers and magazines.

REASON(S) FOR USING A COMPARATIVE FORMAT: Major research about the luxury-car market revealed that the Triumph 2500's potential depended on taking business away from the Volvo 244, Peugeot 504, and Toyota Super Crown. Besides, the target market is made up of conservative, heavy print-readers but very light TV-viewers who are most influenced by "perceived value for money."

ADVANCE CHECKING BY A GOVERNMENT AGENCY: No
SELF-REGULATORY BOARD: No
MEDIA: No

READERSHIP OR TV RATINGS: "It is estimated that 95.8 percent of the target market was reached with a frequency of 10.8, but there was no subsequent research to establish recall, etc."

MARKET RESULTS: During the three months (August through October) of this comparative campaign, retail sales increased by 40 percent over the March–May period when noncomparative ads were used.

COMPLAINTS, HEARINGS, LEGAL ACTION, OTHER REACTIONS: None

This information was provided by Leyland Australia (Sydney).

AN EMBARRASSING EXPOSÉ FOR THREE OF THE BIG LUXURY FOUR.

$10405	$11260	$9950	$8995
Peugeot 504 Automatic	Toyota Super Crown Automatic	Volvo 244 DL Automatic	Triumph 2500 TC Automatic

As the above prices indicate, the Triumph 2500 TC automatic is considerably cheaper than its three main rivals. And as the facts below will demonstrate, it's also embarrassingly better equipped.

An anomaly that owes its origins to two different benefactors.

For the rather generous price advantage we must thank the Bank of England and the favourable exchange rate between the English Pound and the Australian Dollar.

For the high standard of fittings we can thank Triumph's foresight and policy of constant development without compromise.

For the fortunate Australian buyer, the overall result is that he can get considerably more in the way of a luxury car for substantially less.

And not just an ashtray here or a courtesy light there but a list of important components that we think will surprise you.

For only Triumph has a powerful six cylinder engine coupled to a combination of four wheel independent suspension and rack and pinion steering.

Nor is it just any six. The Triumph 2500 TC manual won the 1977 Total Economy Run outright. Getting over five more miles to the gallon than its only four cylinder rival to enter, the Peugeot 504.

The Triumph interior surrounds its driver with polished walnut whilst placing a fully adjustable padded alloy steering wheel in his hands. Adjustable to suit the driver, not vice versa. Our close competitors don't consider that this comfort is important. Neither as a feature, nor an option.

A combination of features that are unmistakeably Triumph. Features that would be worth paying more for, let alone less.

And when it's all said and done, who could want more or settle for less in a luxury car.

Take advantage of the undervalued pound. Take home a Triumph.

TRIUMPH 2500.
More luxury car for your money.

THE GREAT OFFICE EQUIPMENT WAR:
PHOTOCOPIERS, COMPUTERS AND TYPEWRITERS

In terms of aggressivity, few if any comparative campaigns have matched those of the *photocopier* business. Here are a few examples chosen from many bold headlines and claims made against the leaders Xerox and IBM—and Savin must have done something right, since it is now also used as a reference point (at least by Canon).[1]

SAVIN

- "Compared to the new Savin 780—most Xerox copies are overrated."
- "In the time it takes the new Savin 780 to copy these twenty pages—most Xerox machines won't get past page 5."
- "We are where the Xerox used to be" [with a picture showing a Xerox copier being moved out of an office].
- "The Savin 780 [illustration with a shorter paper path]—The Xerox 4000 [with a longer paper path]. The shorter the paper path, the longer the time between service calls."
- "It takes *two* Xerox 3100's to equal the productivity of *one* Savin 780!"
- "What do Xerox and IBM II copiers have most in common? Both are most commonly *replaced* with the Savin 780."
- "What's the largest selling copier in the world today? Wrong! This [Savin 770] is the largest selling copier in the world today.
- "We owe our success to Xerox."
- "Xerox is going to make you an offer you should refuse."

PITNEY BOWES

- "We don't have to make Xerox look bad to look good."
- "Now two [Pitney Bowes PBCs] can copy cheaper than one [Xerox 3600-1]."
- "Now that everyone has taken a shot at Xerox, take a good look at why we don't have to."

ADDRESSOGRAPH MULTIGRAPH

One man: "I rent a Xerox 9200."
Other man: "For the same money, I can rent an AM 4250MR high-volume duplicator, redecorate our offices, hire an additional secretary, and buy two new company cars."

---

[1] According to a Savin spokesman, "Xerox has begun emphasizing large-volume customers, as have AM, Kodak, and IBM. These companies are going after mini-print shop business . . . this has left a hole in the convenience market . . . which may be a crumb for Xerox but a big piece of business for us." "Savin Expanding Anti-Xerox Effort," *Advertising Age* (13 December 1976), p. 4.

The comparative battle has only been a little less vicious in the *computer and word-processing* fields, where IBM is, of course, the choice target but stays away from comparisons.[2]

WANG

- "Buy the idea of word processing from IBM. Buy the system from Wang."

NIXDORF

- "Who dares to offer a 'Computer Buyer's Checklist': IBM? Honeywell? Burroughs? NCR? . . . Only the computer experts from Nixdorf."

In *typewriters,* Olivetti came up with "Olivetti's new Lexicon 92C does more than IBM's Selectric and Executive combined."[3]

[2] A French IBM ad simply says: "There is an IBM photocopier more advanced than yours . . . and probably more economical. Try us."
[3] This ad was substantiated to the satisfaction of the self-regulatory body NAD.

In a number of European countries, some of these ads would be considered to amount to the "unfair" denigration of competitors. In the United States, they have not been challenged by the target companies. Thus, they appear to have met the test of neither being false nor misleading—the major bases for complaints and suits.

242

INDEX